Calvin
for the World

"In the perpetual struggle against historical amnesia, Rubén Rosario Rodríguez's helpful and timely book goes beyond simply demonstrating how Calvin's 'critics got it wrong' with their facile, reductionistic interpretations of the reformer's thought. *Calvin for the World* also offers a corrective to the facile and reductionistic tendencies of many of Calvin's friends. By setting Calvin's theology in its original contexts and following oft-neglected lineages of reception, Rosario Rodríguez illuminates the experiences of dislocation and migration that stand behind Calvin's vision for reform and unveils that vision's liberative potential for theologies during and since the Reformation era. This book invites Reformed believers to consider unexpected ways that their tradition might speak to pressing contemporary issues and center new voices that resonate more deeply with Calvinism's past than is often imagined."

—**Kenneth J. Woo**, Pittsburgh Theological Seminary

"Why would a twenty-first century constructive theologian, especially one from a minority heritage, write a book on John Calvin that invites readers to take a second look? Rosario Rodríguez's *Calvin for the World* offers some thought-provoking answers. The creative fruit of twenty years of teaching, this lively text ranges over many topics that contemporary people would see as their own concerns—from apartheid, to immigration, to Christian engagement in public life, to liberation theology, and more. Professor Rosario Rodríguez shares the exciting surprises that his students have encountered when he has brought voices from many contexts into dialogue with Calvin, and he makes a good case that the so-called dictator of Geneva has something relevant to say today, that this long misread (or rather, unread) pastor is a viable and even worthwhile conversation partner on these 'modern' issues. Rosario Rodríguez never glosses over Calvin's legendary negative reputation. However, by a combination of historical context and fascinating comparisons with figures like Bartolomé de Las Casas, Gustavo Gutiérrez, Thomas More, Allan Boesak, Cotton Mather, and Archbishop Romero, he draws out grounds for reconsidering whether Calvin just might be a more valuable resource for contemporary thought than the old stereotypes would suggest."

—**Elsie McKee**, Princeton Theological Seminary (emerita)

"*Calvin for the World* shows us what it looks like to thoughtfully engage with a theological giant who bears a complicated legacy and yet still says much that may be of value for us today: not pretending or ignoring but also not canceling or forgetting. In Rubén Rosario Rodríguez's capable hands, Calvin is revealed to be a proto-liberationist by the lights of his own convictions as he is interpreted through the genius of his most radical followers."

—**Jonathan Tran**, author of *Asian Americans and the Spirit of Racial Capitalism*

"This book by Rubén Rosario Rodríguez is an excellent contribution to the analysis of the importance of John Calvin as a leader of the emerging Protestant Christian theology. Rosario Rodríguez carefully analyzes the various aspects of Calvinist thought and their implications for the convergences between Calvinism, Lutheranism, and Catholicism. It includes the importance of support for impoverished people and the possibility of coming together in ecumenical relationships that highlight convergences rather than contradictions. I recommend attentive and careful reading of this extraordinary book."

—**Luis N. Rivera-Pagán**, Princeton Theological Seminary (emeritus)

"Rosario Rodríguez has written a comprehensive analysis of Calvin's theology, practical ministry, and recommendations for Christians in social, economic, and political relations. It addresses Calvin's challenge to sixteenth-century Roman Catholic, Lutheran, and Anabaptist theologies while also considering how Calvin's theology and practical ministry have influenced Christian involvement in matters of economic justice, government, immigration, and race policy in Latin America and South Africa from Calvin's time to our own. This book is valuable for scholars, students, pastors, and church classes."

—**Harlan Beckley**, Washington and Lee University (emeritus)

Calvin
for the World

THE ENDURING RELEVANCE *of* HIS POLITICAL, SOCIAL, AND ECONOMIC THEOLOGY

Rubén Rosario Rodríguez

B
Baker Academic
a division of Baker Publishing Group
Grand Rapids, Michigan

Published by Baker Academic
a division of Baker Publishing Group
Grand Rapids, Michigan
BakerAcademic.com

Printed in the United States of America

Library of Congress Cataloging-in-Publication Data
Names: Rosario Rodríguez, Rubén, 1970– author.
Title: Calvin for the world : the enduring relevance of his political, social, and economic theology / Rubén Rosario Rodríguez.
Description: Grand Rapids, Michigan : Baker Academic, a division of Baker Publishing Group, [2024] | Includes bibliographical references and indexes.
Identifiers: LCCN 2024008541 | ISBN 9781540966216 (paperback) | ISBN 9781540967831 (casebound) | ISBN 9781493446292 (ebook) | ISBN 9781493446308 (pdf)
Subjects: LCSH: Calvin, Jean, 1509–1564—Political and social views.
Classification: LCC BX9418 .R59 2024 | DDC 261—dc23/eng/20240409
LC record available at https://lccn.loc.gov/2024008541

Baker Publishing Group publications use paper produced from sustainable forestry practices and postconsumer waste whenever possible.

24   25   26   27   28   29   30   7   6   5   4   3   2   1

To Elsie Anne McKee,
Archibald Alexander Professor of Reformation Studies
and the History of Worship, Emerita,
at Princeton Theological Seminary—
*for cultivating love for Calvin the pastor and
theologian amid all the detractors*

Contents

Preface

This project began as an effort to collect a series of my published essays on the theological, political, and economic impact of John Calvin's thought for contemporary constructive theology. As the book developed, I quickly realized that what began as a series of disparate essays on various topics coalesced into a coherent vision for how to engage Calvin's work for today's world. While drawing on my previously published essays, I reorganized, rewrote, and expanded to such a degree that no chapter now stands as previously published. Hopefully the finished whole is greater than the sum of its dissected and radically reconstituted parts.

In writing this volume I have drawn extensively from the following previously published, peer-reviewed journal articles:

- "Becoming a Church for the Poor: Toward a Reformed Spirituality of Liberation." *KOINONIA* 13, no. 2 (Fall 2001): 152–84.
- "Calvin or Calvinism: Reclaiming Reformed Theology for the Latin American Context." *Apuntes: Reflexiones teológicas desde el margen hispano* 23, no. 4 (Winter 2004): 124–55.
- "Calvin's Influence in Latin America: A Scattered Inheritance." *Ciências da religião: História e sociedade* 4, no. 4 (2006): 136–48.
- "Calvin and 'Communion Ecclesiology': An Ecumenical Conversation." *Theology Today* 66, no. 2 (July 2009): 154–69.
- "*De orilla a orilla*: The Ecumenical Theology of Luis Rivera-Pagán." *Journal of Hispanic/Latino Theology* 18, no. 1 (November 2012): 26–34.

I have also adapted extensive sections from the following previously published chapters:

- "John Calvin." In *Beyond the Pale: Reading Theology from the Margins*, edited by Miguel A. De La Torre and Stacey Floyd-Thomas, 71–78. Louisville: Westminster John Knox, 2011.
- "Calvin's Legacy of Compassion: A Reformed Theological Perspective on Immigration." In *Immigrant Neighbors among Us: Immigration across Theological Traditions*, edited by Leopoldo A. Sánchez M. and M. Daniel Carroll R., 44–62. Eugene, OR: Wipf & Stock, 2015.
- "Immigrants, Refugees, and Asylum Seekers: The Migratory Beginnings of Reformed Public Theology." In *Reformed Public Theology: A Global Vision for Life in the World*, edited by Matthew Kaemingk, 23–34. Grand Rapids: Baker Academic, 2021.

I want to express my gratitude to the journals and editors of the above publications for their kind permission to revisit and republish my work, in revised form, and to Robert Hosack at Baker Academic for suggesting this book in the first place. I would also like to thank my department chair, Dr. Daniel Smith, and my dean, Dr. Donna LaVoie, who in 2022 appointed me to the Clarence Louis and Helen Steber Professorship in Theological Studies. Without the accompanying course reduction, this book might have never reached completion while I juggled teaching with coordinating the master's programs in the Department of Theological Studies at Saint Louis University. Finally, as always, I want to thank my wife, Elizabeth Blake, and our two wonderful children, Isabella and Raphael, for the time they gave me to finish the project.

Introduction:
Why Calvin? Why Now?

Does the world need another book on John Calvin's theology? What could be said that hasn't been said before? More to the point, in the era of dead-White-male backlash, why should we listen to *this* dead White male? In the popular imagination, sixteenth-century Protestant reformer John Calvin (1509–64) is remembered as an authoritarian leader and dogmatic thinker whose legacy is tainted by his teaching on double predestination and his role in the execution by burning at the stake of Michael Servetus in 1553. Red flags on anyone's résumé, to be sure. Therefore, it is not surprising that in our day and age Calvinism is equated with intolerance and Calvin himself viewed as a petty tyrant.

As theologian and public intellectual David Bentley Hart argues in his defense of universalism, *That All Shall Be Saved*, Calvin's assertion that God foreordained the fall of humanity borders on blasphemy: "Nevertheless, to me the God of Calvinism at its worst (as in those notorious lines in Book III of the *Institutes*) is simply Domitian made omnipotent. If that were Christianity, it would be too psychologically diseased a creed to take seriously at all, and its adherents would deserve only a somewhat acerbic pity, not respect. If this is one's religion, then one is simply a diabolist who has gotten the names in the story confused."[1] Still, Hart's barbed comments rejecting double predestination pale in comparison to

1. David Bentley Hart, *That All Shall Be Saved: Heaven, Hell, and Universal Salvation* (New Haven: Yale University Press, 2019), 51.

the bile directed Calvin's way for his role in the Servetus affair, to the point that some have equated Calvin's reforms in Geneva with the rise of global Jihadism: "The parallels between Calvinists and Wahhabists are again evident in their demands for austerity. The Wahhabists, like the Calvinists, require conformity of behavior, including regular public prayer. For both, public comportment reflects genuine religiosity, and—like the citizens of Geneva—Wahhabists are encouraged to report violations of behavioral standards such as modesty in dress, prohibitions on the consumption of alcohol and intoxicants, and bans on most music and dancing."[2]

Ironically, in the United States, a nation founded on Calvinist cultural and intellectual principles, many academics now identify Calvin with anti-American authoritarianism and anti-scientific religious dogmatism. Somewhere along the way, "Calvin became the embodiment of what the new objective historians of the late nineteenth century were fighting against," and his involvement in the Servetus affair was reinterpreted as part of a wider ecclesial suppression of scientific knowledge (i.e., Servetus's discoveries about the human circulatory system) by a religious extremist: "Because of religious bigotry, Calvin executed Servetus, the 'scientist.'"[3] So, despite Calvinism's many contributions to US history and culture—for example, the First Great Awakening (ca. 1730–50) cannot be understood without referencing Calvin's influence on Jonathan Edwards—the recent trend has been to mute Calvin and Calvinism's influence on American culture.

So why another Calvin book? Short answer: the critics got it wrong. Or as Pulitzer Prize–winning novelist Marilynne Robinson so eloquently sums up the matter, "Calvin has a strange reputation that is based very solidly on the fact that nobody reads him."[4] Thus the need for a good introductory textbook for both students and scholars that corrects misconceptions about Calvin while reevaluating his impact on global Christianity. Far from being the "Protestant pope" of popular imagination or the founder of biblical fundamentalism championed by contemporary evangelicalism,

2. Richard Mansbach, "Calvinism as a Precedent for Islamic Radicalism," *Brown Journal of World Affairs* 12, no. 2 (Winter/Spring 2006): 111.

3. Thomas J. Davis, "Images of Intolerance: John Calvin in Nineteenth-Century History Textbooks," *Church History* 65, no. 2 (June 1996): 238.

4. Sarah Pulliam Bailey, "Q&A: Marilynne Robinson on Guns, Gay Marriage, and Calvinism," *Christian Century*, May 12, 2014, https://www.christiancentury.org/article/2014-05/qampa-marilynne-robinson-guns-gay-marriage-and-calvinism.

Calvin remains one of the most influential thinkers in Western history, one whose cosmopolitan vision of a transnational Christianity left its mark on the global church in myriad ways. Long answer: this is not "just another textbook" on Calvin. Rather, this book is an exercise in constructive theology grounded in the belief that Calvin's theological, political, and social thought is still relevant for the Christian churches and has value for the greater society. In other words, this book counterbalances many misconceptions about Calvin in the hopes that readers will discover what Robinson describes as "the visionary quality of his theology."[5]

Without question, Calvin remains a troubling and controversial figure. His supporters praise his transformative influence on the ecclesial, political, and economic spheres of modern life, while his detractors paint him as a ruthless proponent of theocracy comparable to the mullahs of present-day Iran. Historian Carter Lindberg catalogs the many contradictory versions of Calvin: "both a narrow dogmatist and an ecumenical churchperson; a ruthless inquisitor and a sensitive, caring pastor; an ascetic, cold authoritarian and a compassionate humanist; . . . the tyrant of Geneva and a defender of freedom; a dictator and a revolutionary."[6] Yet this very controversy, giving rise to so many conflicting images, suggests there is more to Calvin than meets the eye and that his life and work warrant further investigation. By presenting an account of Calvin's theology in historical context, highlighting key moments in the global dissemination and reception of his works, then proposing avenues for engaging contemporary issues through the lens of Calvin's thought, this book reexamines widespread assumptions and reevaluates clichéd tropes within Calvin studies to present the sixteenth-century reformer as an engaging interlocutor on contemporary matters of social, political, racial, and economic justice.

Whatever one's final judgment on Calvin, responsible scholarship demands a deeper reading that transcends any one-dimensional idealization or demonization. Admittedly, this task is particularly difficult for people of color (like me) given how often Calvin and Calvinism are represented by Eurocentric chauvinism and racially repressive regimes. The Reformed Calvinist tradition has contributed significantly to the oppression of people

5. Bailey, "Q&A."
6. Carter Lindberg, *The European Reformations* (Oxford: Blackwell, 1996), 250.

and communities of color. From the Dutch Reformed Church sanction-
ing the African slave trade in colonial America, to the role of Afrikaner
Calvinism in the founding of the apartheid state of South Africa in the
twentieth century, to the cooperation of Brazilian Presbyterians with
the 1964 military coup d'état and subsequent military dictatorship in
that country, the historical evidence seems incontrovertible concerning
Calvinism's participation in what critics have called "world-repressive"
Christianity.[7] Yet, as a Latino Reformed theologian standing in critical
continuity with Calvin—fully aware of the negative missiological impact
these repressive forms of Calvinism have had throughout the world—I
challenge readers to reevaluate the more emancipatory aspects of Calvin's
thought by highlighting traditions of resistance informed by his theology.

An enduring characteristic of the Christian religion is its sense of social
responsibility in caring for the poor. The New Testament describes Jesus's
ministry as one of compassion and inclusivity, portraying Jesus as a public
figure unafraid to transgress cultural and religious norms for the sake of
a single individual's material or spiritual well-being (Mark 7:24–30; John
4:4–42). Consequently, the religion Jesus inspired has distinguished itself
historically through communal practices of hospitality directed at both
the neighbor *and* the stranger in need. Reformed theology in the twenty-
first century, an inheritor of Calvin's reforming work in sixteenth-century
Geneva, also recognizes and welcomes this civic dimension of the Christian
faith. Theologian and ethicist Douglas Ottati describes Reformed theology
in a "Calvinist key" as "a theology that backs robust participation in the
public realm," as distinguished, for example, from Anabaptist theologies
that consider civil government "outside Christ."[8] In the *Institutes of the
Christian Religion*, Calvin argues that God establishes civil government
so that "humanity may be maintained among men," and he views magistrates as the divinely appointed guardians of public well-being. Civil
government is thus "a calling, not only lawful before God, but also the
most sacred and by far the most honorable of all callings, in the whole life

7. See Mark K. Taylor, "Immanental and Prophetic: Shaping Reformed Theology for Late
Twentieth-Century Struggle," in *Christian Ethics in Ecumenical Context: Theology, Culture,
and Politics in Dialogue*, ed. Shin Chiba, George R. Hunsberger, and Lester Edwin J. Ruiz,
149–66 (Grand Rapids: Eerdmans, 1995); and Nicholas Wolterstorff, *Until Justice and Peace
Embrace* (Grand Rapids: Eerdmans, 1983).

8. Douglas F. Ottati, "What Reformed Theology in a Calvinist Key Brings to Conversations
about Justice," *Political Theology* 10, no. 3 (2009): 447–69.

of mortal men."[9] Not surprisingly, Calvin's ministry in Geneva—a French exile ministering to refugees from France, Poland, Spain, England, and Italy—resembles (and can inform) contemporary debates on issues like immigration and social welfare policies.

Ottati argues that a distinctly Calvinist view of human societies "recognizes that, even as they pursue their legitimate callings, politicians, lawyers, professors, business persons, and the rest will be implicated in the injustices and corruptions that mar all human societies."[10] While all human institutions, the church included, are in need of repentance and reform, Reformed theologies descended from Calvin also confidently affirm "the divine provision for justice and for good."[11] Calvin contends that theological voices belong in the public discourse if for no other reason than to ensure that the fundamental Christian obligation of compassion toward those in need is adequately carried out. For Calvin, and those churches influenced by Calvin, the establishment of a just social order is integral to the Christian life. The call to minister to the poor, the sick, the widow, the orphan, the refugee, and the prisoner (Matt. 25:34–40) is a matter of concern for both church and state because it is first and foremost a spiritual command for all Christians to "take as strong a stand against evil as we can. This command is given to everyone not only to princes, magistrates, and officers of justice, but to all private persons as well."[12]

In this regard, Calvin's public-facing theology has much in common with late twentieth-century theologies of liberation. For Latin America's poor, survival is a daily struggle, material poverty equals death, and death is contrary to the revealed Word of God. The radical disjunction between the God of life who brings good news of salvation (Isa. 61:1; Luke 4:18–19) and the crushing political realities in which the vast "majorities are dispossessed and therefore compelled to live as strangers in their own land" has created a situation in which even "the men and women who try to side with the dispossessed and bear witness to God in Latin America

---

9. John Calvin, *Institutes of the Christian Religion*, ed. John T. McNeill, trans. Ford Lewis Battles, 2 vols. (Louisville: Westminster John Knox, 1960), 4.20.3, 4.20.6. While I am committed to using gender-inclusive language throughout this work, all quotations reflect the culturally and historically bound perspectives of the original authors.

10. Ottati, "Conversations about Justice," 451.

11. Ottati, "Conversations about Justice," 451.

12. John Calvin, *Sermons on 2 Samuel: Chapters 1–13*, trans. Douglas Kelly (Carlisle, PA: Banner of Truth, 1992), 419.

must accept the bitter fact that they will inevitably be suspect."[13] Critical of mainline Protestantism's middle-class comfort, liberation theologian Rubem Alves reminds Christian believers that the Holy Spirit chooses to live and inhabit the most humble of places: "God loves the whole world. But God clearly shows a partiality to those who are suffering. Jesus declares himself present in the prisoner, but is silent about the imprisoners. He says he suffers with the hungry, but has no joy with those who are overstuffed with food. It appears that things are hard for the rich and powerful from the perspective of the Kingdom of God. What do you think about this?"[14] In the context of a repressive military dictatorship backed by the Brazilian Presbyterian church, Alves gave voice to the powerless and marginalized by articulating a neo-Calvinist theology informed by the work of twentieth-century Reformed theologian Karl Barth, in the process becoming the first theologian to employ the term *theology of liberation* in print.[15]

In apartheid South Africa, where Calvinism "[sowed] only the seeds of death" and came to embody White supremacy, Black South Africans still managed to scrutinize it to identify "those aspects of Calvin's theology which [could] contribute to the Black liberation struggle."[16] Reformed theologian Allan Boesak, who became the moderator of the Dutch Reformed Mission Church in South Africa, played a prominent role in the church struggle against apartheid. While not an international celebrity on the level of Anglican archbishop Desmond Tutu, Boesak was the main theological voice behind the Belhar Confession (1982), arguably the most

13. Gustavo Gutiérrez, *We Drink from Our Own Wells: The Spiritual Journey of a People*, trans. Matthew J. O'Connell, 20th anniversary ed. (Maryknoll, NY: Orbis Books, 2003), 11, 12.

14. Rubem Alves, *I Believe in the Resurrection of the Body* (Philadelphia: Fortress, 1986), 56–57.

15. See his 1968 doctoral dissertation for Princeton Theological Seminary, "Towards a Theology of Liberation: An Exploration of the Encounter between the Languages of Humanistic Messianism and Messianic Humanism," published, with a foreword by Harvey Cox, as *A Theology of Human Hope* (Meinrad, IN: Abbey Press, 1969). The press changed the title in an effort to link Alves's book to the hugely popular and influential book by Jürgen Moltmann, *Theology of Hope: On the Ground and the Implications of a Christian Eschatology* (New York: Harper & Row, 1967).

16. Lebakeng Ramotshabi Lekula Ntoane, *A Cry for Life: An Interpretation of "Calvinism" and Calvin* (Kampen: Kok, 1983), 252, quoted in Robert Vosloo, "Calvin and Anti-Apartheid Memory in the Dutch Reformed Family of Churches in South Africa," in *Sober, Strict, and Scriptural: Collective Memories of John Calvin, 1800–2000*, ed. Johan de Niet, Herman Paul, and Bart Wallet (Leiden: Brill, 2009), 237.

important ecclesial statement to emerge from within the Reformed family of churches since the sixteenth-century Reformation.

The Belhar Confession is a crucial text for the reception of Calvin as an anti-apartheid ally in the political struggle against injustice in South Africa. Reflecting on the goals of Belhar, Boesak describes his strategy to employ Calvin against pro-apartheid Calvinists by appealing to Calvin's eucharistic theology, which emphasizes the unity of the church and thereby exposes the heretical nature of apartheid: "Belhar understood Calvin as he spoke of Holy Communion. 'Christ has only one body of which he makes us all partakers.'"[17] While Boesak acknowledges that, at the time, Black South Africans had no desire to unite with White South Africans—who had exploited, tortured, and killed so many of them—Christ calls all believers to justice *and* reconciliation: "So against our self-absorbed instinct for self-absorbed victimhood, the black church confessed God as a God who wants to bring forth peace and justice in the world."[18] Accordingly, despite its unbending insistence on justice, accountability, and restorative justice in South Africa, Boesak affirms that Belhar is "a unifying document" that "stirs us, humbles us, and inspires us."[19] And much like Calvin's 1536 letter to Francis I of France, in which he undermines kingly sovereignty by subjugating it to divine authority, the Belhar Confession challenges the church to follow Christ in all things, "even though the authorities and human laws might forbid them and punishment and suffering be the consequence."[20]

Calvin was arguably the most influential of the sixteenth-century reformers; his theological legacy transcended confessional boundaries to influence the formation of the modern secularized world, its worldview, and its social institutions. This book documents diverse historical narratives that present Calvin and his impact on Christianity's story as complex, compelling, and, yes, sometimes troubling. The primary goal is to affirm Calvin's contemporary relevance while recognizing that, like all thinkers, he remains a product of his times. Exploring Calvin's global impact

17. Gregg Brekke, "Allan Boesak Commends Belhar Confession," Presbyterian Church (USA), June 23, 2016, https://www.pcusa.org/news/2016/6/23/allan-boesak-commends-belhar-confession/.

18. Brekke, "Allan Boesak."

19. Brekke, "Allan Boesak."

20. "Confession of Belhar," in *Book of Confessions*, part 1 of *The Constitution of the Presbyterian Church (U.S.A.)* (Louisville: Office of the General Assembly, 2016), 305.

by examining his views on a broad range of topics, including political theology, migration and dislocation, nationalism, social welfare policies, political resistance and revolution, racism, and religious pluralism, these chapters provide a robust introduction to Calvin that engages his biography in ways that model how church history must attend both to ideals and to concrete contexts to better understand how world-transforming movements emerge. Despite reflecting many of the biases and prejudices of sixteenth-century Christian Europe, Calvin proves a surprisingly cosmopolitan thinker whose theological insights have contributed to the development of Western democratic liberalism and modern conceptions of self and society. In engaging his broad cultural impact, however, these investigations never lose sight of the fact that Calvin remains a religious thinker through and through, whose political, social, and economic thought cannot be understood outside its theological framework.

Without projecting an anachronistic reading of Calvin's thought onto the contemporary conversation, each chapter of the book pursues affinities between Calvin's theology and the pressing issues of the early twenty-first century by analyzing the pressing issues of his day. Chapter 1, "Calvin's Theology of Public Life," examines Calvin's teaching on the roles and responsibilities of the church and the civil government in society, in connection with *Institutes*, book 4, chapter 20, "Civil Government." Chapter 2, "Calvin, Proto-liberationist?," considers the possibility of political resistance and revolution in conversation with Calvin's sermons on 2 Samuel. Chapter 3, "The Undocumented Calvin," examines Calvin's theology of exile as articulated in his commentary on the Psalms, specifically Psalm 137 on the Babylonian captivity, and the *Institutes*' "Prefatory Address to His Most Christian Majesty, the Most Mighty and Illustrious Monarch, Francis, King of the French." Chapter 4, "Calvin's Vision for an Ecumenical and Transnational Church," explores his belief that the church should be free from the authority of the state in its decisions to administer church discipline through a reading of the Ecclesiastical Ordinances of 1541. Chapter 5, "The Cosmopolitan Calvin and Religious Intolerance," engages Calvin's controversial plea for the rights of Turks and Saracens in chapter 2 of the 1536 *Institutes* as a window for examining religious tolerance in sixteenth-century Reformation Europe. Chapter 6, "A Scattered Inheritance—Calvin's Reception in Latin America," explores the impact of Calvin's 1538 catechism on Puritan evangelist Cotton Mather, who in turn wrote his Spanish-language catechism (1699) as part of a concerted effort to spread Calvinist dogma in Latin America. Finally, chapter 7, "Calvin against Apartheid Calvinism," pairs Calvin's "Short Treatise on the Lord's Supper" (1541) with an analysis of the impact his communion theology had on the Black liberationist movement in South Africa.

In an effort to correct many of the misconceptions about Calvin perpetuated by an inadequate knowledge of his works, each chapter ends with a "For Further Reading" section offering a selection (or selections) from Calvin's oeuvre pertaining to the themes featured in that chapter. There is no substitute for consulting these works directly and reading them in full, so I highly encourage the reader to do so.

Public life in the early twenty-first century is plagued by the phenomenon known as cancel culture, where those judged to be speaking or acting in ways contrary to popular opinion are ostracized, boycotted, and even shunned. This has had a chilling effect on public discourse. Celebrities, politicians, and other public figures have been "canceled" and had their careers derailed—in some cases even destroyed. Cancel culture has greatly affected higher education too, prompting a widespread reconsideration of the literary canon, with many asking why figures like Calvin, who burned a heretic at the stake, or Thomas Jefferson, a slave owner, merit inclusion. By engaging Calvin's distinctive biography as a refugee and exile alongside his voluminous published works, this book makes the case that every generation has its share of problems and moral blind spots. Rather than simply "canceling" those ideas or views that offend us, we ought to approach our encounter with troublesome historical figures like Calvin as an opportunity for self-reflection and personal edification, helping uncover and scrutinize our own personal and cultural shortcomings. Calvin's rigid orthodoxy and authoritarian tendencies do not negate all his teaching but merely demonstrate how he—like people in all times and places—got some things seriously wrong amid the many things he got right.

The theology of sin and grace articulated by Calvin is grounded in the New Testament teachings of the apostle Paul, which emphasize that, as human beings, we are each *simul iustus et peccator* (at once righteous and sinner). By taking a careful contextual approach to encountering the past, we come to the realization that in every generation there are those who invoke the name of Christ whose own lives and actions fall far short of the Christian ideal. The problem with canceling problematic figures from the past is that we risk getting rid of all they got right. Instead of canceling Calvin outright, this book advocates risking personal offense by undertaking a serious encounter with his thought, for in seeing how past Christians like Calvin sought to answer the pressing questions and attend to the social problems of their day and age, we just might find answers to the questions and problems we face today.

Calvin's Theology of Public Life

The reason why we ought to be subject to magistrates is because they are constituted by God's ordination. For since it pleases God thus to govern the world, . . . to despise the providence of him who is the founder of civil power, is to carry on war with him.

—John Calvin[1]

The Reformed tradition, a diverse body emerging from the sixteenth-century union of Zwinglians and Calvinists, affirms and maintains the church's social responsibility for the common good as integral to its spiritual mission.[2] Though Calvinism is often identified with middle-class

This chapter draws on, revises, and greatly expands material from two of my previously published works: "John Calvin," in *Beyond the Pale: Reading Theology from the Margins*, ed. Miguel A. De La Torre and Stacey Floyd-Thomas, 71–78 (Louisville: Westminster John Knox, 2011); and "Becoming a Church for the Poor: Toward a Reformed Spirituality of Liberation," *KOINONIA* 13, no. 2 (Fall 2001): 152–84. Both used with permission.

    1. John Calvin, *Calvin's Commentaries*, trans. Calvin Translation Society, 23 vols., 500th anniversary ed. (Grand Rapids: Baker Books, 2009), 19:478–79 (Rom. 13:1).

    2. For a general history of the Reformed/Calvinist theological tradition from its sixteenth-century origins to the height of scholastic orthodoxy, see John T. McNeill, *The History and Character of Calvinism* (New York: Oxford University Press, 1954); and Philip Benedict, *Christ's Churches Purely Reformed: A Social History of Calvinism* (New Haven: Yale University Press,

comfort and the political status quo, the theology of John Calvin provides a useful model for engaging contemporary political realities with a mind toward building the common good. While in the twenty-first century Calvin represents a diachronically distant and alien worldview, in which the work of civil government is seen as advancing God's unfolding plan for salvation, a viable political theology for our more secular age can emerge from an encounter with his theology and pastoral praxis.

Without minimizing criticisms of the Reformed tradition's more repressive tendencies, this chapter argues that meaningful engagement with John Calvin's writings on civil government, his prophetic preaching, and his pastoral work with the poor and the victims of political persecution demands a sober reconsideration of Calvin's thought and its impact on Western culture today. Granted, there are those who point to the intrusive character of Calvin's Ecclesiastical Ordinances (1541) on personal freedoms to argue that the Reformed theological tradition suffers from two major failings: it barely tolerates opposing viewpoints, and it imposes its worldview on others.[3] Still, considering that Calvin's theology was conceived in exile and that he did not balk at confronting the social problems facing sixteenth-century Geneva—from population dislocation, to urban poverty, to public-health crises—a critical retrieval of his public thought is both timely and beneficial.

The Biblical Foundations of Governance

As William Bouwsma contends in his biographical study of Calvin, secular historians and political scientists have largely ignored Calvin's influence in the development of modern law, politics, and church-state relations.[4] The hesitation of secular scholars to engage his thought most likely stems

---

2002). For an examination of Calvinist social ethics, see John H. Leith, *John Calvin's Doctrine of the Christian Life* (Louisville: Westminster John Knox, 1989); and W. Fred Graham, *The Constructive Revolutionary: John Calvin and His Socio-economic Impact* (Richmond, VA: John Knox, 1971). For an introduction to Calvin's impact on the legal and political realms, see Douglas F. Kelly, *The Emergence of Liberty in the Modern World: The Influence of Calvin on Five Governments from the 16th through the 18th Centuries* (Phillipsburg, NJ: P&R, 1992).

3. Mark K. Taylor, "Immanental and Prophetic: Shaping Reformed Theology for Late Twentieth-Century Struggle," in *Christian Ethics in Ecumenical Context: Theology, Culture, and Politics in Dialogue*, ed. Shin Chiba, George R. Hunsberger, and Lester Edwin J. Ruiz (Grand Rapids: Eerdmans, 1995), 154.

4. See William J. Bouwsma, *John Calvin: A Sixteenth-Century Portrait* (New York: Oxford University Press, 1988), 1.

from the fact that anything Calvin says on any matter of importance is always filtered through the lens of Sacred Scripture. Therefore, it is vital that we identify certain foundational assumptions presupposed by Calvin's theological project. While social and economic themes are interwoven throughout his theological corpus, his teachings on social and economic life proceed from a core belief in God as Creator and Redeemer. Calvin also writes for readers who are themselves believers. Consequently, his works ought to be read primarily as instruction and exhortation to believers—employing his language, the elect (to the degree that election is humanly ascertainable)—who share similar views of God and divine providence. Chief among Calvin's theological assumptions is the axiomatic belief that God is good and just; therefore, whatever God wills is, by definition, both good and just. Calvin's doctrine of divine providence affirms that all events are governed by divine edict.[5] Accordingly, the Calvinist view of God is not that of a Creator who sits idly by, content to observe the creation, but that of a God who is an interested participant involved in every aspect of the natural order and every detail of human history. In other words, God truly "directs everything by his incomprehensible wisdom and disposes it to his own end."[6]

Given the underlying assumption that whatever is is God's good will (since God is necessarily good and just), Calvin is constrained by an apparent contradiction: Does ascribing everything to God negate human freedom and responsibility? How then do we account for the reality of evil and innocent suffering in the world? The doctrine of providence burdens believers with accepting that what appears evil from a human perspective is, from God's perspective, in fact good. Yet Calvin does not posit providence as a foundational guiding principle. Rather, he reaches this conclusion because election is a reality first encountered in the Bible. Therefore, Calvin's belief in providence is a practical truth arising from his reading of Scripture, which leads readers to the chief axiom for understanding Calvin's works: his appeal to the Bible as the absolute determiner of human social behavior. Consequently, Calvinists became distinguished by their fervor to "[apply] the Bible to everything. They attempted to shape civil law, secular jurisprudence, politics, national policy, domestic affairs such

5. See John Calvin, *Institutes of the Christian Religion*, ed. John T. McNeill, trans. Ford Lewis Battles, 2 vols. (Louisville: Westminster John Knox, 1960), 1.16.3.
    6. Calvin, *Institutes*, 1.16.4.

as marriage and divorce, and economic matters such as personal consumption and commercial exchange to the Old and New Testaments."[7]

Calvin stands within the tradition of Renaissance humanism insofar as he valued the study of classical sources, especially the study of Latin and Greek, to better understand the Bible. The motto of this first wave of humanism, *ad fontes* (to the sources), implies an abiding trust in the authority of ancient sources, and before Calvin embarked on his theological career, his first published work was a commentary on Seneca's *De Clementia* (ca. 55 CE), a short treatise offering political advice to rulers while differentiating between a good king and a tyrant. Renaissance humanists like Erasmus of Rotterdam shared with Protestant reformers like Luther and Calvin the desire to create an educated citizenry capable of engaging in civic life while persuading others to virtuous and prudent action. Over against the complexity and seeming irrelevance of medieval Scholastic theology (captured in the often-cited debate about how many angels can dance on the head of a pin), humanists like Erasmus praised the New Testament for its simplicity and moral clarity in guiding and shaping the common good. While Calvin, like all humanists, trusted the human capacity for knowledge, he was also apprehensive about the human tendency toward sin and disobedience. Accordingly, while the *Institutes of the Christian Religion* begins with a proclamation of humanity's unique place in God's creation—"Nearly all the wisdom we possess, that is to say, true and sound wisdom, consist of two parts: the knowledge of God and the knowledge of ourselves"[8]—it also concludes, "Man never achieves clear knowledge of himself unless he has first looked upon God's face, and then descends from contemplating him to scrutinize himself."[9]

This knowledge is received from God through the power of the Holy Spirit, who confirms in believers' hearts that Jesus Christ is Savior and that no one can know God properly without first coming to God through Christ. In Christ, believers can trust that God reigns over all—including the temporal realm—for even evil is under God's providential control, and therefore they can set aside all undue anxiety when confronted by

---

7. Mark Valeri, "Calvin and the Social Order in Early America: Moral Ideals and Transatlantic Empire," in *John Calvin's American Legacy*, ed. Thomas J. Davis (Oxford: Oxford University Press, 2010), 22.

8. Calvin, *Institutes*, 1.1.1.

9. Calvin, *Institutes*, 1.1.2.

suffering and evil in the world, as evidenced by Calvin's exhortation to display gratitude, patience, and trust in the benevolent unfolding of divine providence.[10] While Calvin grants the possibility of knowledge of God and the world *independent* of divine revelation, knowledge of God derived from nature is distorted by original sin, which is why for him true and reliable knowledge of God is found *only* in the Scriptures. In other words, the Calvinist stance is that we need God "to take away all cause for enmity and to reconcile us utterly to himself."[11] In Scripture, we encounter the divine visage; and through the inward action of God's Holy Spirit, we receive salvific knowledge of God: "Just as old or bleary-eyed men and those with weak vision, if you thrust before them a most beautiful volume, even if they recognize it to be some sort of writing, yet can scarcely construe two words, but with the aid of spectacles will begin to read distinctly; so Scripture, gathering up the otherwise confused knowledge of God in our minds, having dispersed our dullness, clearly shows us the true God."[12] If, as the Scriptures disclose, the Word of God is revealed by preaching, by implication it must be the case that the Word is still heard this same way today, mediated through human words in the church's proclamation.

Many factors shaped Calvin's theology—social, political, and cultural— but his approach is accurately described as "biblical" insofar as he attempts a faithful exegesis of the whole of Scripture in articulating a normative social ethics. Accordingly, when Calvin's practical theology focuses on matters of social justice and economic equity, it is because these themes are contained within and deemed essential to the biblical message. Critics who argue that liberation theology is imposing a Marxist analysis onto the biblical text ought to read Calvin's extensive commentary on Psalm 82:3–4:

> Give justice to the weak and the orphan;
> > maintain the right of the lowly and the destitute.
> Rescue the weak and the needy;
> > deliver them from the hand of the wicked.

This passage and Calvin's commentary on these verses resonate with the preferential option for the poor.

10. See Calvin, *Institutes*, 1.17.7.
11. Calvin, *Institutes*, 2.16.3.
12. Calvin, *Institutes*, 1.6.1.

We are here briefly taught that a just and well-regulated government will be distinguished for maintaining the rights of the poor and afflicted. By the figure synecdoche, one part of equitable administration is put for the whole; for it cannot be doubted that rulers are bound to observe justice towards all men without distinction. But the prophet, with much propriety, represents them as appointed to be the defenders of the miserable and the oppressed. . . . The end, therefore, for which judges bear the sword is to restrain the wicked, and thus to prevent violence from prevailing among men, who are so much disposed to become disorderly and outrageous. . . . From these remarks, it is very obvious why the cause of the poor and needy is here chiefly commended to rulers; for those who are exposed as easy prey to the cruelty and wrongs of the rich have no less need of the assistance and protection of magistrates than the sick have of the aid of the physician. Were the truth deeply fixed in the minds of kings and other judges, that they are appointed to be the guardians of the poor, and that a special part of this duty lies in resisting the wrongs which are done to them, and in repressing all unrighteous violence, perfect righteousness would become triumphant through the whole world.[13]

While there are crucial differences between liberation theology and Calvin's biblical ideal of "perfect righteousness," there can be no doubt that, according to Calvin, civil government exists to maintain social justice and that those appointed to govern have the specific responsibility to advocate for the poor and powerless over against the rich and powerful who might— and often do—exploit them.

Calvin's teaching on divine providence, especially the doctrine of double predestination, has been criticized for contributing to moral passivity, even outright fatalism, by engendering tolerance and acceptance of unjust social realities. Some of these criticisms are warranted. Calvin was not a political revolutionary. In fact, he repeatedly impresses upon Christians the duty of obedience to God's duly appointed magistrates, a position warranted by his reading of Romans 13:1: "Let every person be subject to the governing authorities; for there is no authority except from God, and those authorities that exist have been instituted by God." Not only does this passage skew Calvin as a social conservative; elsewhere in his writings he goes so far as to demand submission to even the most ty-

13. Calvin, *Commentaries*, 5:332 (Ps. 82:3).

rannical of governments, cautioning the victims of political persecution that "if the correction of unbridled despotism is the Lord's to avenge, let us not at once think that it is entrusted to us, whom no command has been given except to obey and suffer."[14] According to Calvin's vision of civil governance, the governed have neither the duty nor the power to topple tyrants. They are instructed—when under despotic rule—simply to pray.[15]

Calvin on Civil Government

Calvin's counsel to the victims of political oppression—patience and prayer—at crucial moments in history entails the passive acceptance of unjust situations. Nevertheless, before we dismiss Calvin as a resource for articulating a contemporary political theology, we should try to gain a better understanding of the historical context in which he gave this advice. Calvin's cautionary words reflect conditions in France in 1535, when he was writing the first edition of the *Institutes of the Christian Religion* (1536), a time when Protestants were being "cruelly tormented by a savage prince," "greedily despoiled by one who is avaricious," and "vexed for piety's sake by one who is impious and sacrilegious."[16] Consequently, Ford Lewis Battles, who translated the 1536 edition of the *Institutes* into English, suggests reading the entire text—not just the prefatory letter addressed to Francis I of France—as a political treatise: "Taken as a whole, this letter and the theological essay that follows, especially the final chapter ['Christian Freedom, Ecclesiastical Power, and Political Administration'], are a literary whole and hold up to Francis a model of the Christian monarch."[17]

The political circumstances underlying Calvin's authorship help contextualize and explicate his comments on civil government. These words imploring the victims of Francis's persecutions to endure their suffering while praying for divine deliverance from human cruelty are not a justification for moral passivity. Rather, they are practical advice offered to powerless "subjects" motivated by Calvin's pastoral concern for the politically

14. Calvin, *Institutes*, 4.20.31.
15. See Calvin, *Institutes*, 4.20.29.
16. Calvin, *Institutes*, 4.20.29.
17. Ford Lewis Battles, introduction to *Institutes of the Christian Religion, 1536 Edition*, by John Calvin, trans. Ford Lewis Battles (Grand Rapids: Eerdmans, 1975), xxi.

disenfranchised Protestants of France living under the absolute authority of a monarch who—despite political alliances with the Protestant princes of Germany against his rival, Charles V, Holy Roman emperor and arch- duke of Austria—persecuted the Reformed churches of France as doctrin- ally heretical and politically subversive. By 1525, fewer than a dozen cities in France had held heresy trials, but by 1540 every region in France had conducted them, and the number of trials continued to increase every decade through 1560. In fact, the intensification of public persecution of French Protestants in the 1540s prompted the first of several waves of Hu- guenot refugees fleeing to Geneva at a time when Calvin's published works were consistently the most cited in the French index of prohibited books.[18] Given that the quashing of the Peasants' Revolt in Germany (1524–25), Europe's largest democratic uprising prior to the French Revolution of 1789, loomed large in the collective memory,[19] Calvin's advice to the Prot- estant subjects of Francis I makes perfect sense. It is universally agreed that Martin Luther's condemnation of the uprising contributed to its defeat and not surprising that many veterans of the Great Peasants' Revolt even- tually became leading figures in the more radical Anabaptist movement.[20] Furthermore, it is important to recall that Calvin wrote this advice while in exile, having fled France for fear of being executed for heresy.

On October 18, 1534, in a number of French cities, members of the Protestant minority posted copies of a handbill containing crude attacks on the Catholic mass. This "Affair of the Placards," as it came to be known, so angered Francis I (a copy had been posted on the door of his own bed- chamber) that he proclaimed that anyone concealing the person or persons responsible for posting the placards would burn at the stake. Given Calvin's previous connection to Nicolas Cop's All Saints' Day address of 1533, a sermon on the Beatitudes critical of Catholic persecution of "Lutheran" ideas, he fled to Basel to avoid persecution by the authorities.[21] In the

---

18. For an overview and history of the clandestine Reformed churches of France, see Benedict, *Christ's Churches Purely Reformed*, 127–48.

19. By different estimates, from 100,000 to 300,000 poorly armed farmers were slaughtered by the German princes' well-armed (with cavalry and artillery) and well-trained military forces.

20. See Michael G. Baylor, *The German Reformation and the Peasants' War: A Brief History with Documents* (Boston: Bedford/St. Martin's, 2012).

21. See Battles, introduction to *Institutes of the Christian Religion, 1536 Edition*, xvii–xviii, where he cites Calvin's successor in Geneva and later his biographer, Theodore of Beza, at- tributing authorship of Cop's address to Calvin.

aftermath of the placard incident, many Protestants were imprisoned and executed, and the king's attitude toward Protestant subjects became increasingly hostile. Calvin's prefatory letter to Francis I of France, first published in the 1536 edition of the *Institutes* (and included in every subsequent edition), was written as an *apologia* (defense) on behalf of the persecuted French Protestant minority accused of heresy and sedition. Fearful that the "Lutheran" cause would be discredited, especially after the brutal end to the 1535 Anabaptist revolution in Münster,[22] Calvin pleaded with the king for patience and understanding: "So that no one may think we are wrongly complaining of these things, you can be our witness, most noble King, with how many lying slanders it is daily traduced in your presence."[23] Arguing that "falsehoods, subtleties, and slanders" have been spread by the enemies of French evangelicals, Calvin demanded not just toleration but official protection for the French agents of "Lutheran" ecclesial reforms. His goal was to demonstrate to the king that Protestants were law-abiding citizens loyal to the duly appointed magistrates and that their actions (reforming ecclesial worship and sacraments) ought not to be compared to those of political revolutionaries like the Anabaptists of Münster, who wanted to overthrow the yoke of both Catholic and Lutheran civil governments in favor of a polygamous theocracy.[24] King Francis never replied to Calvin's letter, and it is not known whether Francis ever even read it—for what it's worth, the king's policies toward Protestants did not change significantly—but the 1536 letter stands as a clear statement of the Reformed/Calvinist understanding of the relationship between church and state.

In the final chapter of the *Institutes*, much of what Calvin says concerning civil government was written in polemical opposition to either the Anabaptist reformers, who advocated complete withdrawal from the "unregenerate" world, or the Roman Catholic establishment, under which princes were subject to ecclesial authority. In the prefatory letter to Francis, it is the more radical wing of the Reformation that Calvin identifies as undermining France's governing authorities, even as he embraces the

---

22. See Benedict, *Christ's Churches Purely Reformed*, 66–67.

23. Calvin, "Prefatory Address to King Francis I of France," in *Institutes*, 1:30.

24. For a well-balanced history of the Münster rebellion, see Anthony Arthur, *The Tailor-King: The Rise and Fall of the Anabaptist Kingdom of Muenster* (New York: St. Martin's Press, 2011). For a collection of documents from the various leaders associated with the Münster rebellion, see Paul Ham, *New Jerusalem: The Short Life and Terrible Death of Christendom's Most Defiant Sect* (Melbourne: Penguin Random House Australia, 2018).

common Protestant belief in the priesthood of all believers (1 Pet. 2:9), which gave higher status to princes and monarchs over against Rome's ecclesial hierarchy while simultaneously encouraging the leveling of all ranks in civil society. The position of most radical, including Anabaptist, reformers on church and state was encapsulated in the fourth article of the Confession of Schleitheim (1527), written by Michael Sattler: "We have been united concerning the separation that shall take place from the evil and wickedness which the devil has planted in the world. . . . We have no fellowship with them in the confusion of their abominations."[25] Article 6, concerning the state's use of coercive power, explicitly rejects any Christian involvement in civil government, for "it does not befit a Christian to be a magistrate: the rule of the government is according to the flesh, that of the Christian according to the spirit."[26] Calvin was thus quick to distance the French evangelicals from the Anabaptist sects that advocated complete separation from, and even disobedience to, the state: "We are unjustly charged . . . [with] contriving the overthrow of kingdoms—we, from whom not one seditious word was ever heard."[27]

Aside from the argument in the prefatory letter, relevant discussions on civil governance are found in book 3, chapter 19, and book 4, chapter 20, of the 1559 *Institutes*, along with a related conversation in 4.11.1–5 on the power of the keys (Matt. 16:17–19), all of which clearly demarcate ecclesiastical and civil jurisdictions in marked contrast to the Roman Church. *Institutes* 3.19, "Christian Freedom," discusses believers' freedom of conscience, while 4.20, "Civil Government," clearly defines the duties and responsibilities of both magistrates and citizens. While in the 1559 edition these two passages are far apart and appear unrelated, in the 1536 edition they appear together in close proximity, separated only by a small section on ecclesiastical power. Given that the final edition of Calvin's *Institutes* is five times larger than the 1536 edition, it is important to recall the original relationship of these two chapters and resist reading Calvin's discussion of civil government in the closing chapter of the 1559 edition as a mere afterthought. Rather, a careful reader of Calvin's 1559

25. Michael Sattler, "Brotherly Union of a Number of Children of God concerning Seven Articles," in *The Legacy of Michael Sattler*, trans. and ed. John H. Yoder (Scottdale, PA: Herald, 1973), 37–38.
26. Sattler, "Brotherly Union," 40.
27. Calvin, "Prefatory Address to King Francis I of France," in *Institutes*, 1:30.

Institutes locates his comments on responsible citizenship in book 4 *within* the earlier discussion of the Christian life in book 3.

In contrast to that of the Anabaptists, Calvin's theology *must* address the question of civil government because, in his understanding, it is God who establishes the state and defines its jurisdiction and purpose.[28] Given humanity's sinful and fallen state, God has ordered civil government to serve two purposes, both of them ultimately intended to build the common good: "It provides that a public manifestation of religion may exist among Christians, and that humanity may be maintained among men."[29] To this end, temporal governments are granted the power of the sword— that is, the authority to use coercion to enforce their laws. God ordained the secular order (the state) to maintain peace and justice in the world, by force if necessary, while the church operates as the spiritual government, "initiating in us upon earth certain beginnings of the Heavenly Kingdom."[30]

Like Martin Luther (1483–1546), Calvin emphasized God's sovereignty over all of creation while recognizing that God rules in two distinct ways. However, Calvin modified Luther's "two kingdoms" theology by insisting that the church maintain its autonomy over against the state in administering the church's life together, especially when disciplining its members. According to Calvin, Christ himself declares that "there is no disagreement between his kingdom and political government or order."[31] Nevertheless, while a distinction is maintained between the spiritual and temporal realms, they are two aspects of a single "twofold government" in which the spiritual oversees the inner spiritual life while the temporal works for the establishment of a just social order.[32] Thus, unlike with the modern separation of church and state, there is no inherent conflict between the spiritual and temporal realms since they are manifestations of the one divine will. According to Calvin, each realm has clearly demarcated jurisdictions: the state makes and enforces laws that maintain the social order, while the church educates and disciplines its members. Calvin's version of the "two kingdoms" not only provides a contrast to Anabaptist

28. See Calvin, *Institutes*, 4.20.2.
29. Calvin, *Institutes*, 4.20.3.
30. Calvin, *Institutes*, 4.20.2.
31. Calvin, *Commentaries*, 18:209 (John 18:36).
32. See Calvin, *Institutes*, 4.20.1.

sectarianism, but it also opposes the late-medieval view that the church is the highest temporal authority, while still affirming both jurisdictions as religious vocations. For Calvin, who took his vocation as preacher and doctor of the church quite seriously, the vocation of magistrate is also divinely ordained.[33]

The question for Reformed theology in its Calvinist strain is not whether the church has the right to enter the public arena and exert its political influence. Rather, the question is how, and to what end. Governance is a high calling that comes with great responsibility. Calvin repeatedly stresses the duties of rulers toward their subjects even as he remains steadfast about the obedience the governed owe their rightful rulers, no matter how incompetent or cruel.[34] The governed must obey those appointed to rule by God, even if they prove to be tyrants. Conversely, magistrates—even absolute monarchs like King Francis of France—are subject to the teaching and discipline of the church as members of the one body (in a Christian society). Calvin exhorts rulers to remain faithful to God's commands: "To sum up, if they remember that they are vicars of God, they should watch with all care, earnestness, and diligence, to represent themselves to men some image of divine providence, protection, goodness, benevolence, and justice."[35] Civil government exists to exercise its God-given power to "restrain the sinful tendencies of the strong to take advantage of the weak, and to secure a certain measure of social justice in human transactions."[36] Late in his career, Calvin preached a series of sermons on 2 Samuel, in which he offered an interpretation of kingship that challenged the legitimacy of any monarch who hampers or impedes the preaching of the Word of God. Such a king, like Saul in the Old Testament, would be replaced by one who "hears and obeys the prophetic Word."[37] While holding rulers accountable for their stewardship and warning them that God works in human history to topple and replace tyrants, Calvin repeatedly impresses on Christian citizens the duty to obey their appointed leaders

33. See Calvin, *Institutes*, 4.20.2.
34. See Calvin, *Institutes*, 4.20.29.
35. Calvin, *Institutes*, 4.20.6.
36. Guenther H. Hass, *The Concept of Equity in Calvin's Ethics* (Waterloo, ON: Wilfrid Laurier University Press, 1997), 108.
37. David Willis-Watkins, "Calvin's Prophetic Reinterpretation of Kingship," in *Probing the Reformed Tradition: Historical Studies in Honor of Edward A. Dowey, Jr.*, ed. Elsie Anne McKee and Brian G. Armstrong (Louisville: Westminster John Knox, 1989), 125.

as "vice regents" of God, even demanding obedience to tyrannical rulers. Considering the violent times in which he lived and the atrocities committed against the French Protestant minority (Calvin himself was forced to flee France in 1534, never to return), Calvin's often-repeated appeal for subjects to obey even corrupt rulers was clearly motivated by pastoral concern for the well-being of the "little people," the pawns of history consigned to serve as cannon fodder in the machinations of monarchs and nations: "By this, humility will restrain our impatience. Let us then also recall this thought to mind, that it is not for us to remedy such evils; that only this remains, to implore the Lord's help."[38]

The Reception of Calvin's Political Thought

In what is arguably the most influential book written about American politics, *Democracy in America* (1835), Alexis de Tocqueville describes the United States as an experiment in democracy made possible by a certain set of shared values, or family resemblances, uniting the various English colonies since their inception: "From the first, all seem destined to encourage the growth of liberty: not the aristocratic victory of the mother country but bourgeois and democratic liberty, of which history as yet offered no fully developed model."[39] Noting major differences between the primarily profit-driven Jamestown colonists and the more ideologically driven New England settlers, Tocqueville attributes the political differences that came to divide North and South to the introduction of slavery in Virginia: "No sooner was the colony created than slavery was introduced. This capital fact was to exert an immense influence on the character, laws, and entire future of the South."[40] By contrast, Tocqueville contends that the English colonies of the North, while not tone deaf to the importance of trade and mercantilism, were founded on a set of noble principles that provided "the two or three principal ideas which today form the basis of the social theory of the United States."[41] These principles spread to nearby states, and their "influence extended beyond New England's borders . . . like a

---

38. Calvin, *Institutes*, 4.20.29.

39. Alexis de Tocqueville, *Democracy in America*, ed. Olivier Zunz, trans. Arthur Goldhammer (New York: Library of America, 2004), 34.

40. Tocqueville, *Democracy in America*, 35.

41. Tocqueville, *Democracy in America*, 36.

bonfire on a hilltop, which, having spread its warmth to its immediate vicinity, tinges even the distant horizon with its glow."[42]

The settlers of New England appropriately called themselves "pilgrims" because they came to the "New World" in pursuit of religious freedom, not economic gain. In fact, most who settled New England "belonged to the well-to-do classes," having immigrated with their entire families, as opposed to being "adventurers without families," and what "distinguished them most of all from other colonizers was the very purpose of their enterprise."[43] According to Tocqueville, these pilgrims did not come with hopes of "improving their situation or enhancing their wealth" but left the relative comfort of their native lands "in obedience to a purely intellectual need. They braved the inevitable miseries of exile because they wished to ensure the victory of *an idea*."[44] The two ideas central to the New England project, what Tocqueville labels the "spirit of religion" and the "spirit of liberty," found support and approval throughout the English colonies in America. While seemingly contradictory drives, these two "spirits" complemented each other and allowed religious *and* democratic freedom to develop together: "Religion looks upon civil liberty as a noble exercise of man's faculties, and on the world of politics as a realm intended by the Creator for the application of man's intelligence. . . . Liberty looks upon religion as its comrade in battle and victory, as the cradle of its infancy and divine source of its rights. It regards religion as the safeguard of mores, and mores as the guarantee of law and surety for its own duration."[45] Underlying these interrelated ideas in American political thought is John Calvin's understanding of the interrelationship between church and state and its impact on the theologically Reformed settlers of the American colonies, including the Puritans of New England, the Presbyterians of Philadelphia, the Dutch Reformed of New York, and the French Huguenots of Charleston.

It is not coincidental that John Witherspoon, a Presbyterian pastor and president of the College of New Jersey (now Princeton University), joined eleven other Presbyterians in signing the Declaration of Independence and that all of them went on to become leaders in the Continental Congress

---

42. Tocqueville, *Democracy in America*, 36.
43. Tocqueville, *Democracy in America*, 36–37.
44. Tocqueville, *Democracy in America*, 37 (emphasis original).
45. Tocqueville, *Democracy in America*, 49.

during the American Revolution, which King George III's loyalist supporters disparagingly called the "Presbyterian Rebellion."[46] By labeling the American independence movement the Presbyterian Rebellion, English loyalists hoped to undermine the war effort by linking it to a widely disliked group of religious extremists, those anti-monarchists under the influence of Calvin and Calvinism, such as the Presbyterians descended from John Knox (ca. 1514–72) of Scotland. While the term *Presbyterian* was applied widely in the eighteenth century, it was most often used as a synonym for *Calvinist*. And in the English context, Calvinism had become equated with anti-monarchical republicanism: "Calvinists and Calvinism permeated the American colonial milieu, and the king's friends did not wish for this fact to go unnoticed."[47]

After the death of Edward VI in 1553, Mary Tudor ascended to the throne, outlawing Protestantism and reimposing Catholic rule over England and Ireland, forcing John Knox to resign his position as royal chaplain in the Church of England and seek refuge in Geneva. During his absence from Scotland, Knox kept informed of the political events in his homeland, hoping and planning for an eventual return. Following his exile in Calvin's Geneva, he commented, "[Geneva] is the most perfect school of Christ that ever was in the earth since the days of the apostles."[48] Knox's views on the relationship between church and state were inevitably shaped by his time with Calvin. On his return to Scotland after Mary Tudor's death in 1558, Knox led the Protestant Reformation in Scotland with the aid of the Scottish Protestant nobility and eventually founded the Presbyterian Church of Scotland. The movement was labeled a revolution by his opponents because it led to the ousting of the Catholic regent Mary of Guise, who had been governing the country in the name of her young daughter Mary, Queen of Scots. But in essence, Knox, like Calvin, was not calling for an armed rebellion of the masses (as in Münster) but demanding that divinely appointed magistrates carry out their duty to maintain right doctrine in the face of apostasy: "But now, shall some

---

46. See Richard Gardiner, "The Presbyterian Rebellion?," *Journal of the American Revolution*, September 5, 2013, https://allthingsliberty.com/2013/09/presbyterian-rebellion/.

47. See Richard Gardiner, "The Presbyterian Rebellion: An Analysis of the Perception That the American Revolution Was a Presbyterian War" (PhD diss., Marquette University, 2005), 1.

48. John Knox, "Letter XIII (To Mr. Locke)," in *Writings of the Rev. John Knox: Minister of God's Word in Scotland* (London: Religious Tract Society, 1842), 454.

demand, 'What then? Shall we go to and slay all idolaters?' That were the office, dear brethren, of every civil magistrate within his realm. But of you is required only to avoid [the] participation and company of their abominations, as well in body as in soul."[49] Regardless, many in England and Scotland labeled Knox a revolutionary, and for them Presbyterianism became synonymous with political sedition. As historian Richard Gardiner has argued, while the uses of the term *Presbyterian* in eighteenth-century England and America were varied, the same English prejudice against Calvinists was also common in the thirteen colonies. He cites a 1765 letter from Ezra Stiles to Benjamin Franklin about British loyalists' efforts to suppress opposition to the Stamp Act: "The last effort to prevent it was to render it popularly obnoxious by casting it on the Presbyterians."[50] One Methodist clergy writing in England during the American Revolution commented, "The American controversy is closely connected with Christianity in general, and with Protestantism in particular; . . . it is of a *religious* as well as of a civil nature."[51] Whatever the particulars, the widespread understanding was that the American Revolution was a distinctly Protestant—and specifically Calvinist—movement, which in turn inspired the opinion popularized by Tocqueville that the United States is a nation founded on Puritan values.

Despite a creeping cultural secularization, most notable with the rise of the religious "nones" (those who identify as religiously unaffiliated),[52] the United States still has the reputation, disseminated by Tocqueville, of being a predominately Anglo-Protestant nation. In the last decade, mainline Protestantism and evangelicalism have seen massive declines in membership, with one in three young people raised within evangelical homes choosing "no religious affiliation," while over the same decade the Catholic Church has seen its membership remain relatively stable because of immigration from Latin America. Given the historical dominance of

---

49. John Knox, "A Godly Letter of Warning or Admonition to the Faithful in London, Newcastle, and Berwick (1553)," in *The Works of John Knox*, ed. David Laing (Edinburgh: Bannatyne Society, 1848), 3:157.

50. Gardiner, "Presbyterian Rebellion," xvi. The author cites the correspondence in *The Papers of Benjamin Franklin*, ed. Leonard W. Labaree (New Haven: Yale University Press, 1968), 12:333.

51. John Fletcher, *The Works of the Rev. John Fletcher* (New York: Phillips and Hunt, 1883), 4:439.

52. See "The 2020 PRRI Census of American Religion," PRRI, July 8, 2021, https://www.prri.org/research/2020-census-of-american-religion/.

Catholicism in Latin America, dating back to the conquest and colonization by sixteenth-century Iberian (Spanish and Portuguese) monarchs, it is no surprise that today nearly 40 percent of US Catholics are of Latin American or Latinx descent.[53] Probing beneath the surface, we find that while there is a drop in the numbers of registered parish members, in absolute numbers there has been an increase in self-identified Catholics in the United States over the last decade that is almost entirely attributable to Latin American immigration,[54] even as Catholic dioceses in the United States closed over eleven hundred churches.[55] Along with this increased Latin American Catholic presence, the United States has seen an increase in anti-immigrant nativism, much of it targeting immigrants from Latin America. Accordingly, any attempt to measure the impact of Latin American immigration on the increased demographic presence of Latinx people in the United States and how this affects North American Christianity—especially Catholicism—must come to terms with the far-reaching legacy of Samuel Huntington's controversial book *Who Are We? The Challenges to America's National Identity* (2004).

In 1993, Huntington, a Harvard professor and political advisor to multiple presidential administrations, published an essay, "The Clash of Civilizations," that claimed future conflicts would not be driven by economic or ideological differences but would originate in almost unbridgeable cultural differences. While no one could have predicted the events of 9/11, Huntington's claim that one such civilizational clash existed between Islam and the Christian West informed US foreign policy for the next twenty years. A decade later, in 2004, Huntington offered another divisive and equally harmful thesis in *Who Are We?*, arguing that the largest threat to US national identity (and by implication national security) was not radical Islam but Latin American immigration. According to Huntington, American culture is inherently Protestant, so continuing migration from

53. See Jens Manuel Krogstad, Joshua Alvarado, and Besheer Mohamed, "Among U.S. Latinos, Catholicism Continues to Decline but Is Still the Largest Faith," Pew Research Center, April 13, 2023, https://www.pewresearch.org/religion/2023/04/13/among-u-s-latinos-catholicism-continues-to-decline-but-is-still-the-largest-faith/.

54. Lydia Saad, "Catholics' Church Attendance Resumes Downward Slide," Gallup, April 9, 2018, https://news.gallup.com/poll/232226/church-attendance-among-catholics-resumes-downward-slide.aspx.

55. See Claire Giangravé, "Vatican Census: The Catholic Church Is Growing Everywhere—Except Europe," *America: The Jesuit Review*, October 21, 2021, https://www.americamagazine.org/faith/2021/10/21/vatican-census-catholic-church-growing-241696.

predominately Catholic Latin American countries constitutes yet another locus of civilizational clash—one that already threatens Anglo-Protestant culture given the proliferation of mostly undocumented workers from Latin America filling jobs in agriculture, the service industry, and construction. Sadly, this same rhetoric was employed by then presidential candidate Donald Trump in 2016, who rode a wave of White nativist populism into office by labeling Latin American immigrants "rapists," "criminals," and "bad hombres."[56]

In *Who Are We?* Huntington argues that immigrants—especially from Latin America—are undermining the "Anglo-Protestant" creed on which this nation was founded, advancing the demise of the shared identity that defines us as Americans. Not only does Huntington mistakenly reduce US national identity to Anglo-Protestant culture; he also overestimates the influence of Protestantism in today's increasingly secular culture and ignores the demographic reality that by the third generation Latin American immigrants are fully integrated into the dominant culture, no longer learn the Spanish language, and are no more or less likely to choose "no religious affiliation" than any other segment of the US population. The pervasiveness of this Anglo-Protestant narrative is problematic for a variety of reasons.

Previous waves of foreign migration were met with similar prejudice, but unlike the German, Polish, Irish, and Italian immigrants of years past, Huntington contends that Spanish-speaking, Latin American Catholics are adamantly holding on to their cultural identity as Latin American and Catholic and refusing to integrate into the dominant culture. German, Polish, Irish, and Italian immigrants successfully integrated into the dominant culture, yet most retained their Catholic religious identity. This necessitates an exploration as to why this new wave of Catholic immigrants has been particularly singled out by Huntington and nativist policymakers. My suspicion is that what differentiates this wave of Catholic immigration is not linguistic heritage or religious identity but racial prejudice based on observable phenotypical differences.

What Huntington termed the "Hispanic Challenge" has affected domestic and foreign policy in the United States while feeding the rise of

---

56. Janell Ross, "From Mexican Rapists to Bad Hombres, the Trump Campaign in Two Moments," *Washington Post*, October 20, 2016, https://www.washingtonpost.com/news/the-fix /wp/2016/10/20/from-mexican-rapists-to-bad-hombres-the-trump-campaign-in-two-moments/.

Christian nationalism. In 2020, 84 percent of White evangelical Protestants voted for Donald Trump.[57] In the aftermath of the Capitol riot on January 6, 2021, many of these same White evangelical Christians continued to support Trump, fueling "Trump's baseless allegations of widespread voter fraud."[58] For them, Trump is a savior. In the words of presidential advisor Kellyanne Conway, Trump was the "most pro-life president in history,"[59] a belief that proved well-founded, given the recent decision to overturn *Roe v. Wade* by a US Supreme Court that included three Trump-appointed justices.[60] The events witnessed on January 6 confirm what many on the left have worried about for years: there is a push by many loosely connected popular organizations to impose Christian theocracy on the nation. Most alarming, these Christian groups are proclaiming a White racist nationalism in the name of Christ.[61]

Despite a constitutionally mandated separation of church and state that prohibits the establishment of a state religion, the myth that the United States of America is a Christian nation persists. This myth has roots in the nation-building discourse of New England Puritanism. Biblical prophetic imagery undergirded the Puritan narrative of a nation founded on religious freedom after fleeing Anglican persecution,[62] energized the nation building

57. Jennifer Rubin, "Why Are White Evangelicals Embracing an Anti-Democratic Movement? Because They're Panicking," *Washington Post*, July 12, 2021, https://www.washingtonpost.com/opinions/2021/07/12/white-evangelicals-decline-spurs-an-anti-democratic-movement/.

58. Rick Jervis, Marc Ramirez, and Romina Ruiz-Goiriena, "'No Regrets': Evangelicals and Other Faith Leaders Still Support Trump after Deadly US Capitol Attack," *USA Today*, January 12, 2021, https://www.usatoday.com/story/news/nation/2021/01/12/evangelicals-donald-trump-capitol-riot-voter-fraud/6644005002/.

59. Elizabeth Dias, Annie Karni, and Sabrina Tavernise, "Trump Tells Anti-Abortion Marchers, 'Unborn Children Have Never Had a Stronger Defender in the White House,'" *New York Times*, January 24, 2020, https://www.nytimes.com/2020/01/24/us/politics/trump-abortion-march-life.html.

60. Adam Liptak, "In 6-to-3 Ruling, Supreme Court Ends Nearly 50 Years of Abortion Rights," *New York Times*, June 24, 2022, https://www.nytimes.com/2022/06/24/us/roe-wade-overturned-supreme-court.html.

61. Guthrie Graves-Fitzsimmons and Maggie Siddiqi, "Christian Nationalism Is 'Single Biggest Threat' to America's Religious Freedom," interview with Amanda Tyler of the Baptist Joint Committee, Center for American Progress, April 13, 2022, https://www.americanprogress.org/article/christian-nationalism-is-single-biggest-threat-to-americas-religious-freedom/.

62. See John M. Barry, *Roger Williams and the Creation of the American Soul: Church, State, and the Birth of Liberty* (New York: Penguin, 2012); Robert Louis Wilken, *Liberty in the Things of God: The Christian Origins of Religious Freedom* (New Haven: Yale University Press, 2019); and Michael P. Winship and Mark C. Carnes, *The Trial of Anne Hutchinson: Liberty, Law, and Intolerance in Puritan New England* (New York: Norton, 2013).

of the original thirteen colonies while resisting English despotism,[63] and fueled the westward expansion that gave rise to the ideology of Manifest Destiny.[64] In the collective unconscious of US populism, this biblical language became conflated with the American exceptionalism of Ronald Reagan, who successfully borrowed Puritan preacher John Winthrop's "city on a hill" speech for his 1980 election eve address: "I have quoted John Winthrop's words more than once on the campaign trail this year—for I believe that Americans in 1980 are every bit as committed to that vision of a shining 'city on a hill,' as were those long-ago settlers."[65]

This book, while emphasizing the cultural impact of Calvin's theology on the formation of American democracy, refutes the grossly mistaken assumption that Calvin was a proponent of Christian theocracy. As demonstrated above, Calvin defended the division between civil and ecclesial governance, setting clear parameters to limit the encroachment of civil authorities on church governance. Given Calvin's vision of a transnational and ecumenical church, he would have balked at the idea of a national church even as he assumed a central role for the church in society and took for granted that the culture would be predominately Christian. In that regard, he was very much a man of his times.

Nevertheless, despite Calvin's call for obedience to lawfully appointed rulers, there is in his theology such a high demand for justice that in his later writings he articulates a theological argument in favor of lawful opposition to tyrants. Consequently, a strong argument can be made that Calvin would oppose the tyranny of Christian nationalism in the United States—especially its most racist and nativist strains that preserve political power through the marginalization and oppression of minoritized voices—as evidenced by this passage from his *Commentary on the Acts of the Apostles* (published between 1552 and 1554): "For it is tyrannous if

63. See James P. Byrd, *Sacred Scripture, Sacred War: The Bible and the American Revolution* (New York: Oxford University Press, 2013); James Darsey, *The Prophetic Tradition and Radical Rhetoric in America* (New York: New York University Press, 1999); and Nicholas Guyatt, *Providence and the Invention of the United States, 1607–1876* (Cambridge: Cambridge University Press, 2007).

64. See Anders Stephanson, *Manifest Destiny: American Expansion and the Empire of Right* (New York: Hill & Wang, 1995); and Reginald Horsman, *Race and Manifest Destiny: The Origins of American Racial Anglo-Saxonism* (Cambridge, MA: Harvard University Press, 2009).

65. Ronald Reagan, "Election Eve Address 'A Vision for America'" (November 3, 1980), The American Presidency Project, UC Santa Barbara, https://www.presidency.ucsb.edu/documents/election-eve-address-vision-for-america.

any one man appoint or make ministers at his pleasure. Therefore, this is the (most) lawful way, that those be chosen by common voices who are to take upon them any public function in the Church."[66] In the next chapter, I will make the case that Calvin can be read as a proto-liberationist who advocated for the overthrow of illegitimate governments that act contrary to the Word of God and seek to force their citizens to obey the state over against the Creator.

For Further Reading

Calvin, John. "Christian Freedom." In *Institutes of the Christian Religion*, vol. 1, edited by John T. McNeill, translated by Ford Lewis Battles, bk. 3, chap. 19, 833–49. Philadelphia: Westminster John Knox, 1960.

———. "Christian Freedom, Ecclesiastical Power, and Political Administration." In *Institutes of the Christian Religion, 1536 Edition*, translated by Ford Lewis Battles, chap. 6, 176–226. Grand Rapids: Eerdmans, 1975.

———. "Civil Government." In *Institutes of the Christian Religion*, vol. 2, edited by John T. McNeill, translated by Ford Lewis Battles, bk. 4, chap. 20, 1485–521. Philadelphia: Westminster John Knox, 1960.

———. "Epistle Dedicatory to Francis, King of the French." In *Institutes of the Christian Religion, 1536 Edition*, 1–14.

———. "The Jurisdiction of the Church and Its Abuse as Seen in the Papacy." In *Institutes of the Christian Religion*, vol. 2, bk. 4, chap. 11, 1211–29.

———. "Reply by John Calvin to the Letter by Cardinal Sadolet to the Senate and People of Geneva." In *Calvin: Theological Treatises*, edited and translated by J. K. S. Reid, 219–56. Philadelphia: Westminster, 1954.

---

66. Calvin, *Commentaries*, 18:235 (Acts 6:3).

Calvin, Proto-liberationist?

God commandeth us to bear witness of Christ; therefore it is in vain for you to command us to keep silence. . . . We must obey God's ministers and officers if we will obey him. But so soon as rulers do lead us away from the obedience of God, because they strive against God with sacrilegious boldness, their pride must be abated, that God may be above all in authority. Then all smokes of honour vanish away. For God doth not vouchsafe to bestow honourable titles upon men, to the end they may darken his glory.

—John Calvin[1]

When my first book, *Racism and God-Talk: A Latino/a Perspective* (2008), was published, one reviewer noted, "Any text that suggests that John Calvin is a liberation theologian deserves a closer look."[2] And Protestant pastors and theologians in Latin America certainly took an interest in it,

An earlier version of this chapter was previously published as "Calvin or Calvinism: Reclaiming Reformed Theology for the Latin American Context," *Apuntes: Reflexiones teológicas desde el margen hispano* 23, no. 4 (Winter 2003): 124–55. Used with permission.

1. John Calvin, *Calvin's Commentaries*, trans. Calvin Translation Society, 23 vols., 500th anniversary ed. (Grand Rapids: Baker Books, 2009), 18:214–15 (Acts 5:29).

2. John Francis Burke, review of *Racism and God-Talk: A Latino/a Perspective*, by Rubén Rosario Rodríguez, *Politics and Religion* 3, no. 1 (February 19, 2010): 195–97.

as they did in my previous article "Calvin or Calvinism: Reclaiming Reformed Theology for the Latin American Context."[3] But in the mainstream of North American academic theology, my thesis has so far received little notice. Still, I stand by the claim—with some caveats—that John Calvin should be read as a proto–liberation theologian.

One major difference, worth noting from the outset, between liberation theology and Calvin's theology is that while liberation theology seeks to undermine and overthrow hierarchical social orders, Calvin seems to accept a rigid, top-down social hierarchy in which most members of society are called to be obedient subjects while a few (very few!) are called to be benevolent rulers. Furthermore, some liberation theologies have advocated revolutionary violence in overcoming repression, but Calvin offers little practical advice on what to do when the powerless suffer because rulers are unfaithful in their God-appointed duties. Still, it cannot be denied that Calvin placed the needs of the poor and politically vulnerable in sixteenth-century Geneva at the forefront of his efforts at ordering both political and ecclesial life. Consequently, the theological tradition he inspired has distinguished itself through communal practices of hospitality targeting the neighbor in need. Reformed theology today ought not forget that despite the social conservatism associated with Calvinist piety, Calvin never evaded Scripture's demand that believers act for justice at great cost to themselves.

Those critics who seek to keep spiritual matters separate from temporal affairs should recall that upon his return to Geneva after three years in Strasbourg (1538–41), following his earlier expulsion, not only was Calvin invited to write the rules of church governance for the Genevan church (which became the Ecclesiastical Ordinances of 1541), but he was also "responsible for leading the committee to write what would become Geneva's first, postrevolutionary constitution."[4] It says a lot about the council's estimation of Calvin's skills and abilities that—despite strong personal dislike for Calvin, as evidenced by repeated references to him as

---

3. Rosario Rodríguez, "Calvin or Calvinism." In addition to its being revised for this chapter, this article has been reprinted, translated into Spanish and Portuguese, and anthologized multiple times over the years.

4. William Naphy, "Calvin's Church in Geneva: Constructed or Gathered? Local or Foreign? French or Swiss?," in *Calvin and His Influence, 1509–2009*, ed. Irena Backus and Philip Benedict (Oxford: Oxford University Press, 2011), 102.

"that Frenchman" (*ille Gallus*) in the city council minutes in 1541—"this foreigner only recently returned from exile was given so great a role" in the reformation of both the Genevan church and the city's civil government.[5] An analysis of how the Word of God exhorts, judges, and continually reforms public life on behalf of the poor and powerless, primarily through the preaching of the prophets, provides an antidote to the more "repressive" manifestations of the Reformed tradition. But first, a quick introduction to Latin American liberation theology is warranted before comparing it to the theology of political resistance articulated by Calvin.

Understanding Latin American Liberation Theology

Liberation theology is arguably the most influential Christian theological movement of the last fifty years. Its impact has altered the canon of theological education in universities and seminaries, changed the language of authoritative ecclesial statements, and even crossed over into popular culture. Still, despite its global reach, no single event marks the origin of liberation theology. One recurrent narrative is that liberation theology began in Latin America with similar developments percolating throughout the Third World wherever the realities of absolute poverty sharply focused Christian theological reflection on the experiences of oppression, exploitation, and marginalization that give rise to poverty on such a large scale.[6] However, this ignores the independent-yet-conceptually-similar articulation of a Black theology of liberation by James H. Cone in a First World context of Black resistance to White supremacy in the United States.[7] Nevertheless, the 1968 meeting of the Latin American Episcopal Council (CELAM) in Medellín, Colombia, put forward the first magisterial statements employing the language and analysis of liberation theology.[8]

5. Naphy, "Calvin's Church in Geneva," 102.

6. See the agreements and final documents of the UN World Summit for Social Development held in 1995 in Copenhagen: "World Summit for Social Development 1995," United Nations Department of Economic and Social Affairs, https://www.un.org/development/desa/dspd/world-summit-for-social-development-1995.html. *Absolute poverty* is the UN term to describe conditions in which people lack the basic necessities of life (food, shelter, clean water) on a day-to-day basis.

7. See James H. Cone, *Black Theology and Black Power* (New York: Seabury, 1969) and *A Black Theology of Liberation* (Maryknoll, NY: Orbis Books, 1970).

8. The final documents from this council can be found in Alfred T. Hennelly, ed., *Liberation Theology: A Documentary History* (Maryknoll, NY: Orbis Books, 1990), 89–119.

Many view the Medellín council as the first concerted effort by the Latin American bishops to move the church toward a more progressive stance immediately following the epochal changes wrought by the Second Vatican Council (1962–65). The central themes of Medellín were the Latin American reality of absolute poverty, the struggle for peace and justice under regimes of institutionalized violence, and a renewed embrace of the political dimension of faith. The council's work was deeply influenced by the 1963 encyclical statement *Pacem in terris* (Peace on earth) of Pope John XXIII, the statements proceeding from Vatican II, and the 1967 encyclical statement *Populorum progressio* (On the development of peoples) of Pope Paul VI. Among the pastoral conclusions articulated by the bishops in the final documents was a commitment to work together to create conditions that make life "more human" for all by defending "the rights of the poor and oppressed according to the gospel commandment, urging our governments and upper classes to eliminate anything which might destroy social peace: injustice, inertia, venality, insensibility."[9]

This narrative soon unravels for the simple reason that liberation theology did not proceed from official ecclesial statements or originate within academic theology. Rather, it existed as an organic, haphazard, and decentralized movement in a variety of local contexts primarily through lay-led Christian base communities.[10] Not only were the seeds of liberation theology planted in the fertile soil of the ultimately doomed theology of revolution,[11] but the very concept of liberation within Latin America was

9. Hennelly, *Liberation Theology*, 112.

10. See Leonardo Boff, *Ecclesiogenesis: The Base Communities Reinvent the Church*, trans. Robert R. Barr (Maryknoll, NY: Orbis Books, 1986); Andrew Dawson, "The Origins and Character of the Base Ecclesial Community: A Brazilian Perspective," in *The Cambridge Companion to Liberation Theology*, ed. Christopher Rowland, 2nd ed. (Cambridge: Cambridge University Press, 2007); Margaret Hebblethwaite, *Base Communities: An Introduction* (London: Geoffrey Chapman, 1993); John Burdick and Warren Edward Hewitt, eds., *The Church at the Grassroots in Latin America: Perspectives on Thirty Years of Activism* (Westport, CT: Praeger, 2000); and Raimundo C. Barreto, "The Prophet and the Poet: Richard Shaull and the Shaping of Rubem Alves's Liberative Theopoetics," *Religions* 12, no. 4 (2021): 251–64. Christian base communities (Comunidades Eclesiales de Base [CEB]) are lay-led church communities in remote and poor regions of Latin America that lack a permanent clergy presence and rely on lay leadership. This means that at times, against Roman Catholic doctrine, the sacraments are consecrated and distributed by laypersons.

11. A historic moment for what eventually became the theology of liberation took place at the third plenary session during the World Conference on Church and Society held in Geneva on July 14, 1966, when many in the global ecumenical church felt strongly that the "theology of revolution" seemed incommensurate with the nonviolent Christian gospel. In Latin America, two

being articulated in a variety of ways by both Catholic and Protestant thinkers.[12] Consequently, when discussing the impact of Latin American liberation theology on the broader theological conversation, especially in light of the renewed interest in political theology after Auschwitz, it makes sense to narrow the discussion to the contributions of Gustavo Gutiérrez (1928–), widely considered the father of liberation theology, while acknowledging the contributions of other voices. Furthermore, I will argue that the greatest impact made by liberation theology came not from a theologian but from a priest—Óscar Romero of El Salvador— whose three years as archbishop elevated liberation theology onto the world stage and whose four pastoral letters continue to serve as a road map for reimagining the church in a new key, as a church no longer *for* the poor but *of* the poor.

Liberation theology, while born from the same troubled waters as the European political theologies of Johann Baptist Metz, Dorothee Sölle, and Jürgen Moltmann, sought to articulate its own distinct genealogy on the assumption that the Christian tradition is broader and deeper, offer- ing far richer resources than the "soulless subjectivity of Enlightenment

---

key figures in this movement were Presbyterian theologian and missionary Richard Shaull and Roman Catholic priest Camilo Torres. Richard Shaull (1919–2002), a longtime contributor to the journal *Iglesia y sociedad en América Latina* (Church and society in Latin America), was hugely influential in the early Christian base-community movement, impacting both Protestants in Brazil and Catholics in Colombia, but he is best known for articulating the Christian "theology of revolution" so hotly debated in Geneva. See M. Richard Shaull, *Encounter with Revolution* (New York: Association Press, 1955); Angel D. Santiago-Vendrell, *Contextual Theology and Revolutionary Transformation in Latin America: The Missiology of M. Richard Shaull* (Eugene, OR: Wipf & Stock, 2010); and J. M. Lochman, "Ecumenical Theology of Revolution," *Scottish Journal of Theology* 21, no. 2 (June 1968): 170–86. Camilo Torres (1929–66), a folk hero among Latin American revolutionaries, second only to Che Guevara in popular appeal, left the priesthood to become a guerrilla in the Colombian National Liberation Army. A few weeks into his life as a guerrilla, Torres was killed in his first military action. See Camilo Torres, *Revolutionary Priest: The Complete Writings and Messages of Camilo Torres*, ed. John Gerassi (New York: Vintage Books, 1971); and Joe Broderick, *Camilo Torres: A Biography of the Priest-Guerrillero* (New York: Doubleday, 1975).

12. Among first-generation Latin American liberation theologians, Brazilian Presbyterian Rubem Alves is credited with first coining the term *theology of liberation* in his 1968 PhD dissertation for Princeton Theological Seminary, "Toward a Theology of Liberation," two years before Gutiérrez published his landmark book *A Theology of Liberation*. However, that same year Gustavo Gutiérrez gave a talk (unpublished) to a gathering of priests in Chimbote, Peru (July 21–25, 1968), titled "Hacia una teología de la liberación" (Toward a theology of liberation), which greatly impacted what took place at the Medellín conference one month later. Other first-generation voices include Catholics Juan Luis Segundo, Leonardo Boff, and Jon Sobrino, and Protestants José Míguez Bonino and Jorge (George) Pixley.

rationality" for combating the "social ravages of unfettered . . . capitalism."[13]
Upon returning from the "theological grand tour" that included study in
Belgium, France, and Rome (at the time popular wisdom in Latin America
viewed a European education as necessary for the formation of promising
young candidates for ordination), Gustavo Gutiérrez found even the best
of the *nouvelle théologie* ultimately lacking. So he began to articulate
an indigenous theology better suited to address the pastoral needs and
social realities of the church in Latin America. The introduction to the
original edition of *Teología de la liberación* (1971; published in English
as *A Theology of Liberation* in 1973) begins with this simple statement of
intent: "This book is an attempt at reflection, based on the gospel and the
experiences of men and women committed to the process of liberation in
the oppressed and exploited land of Latin America."[14] In the 1960s, the
majority of Christians in Latin America were, for the most part, poor and
struggling for basic subsistence. Yet the church in Latin America operated
under models developed in a First World context where churches were
financially well endowed, resisted change, and ministered to the needs of
the middle and upper classes. In keeping with this precedent, the church
in Latin America became so integrated into the dominant socioeconomic
system that it rarely took stands against its own financial interests, except
when the rights of the church were threatened (the Catholic Church is
one of the largest nongovernmental landowners in Latin America, if not
the largest).[15] This establishment church "moves within the world of the
Enlightenment and is preoccupied with harmonizing faith and reason,
proving the rationality of religious experience, and establishing rational
foundations for their theological affirmations."[16] By contrast, the prophetic urgency among the poor Christians of Latin America reflects their
daily struggle for survival, so that the need to articulate a theology of
liberation—to paraphrase Gutiérrez—proves the oldest, most persistent
challenge facing the church: how to tell the wretched of this world that
God loves them.

13. Gary Dorrien, *Imagining Democratic Socialism: Political Theology, Marxism, and Social
Democracy* (New Haven: Yale University Press, 2019), 3.
14. Gustavo Gutiérrez, *A Theology of Liberation: History, Politics, and Salvation*, trans. and
ed. Sister Caridad Inda and John Eagleson, rev. ed. (Maryknoll, NY: Orbis Books, 1988), xiii.
15. Juan José Tamayo, *Presente y futuro de la teología de la liberación* (Madrid: San Pablo,
1994), 176.
16. Tamayo, *Presente y futuro*, 176 (my trans.).

The church faces an existential decision, and liberation theology insists it must choose sides. Though the phrase "preferential option for the poor" was not officially endorsed by any magisterial document until the third Latin American Episcopal Council, held in Puebla, Mexico, in 1979, Gutiérrez is quick to point out that Medellín contained in its final documents a call for the church to give "preference to the poorest and most needy sectors and to those segregated for any cause whatsoever."[17] Medellín "made clear that poverty expresses solidarity with the oppressed and a protest against oppression," so much so that instead of "talking about the Church of the poor, we must be a poor Church."[18] Accordingly, the Latin American church had to confront the historical reality of a deeply divided church in which fellow Christians were "among the oppressed and persecuted and others among the oppressors and persecutors, some among the tortured and others among the torturers or those who condone torture. This gives rise to a serious and radical confrontation between Christians who suffer from injustice and exploitation and those who benefit from the established order."[19]

The consequent scandal breaches the very union in Christ that makes *ecclesia* (assembly, gathering) possible: "Participation in the Eucharist, for example, as it is celebrated today, appears to many to be an action which . . . becomes an exercise in make-believe."[20] These are shocking words coming from Gutiérrez, a Catholic priest guided by the communion ecclesiology of Vatican II who views the sacrament as a universal invitation, "the efficacious revelation of the call to communion with God and to the unity of all humankind."[21] Yet, when confronted by the historical realities in Latin America, he is driven to conclude, "Without a real commitment against exploitation and alienation and for a society of solidarity and justice, the Eucharistic celebration is an empty action, lacking any genuine endorsement by those who participate in it."[22] Thus, the church has no choice but to divest itself from the centers of political and economic

17. Gutiérrez, *Theology of Liberation*, xxv. Gutiérrez here cites paragraph 9 of the "Document on the Poverty of the Church" from the Medellín conference. See Hennelly, *Liberation Theology*, 114–19.

18. Gutiérrez, *Theology of Liberation*, 70.

19. Gutiérrez, *Theology of Liberation*, 75.

20. Gutiérrez, *Theology of Liberation*, 75.

21. Gutiérrez, *Theology of Liberation*, 146.

22. Gutiérrez, *Theology of Liberation*, 150.

power and put its social capital behind the social transformation of Latin America on the side of the poor and oppressed. Inevitably, "the groups that control economic and political power will not forgive the Church for this."[23]

Gutiérrez challenges the institutional church to make a choice for the poor over against the oppressors and exploiters of the poor, in effect condemning those who unrepentantly continue to profit from this exploitation and keep the poor trapped in certain death, because such oppressors are not genuine followers of Christ. For the church "must make the prophetic denunciation of every dehumanizing situation, which is contrary to fellowship, justice, and liberty. At the same time, it must criticize every sacralization of oppressive structures to which the Church itself might have contributed. Its denunciation must be public, for its position in Latin American society is public."[24] The radical disjunction between the good news of salvation and the crushing political realities "in which the vast Latin American majorities are dispossessed and therefore compelled to live as strangers in their own land" has created a situation in which even "the men and women who try to side with the dispossessed and bear witness to God in Latin America must accept the bitter fact that they will be inevitably suspect."[25]

Regardless, the church and its people must take this risk—enduring suspicion from the poor and oppression and retribution from the rich and powerful—for "only a radical break from the status quo, that is, a profound transformation of the private property system, access to power of the exploited class, and a social revolution . . . would allow for the change to a new society."[26] This risk—a risk that includes the possibility of martyrdom—explains why, when writing the introduction to the revised fifteenth anniversary edition of *A Theology of Liberation*, Gutiérrez came to focus on the assassination of Archbishop Óscar Romero in 1980 as a major turning point for liberation theology:

> This great bishop risked his life in his Sunday homilies . . . and in interventions that responded to First World pressures by continually calling for a

23. Gutiérrez, *Theology of Liberation*, 151.
24. Gutiérrez, *Theology of Liberation*, 153.
25. Gustavo Gutiérrez, *We Drink from Our Own Wells: The Spiritual Journey of a People*, trans. Matthew J. O'Connell, 20th anniversary ed. (Maryknoll, NY: Orbis Books, 2003), 11, 12.
26. Gutiérrez, *Theology of Liberation*, 17.

peace founded on justice. He received several death threats. . . . A month before his own death he said with reference to those in power in his country: "Let them not use violence to silence those of us who are trying to bring about a just distribution of power and wealth in our country." Calmly and courageously he continued: "I speak in the first person because this week I received a warning that I am on the list of those to be eliminated next week. But it is certain no one can kill the voice of justice."

He died—they killed him—for bearing witness to the God of life and to his predilection for the poor and oppressed. It was because he believed in this God that he uttered an anguished, demanding cry to the Salvadoran army: "In the name of God and of this suffering people whose wailing mounts daily to heaven, I ask and beseech you, I order you: stop the repression!" The next evening his blood sealed the covenant he had made with God, with his people, and with his church.[27]

Romero's funeral drew a quarter of a million people to the capital of El Salvador, filling the cathedral and crowding the plaza, with Gutiérrez among those in attendance. As people were leaving the cathedral after Mass, members of the National Guard began firing on the crowd in the plaza, killing numerous civilians and creating a panic that almost crushed the diminutive Gutiérrez, who "made it safely into the cathedral and administered the last rites of the church to a woman who had been shot and was bleeding to death."[28] Romero's death exemplified the political repression so commonplace in Latin America, but it brought the crisis into the international spotlight. Gutiérrez commented in an interview with Archbishop Romero's biographer, James Brockman, SJ, "The most important event since the Puebla conference was the assassination of Archbishop Óscar Romero of San Salvador. I think that his martyrdom . . . [illumines] something [that] has been happening in Latin America that some people refuse to recognize: the fact that many Christians are giving their lives, witnessing unto death to the gospel, to the God of love and the God of the poor."[29]

In many ways, 1979 proved the high point for Latin American liberation theology with the convening of the Third General Conference of the

---

27. Gutiérrez, *Theology of Liberation*, xliii.

28. Robert McAfee Brown, *Gustavo Gutiérrez: An Introduction to Liberation Theology* (Maryknoll, NY: Orbis Books, 1990), 39.

29. James Brockman, SJ, "The Prophetic Role of the Church in Latin America: A Conversation with Gustavo Gutiérrez," *Christian Century*, October 19, 1983, 931–35.

Latin American Episcopate in Puebla de Los Angeles, Mexico. Pope John Paul II, in his first papal visit, convened the Puebla conference on January 28, 1979, and in March 1979 approved its final documents, which employ the language of liberation and God's preferential option for the poor while providing a critical analysis of liberation theology.[30] The bishops' final statement acknowledged the movement's progress and reaffirmed the church's commitment to historical liberation, even if tempered with some degree of compromise: "With its preferential but not exclusive love for the poor, the church present in Medellín was a summons to hope for more Christian and humane goals. . . . This Third Episcopal Conference in Puebla wishes to keep this summons alive and to open up new horizons of hope."[31] If Puebla marked the high point for liberation theology, then the assassination of Archbishop Romero in March 1980, followed soon thereafter by the rape and murder of two Maryknoll sisters, Maura Clarke and Ita Ford, Ursuline sister Dorothy Kazel, and lay missionary Jean Donovan by five members of the Salvadoran National Guard, marked its low point.

The Pastoral Praxis of Archbishop Romero

Following three years of persistent, nonviolent resistance against the right-wing government of El Salvador that was running a covert assassination campaign of its political opponents, Romero pleaded with government forces from the pulpit. The day after commanding Christian soldiers serving in the Salvadoran Army to disobey orders and stop the repression of innocent Salvadorans, Romero was assassinated while celebrating Mass by an off-duty army marksman acting under orders from Major Roberto D'Aubuisson, the acknowledged leader of the right-wing death squads that tortured and killed tens of thousands of civilians before and during the Salvadoran Civil War (1979–92). Presciently, in Romero's last homily, mere moments before the assassin's bullet took his life, he remarked, "Those who out of love for Christ give themselves to the service of others will live, like the grain of wheat that dies, but only apparently. If it did not die, it would remain alone. The harvest comes about because it dies, allowing

30. For the final documents of the Puebla conference, see Hennelly, *Liberation Theology*, 225–58.
31. Hennelly, *Liberation Theology*, 258.

itself to be sacrificed in the earth and destroyed. Only by undoing itself does it produce the harvest."[32]

Archbishop Romero often extolled the virtues of martyrdom from the pulpit, reminding us that "Christ invites us not to fear persecution because, believe me, brothers [and sisters], the one who is committed to the poor has to face the same fate as the poor. In El Salvador we know what it means to share the same fate as the poor: to be among the disappeared, tortured, imprisoned, to turn up as corpses."[33] The persecuted church of El Salvador became a martyr church, as can be gleaned from Romero's weekly descriptions of the atrocities endured by his flock: "It is my duty to collect the mutilated bodies, corpses, and everything else left behind by the persecution of the Church."[34] Their archbishop reminded them that "persecution is necessary for the Church. Do you know why? Because truth is always persecuted."[35] Jon Sobrino, Jesuit priest, theologian, and one-time colleague of Archbishop Romero, reflecting on the political realities of Latin America in which the struggle for human liberation has produced so many martyrs, affirms Romero's assertion that liberation and martyrdom walk hand in hand while questioning whether the persecution has made a "virtue of necessity: 'Since there is no liberation, let us praise martyrdom.'"[36] But Romero preparing the persecuted church for martyrdom, and Ignacio Ellacuría pleading on behalf of the "crucified people" of the Third World,[37] do not entail "abandoning liberation in favor of martyrdom"; rather, they speak to the interconnectedness of both realities—"because liberation is weakened if it is separated from the reality of martyrdom, and the reverse is also true."[38]

32. Óscar Romero, "Last Homily of Archbishop Romero," in *Voice of the Voiceless: The Four Pastoral Letters and Other Statements*, trans. Michael J. Walsh (Maryknoll, NY: Orbis Books, 1985), 191–92.

33. Monseñor Óscar A. Romero, *Su pensamiento*, 8 vols. (San Salvador: Publicaciones pastorales del Arzobispado, 1980–89), 1–2:236 (February 10, 1980). Unless otherwise noted, all passages from Romero's homilies are my own translation.

34. Romero, *Su pensamiento*, 1–2:97 (June 19, 1977).

35. Romero, *Su pensamiento*, 1–2:73 (May 29, 1977).

36. Jon Sobrino, "From a Theology of Liberation Alone to a Theology of Martyrdom," in *Witnesses to the Kingdom: The Martyrs of El Salvador and the Crucified Peoples* (Maryknoll, NY: Orbis Books, 2003), 102.

37. Ignacio Ellacuría, SJ, "The Crucified People," in *Mysterium Liberationis: Fundamental Concepts of Liberation Theology*, ed. Ignacio Ellacuría, SJ, and Jon Sobrino, SJ (Maryknoll, NY: Orbis Books, 1993), 580–603.

38. Sobrino, "Theology of Martyrdom," 103.

For Romero, the struggle of the Salvadoran church had to be interpreted christologically: "Had Christ realized his incarnation today, in 1978, he would be a man thirty years old, a peasant [*campesino*] from Nazareth, looking like any one of the peasants from our surrounding cantons so that the Son of God would be in the flesh and we would not recognize him, he would so resemble us!"[39] By emphasizing an incarnational Christology, Romero is claiming that Jesus Christ is alive in the persecuted church of El Salvador, that he is daily arrested, beaten, and killed: "I am not saying that we postpone the liberation of the people until the afterlife. I am saying that the risen Christ belongs to the present and is the font of liberation and human dignity in history. . . . Christ is Salvadoran for the Salvadorans. Christ is risen, here in El Salvador, for us, to help us realize through the power of the Holy Spirit our proper nature, our proper history, our proper liberty, our proper dignity as Salvadoran people."[40] The church can endure persecution because it participates in the mystical body of Christ, not a mere moral *imitatio Christi*, but a true communion of saints, which is why Romero remained adamant throughout his active struggle against the forces of dehumanization, exploitation, and death that the only truly Christian option is nonviolence. Romero's clarity on the necessity of nonviolence originates with the Christ encountered in the Gospels: "The only violence permissible in the Gospel is that which one allows to be done to oneself, like when Christ allowed himself to be killed. The only legitimate violence is to let oneself be killed. . . . It is easy to kill, especially when one is armed, but how hard it is to allow oneself to be killed for the love of humanity."[41] The majority of El Salvador's progressive Catholics who took part in El Salvador's struggle for human rights and democratic freedoms in the 1970s and 1980s committed themselves to resisting their corrupt government through nonviolence: "They have done so to the end, to death, and without making use of violence."[42]

Óscar Romero's all-too-brief tenure as archbishop of San Salvador will always be remembered for his courageous stance for social justice and eventual martyrdom, but this does not overshadow the fact that Romero was

39. Romero, *Su pensamiento*, 6:38 (December 17, 1978).
40. Romero, *Su pensamiento*, 8:263 (February 24, 1980).
41. Romero, *Su pensamiento*, 7:168 (August 12, 1979).
42. Jon Sobrino, "Our World: Cruelty and Compassion," in *Concilium: Rethinking Martyrdom*, ed. Teresa Okure, Jon Sobrino, and Felix Wilfred (London: SCM, 2003), 18–19.

also one of the most remarkable and successful pastoral leaders in recent memory. Romero lived in an era of growing violence in El Salvador, which, despite his efforts at nonviolent conflict resolution, ultimately escalated into an all-out civil war that lasted until 1992. In the 1970s, El Salvador's executive branch was controlled by the military, and after two fraudulent elections in 1972 and 1976, institutionalized violence became the government's primary means of maintaining power against the proliferation of popular revolutionary movements. Faced with this volatile political reality, in which Christians on both sides of the political spectrum were advocating violence, Romero advocated justice, dialogue, increased democratization, and the redistribution of wealth as guiding virtues for a national conversation he hoped and prayed would result in genuine social transformation.

Employing timely pastoral letters, prophetic sermons from the pulpit, acts of direct intervention, and pioneering legal advocacy, Romero utilized the office of archbishop to bring the church's full resources—not to mention elicit international attention—to the crisis in El Salvador. He left behind a legacy of compassionate humanitarian aid focused on preserving the basic dignity of the victims of unjust social structures, while acting creatively to positively transform those very structures. One of the most unheralded aspects of Romero's ministry was the establishment of the archdiocesan Office of Legal Aid, "made up of lawyers, law students, and consultants who considered that the legal system should be at the service of the very poorest" and who stayed at Romero's side, supporting his vision of "legal help for the very poor" until his death.[43] The Office of Legal Aid not only provided immediate legal help to those most in need; it also developed a system of documenting human rights violations that has become the norm in truth commissions and nongovernmental human rights organizations around the world. Archbishop Romero promoted human rights for all persons without discrimination and worked tirelessly for increased democratization, yet he never bound himself to any single political party or agenda—he was always willing to speak with all sides in the conflict. He acted concretely out of a deep commitment to Christian nonviolence to condemn "any strategy or method based on violence."[44]

43. Roberto Cuéllar, "The Legal Aid Heritage of Oscar Romero," in *Archbishop Romero and Spiritual Leadership in the Modern World*, ed. Robert S. Pelton (Lanham, MD: Lexington Books, 2015), 147.
44. Cuéllar, "Legal Aid Heritage," 151.

Eventually, Romero's fellow bishops wrote to Rome asking that he be removed as archbishop, necessitating he travel to Rome several times to defend himself. But he always acted, wisely and consistently, under the guidance of official church doctrine, as evidenced by his four pastoral letters. At a time when political tensions were on the rise in El Salvador—exacerbated by a proliferation of popular revolutionary movements organizing farmers, laborers, and students against the repressive government—Archbishop Romero published his third pastoral letter, "The Church and Popular Political Organizations" (with help from Jesuit theologian Jon Sobrino), on August 6, 1978. The letter has a straightforward intent: "In this pastoral letter we . . . [want] to restate the right to organize and to denounce the violation of that right in our country."[45] And it deals with two basic questions: What constitutes an authentic Christian response to the antidemocratic repression by the state? And, considering Catholic social teaching, what is the church's relationship to popular political movements advocating for more democratic freedoms for all Salvadorans? Romero answers with moral clarity, pastoral compassion, and unquestioned integrity: "It is here, faced with the absence of this real freedom, that we have to denounce this violation of this human right of association proclaimed by our Constitution and by an international declaration of human rights accepted by our country."[46] He then identifies three abuses perpetrated by the Salvadoran regime: (1) some citizens are granted the right of association, while others are denied it; (2) the elite groups make up a minority of the population yet are granted more freedoms than the majority; and (3) the state has sown disorder and fostered conflict between *campesino* groups in order to prevent them from uniting for social change.

Romero used the office of archbishop to name the false idols plaguing Salvadoran society—materialist greed, unchecked militarism, and antidemocratic political practices—and critiqued any group or agent who impeded democratic reforms that could bring about positive social change. In practical terms, this meant the archbishop was making political enemies on both the right and the left, because while the right-wing government and its capitalist supporters were responsible for the repression and

45. Óscar Romero, "Third Pastoral Letter, The Church and Popular Political Organizations," in *Voice of the Voiceless*, 89–90.
46. Romero, "Third Pastoral Letter," 90.

dehumanization of the Salvadoran people, those political movements on the left that claimed to speak for the people yet refused to abandon violence in order to bring about a genuine national dialogue were also to blame. Romero insisted that an "essential element of this dialogue is that an end be put to all kinds of violence," for "it is absurd to talk about dialogue" until all sides set aside political violence.[47]

Though Romero never advocated violence, he recognized the right of people to defend themselves in situations of political repression, when the state—ideally the guarantor of the people's freedoms—becomes the agent of tyranny and injustice. Therefore, in his fourth pastoral letter, Romero acknowledges the right of self-defense, but only under very unique circumstances. After "every other possible peaceful means has been tried," the Christian tradition allows for a just war in defense of others, insurrectional violence in the case of "prolonged tyranny," and a war of self-defense in response to unjust aggression.[48] However, recognizing the right of oppressed peoples to defend themselves is a far cry from arguing that political violence is a divinely ordained means of social change. Though appealing to just war theory, Archbishop Romero is not legitimizing Christian political violence. Rather, he is advocating for the right of revolutionary political movements to take on the role of guardian of the people's interests to represent them in peaceful negotiations, but *only* when the government has become tyrannical and is persecuting its own people. In other words, it is the breakdown of just governance that gives birth to violent revolutionary movements: "The most reasonable and effective thing for a government to do, therefore, is to use its moral and coercive force not to defend the structural violence of an unjust order, but to guarantee a truly democratic state, one that defends the fundamental rights of all its citizens, based on a just economic order. Only in this way will it be possible to make those instances distant and unreal in which recourse to force, by groups or by individuals, can be justified by the existence of a tyrannical regime and an unjust social order."[49] Here we find a major point of agreement between Latin American liberation theology and Calvin's theology of civil governance: governments do not exist to exercise the power of coercion,

47. Óscar Romero, "Fourth Pastoral Letter, The Church's Mission amid the National Crisis," in *Voice of the Voiceless*, 147.
48. Romero, "Fourth Pastoral Letter," 144–45.
49. Romero, "Fourth Pastoral Letter," 145.

including the power of the sword; rather, governments exist to maintain a stable social order that preserves the basic human rights of its citizens.

Calvin's Emancipatory Theology

Richard Shaull (1919–2002), a Presbyterian theologian and missionary deeply steeped in Calvinist theology, experienced a dramatic encounter with extreme poverty and political repression in Colombia that led to a personal conversion to solidarity with the poor. In turn, Shaull influenced an entire generation of pastors and theologians in Brazil and Colombia. Identifying important similarities between the sixteenth-century reformers and the lay-led liberation movement within primarily Catholic base communities in Latin America, he described the theological revolutions of the 1960s and 1970s in Latin America as a second Reformation.[50] While lauded for his ecumenical leadership, he developed these ideas in ecumenical (Protestant and Catholic) conversation with lay and ordained leaders throughout Central and South America. To his credit, "Shaull did not see himself as the initiator of any movement. On the contrary, for him, the Brazilian situation at the time of his arrival in the country was already ripe for what he would come to offer, and he only played the role of a catalyst."[51] If the Protestant Reformation was a movement of *spiritual* liberation that fostered major social change, including the empowerment of lay Christians and the undermining of monarchy in favor of representative democracy, liberation theology emphasizes concrete *political* liberation in the name of the gospel. Sixteenth-century reformers and Latin American liberationists start in different locations but soon reach common ground. Speaking to those within the Calvinist Reformed tradition, Shaull praised liberation theology for continuing the reformers' commitment to continually reforming church teaching and practice (*ecclesia semper reformanda*), emphasizing the priesthood of all believers (1 Pet. 2), and applying these "Protestant" principles to the historical struggle for human liberation.

Calvin embodies these same principles, and while he repeatedly stresses obedience to rulers and magistrates as "vice regents" of God—to the

---

50. See Richard Shaull, *The Reformation and Liberation Theology: Insights for the Challenges of Today* (Louisville: Westminster John Knox, 1991).

51. Barreto, "The Prophet and the Poet," 257n14.

point of demanding obedience to tyrannical rulers—he shares with liberation theology a commitment to historical struggles for political liberation. Contrary to the prevailing opinion that Calvin is opposed to political revolution, a careful reading of his theology of civil governance finds that he argues in favor of the possibility of Christian resistance to unjust rulers: "But in that obedience which we have shown to be due the authority of rulers, we are always to make this exception, indeed to observe it as primary, that such obedience is never to lead us away from obedience to him [God], to whose will the desires of all kings ought to be subject, to whose decrees all their commands ought to yield, to whose majesty their scepters ought to be submitted. And how absurd would it be that in satisfying men you should incur the displeasure of him for whose sake you obey men themselves!"[52] Is Calvin contradicting himself? He consistently argues that it is not the place of subjects to overthrow tyrannical rulers, yet it seems that he also urges some level of resistance to the state when it acts contrary to the will of God, since we must always "obey God rather than any human authority" (Acts 5:29).

Like Archbishop Romero, Calvin seems to favor Christian nonviolence. So how ought Christians to withstand the rule of impious despots? Given his acceptance of a hierarchical social order, Calvin suggests different options are available to different types of Christians depending on the role they serve in the social order. Early in chapter 20 of book 4 of the *Institutes*, Calvin addresses subjects; then later in the same chapter he acknowledges that God sometimes "raises up open avengers from among his servants, and arms them with his command to punish the wicked government and deliver his people, oppressed in unjust ways, from miserable calamity."[53] Calvin appears conflicted on this matter, desiring a stable social order even at the cost of innocent suffering, while affirming (like the liberationists) that God acts in human history to overcome tyranny. But we see that Calvin is consistent throughout once we recognize he offers different instructions to different persons.

Speaking to private citizens, he warns, "If the correction of unbridled despotism is the Lord's to avenge, let us not at once think that it

----

52. John Calvin, *Institutes of the Christian Religion*, ed. John T. McNeill, trans. Ford Lewis Battles, 2 vols. (Louisville: Westminster John Knox, 1960), 4.20.32.
53. Calvin, *Institutes*, 4.20.30.

is entrusted to us, to whom no command has been given except to obey and suffer."[54] Yet when addressing the lawfully appointed magistrates of the people, Calvin burdens them with the duty of restraining the abuses of tyrannical rulers: "I am so far from forbidding them to withstand, in accordance with their duty, the fierce licentiousness of kings, that, if they wink at kings who violently fall upon and assault the lowly common folk, I declare that their dissimulation involves nefarious perfidy, because they dishonestly betray the freedom of the people, of which they know that they have been appointed protectors by God's ordinance."[55] Calvin urges appointed political leaders to protect the liberties of the subjects entrusted to their care. This controversial passage—calling for political revolution against tyrannical rulers—alongside the explicit warning in the closing paragraph of the *Institutes* that obedience to earthly rulers must not lead to disobeying God, provides the Reformed tradition with the basic tools for political resistance.

While Calvin never condones a people's revolution, he provides a theological foundation for resisting social injustice and political oppression. If most believers are called to be obedient subjects, with patient prayer their only means of political resistance, and a smaller number are set above them as magistrates responsible for the just administration of human society and granted corresponding power by God, then an even smaller number are called to wield the power that stands in judgment of all, the Word of God. According to Calvin, preachers occupy an exalted place in society since from the pulpit they wield great power to guide and transform the life of church and society.

Calvin's understanding of the preaching office begins with his reading of the Old Testament, specifically his reading of the Hebrew prophets who spoke with God's voice and authority: "The word goeth out of the mouth of God in such a manner that it likewise 'goeth out of the mouth' of men; for God does not speak openly from heaven, but employs men as his instruments, that by their agency he may make known his will."[56] In Calvin's estimation, preaching is so vital for the life of the church (and, by implication, the rest of society) that we who hear the Word of God preached "ought to be so much affected by it, whenever he [God] speaks

---

54. Calvin, *Institutes*, 4.20.31.
55. Calvin, *Institutes*, 4.20.31.
56. Calvin, *Commentaries*, 8:172 (Isa. 55:11).

by his servants, as though he were nigh to us, face to face."[57] Accordingly, preaching serves a dual purpose—revealing God's will to humanity and providing believers with an opportunity to demonstrate their obedience to God.[58]

Of course, this understanding of the preaching office presumes an ecclesiology in which we are called to live in community as the one body, nurtured by Mother Church through the preaching of God's Word, in faithful obedience to those placed over us as leaders of the church. While affirming the priesthood of all believers, Calvin also recognizes differing vocations within the body of Christ and emphasizes the importance of preaching. At the same time, he is quick to admonish pastors to keep them humble by reminding them that it is only by an act of the Holy Spirit that the human word becomes the Word of God. Of course, the same can be said for the receptiveness of the hearers of the Word, for "when God separates himself from his ministers, nothing remains in them."[59]

In faith, believers accept it is Christ who speaks through preaching, and they also accept that preaching is how Christ rules the church. Commenting on a line from the prophet Isaiah, "He made my mouth like a sharp sword" (Isa. 49:2), Calvin explains how Christ reigns (and how Christ's kingdom differs from human governments) because he has been "appointed by the Father, not to rule, after the manner of princes . . . but his whole authority consists in doctrine, in the preaching of which he wishes to be sought and acknowledged; for nowhere else will he be found."[60] Through his ministers on earth, Jesus Christ exercises power and authority over the church and the world, but this is not a restoration of medieval Christendom where the church has temporal authority over the state. Rather, "the sword now put into our hand is of another kind, that of the word and spirit."[61] In Calvin's understanding of church and state, the power of the sword is granted by God to temporal governments as an accommodation to human sinfulness in order to maintain some degree of social order, which means this power is not granted to the church, whose domain is spiritual governance: "Since the church does not have the power

57. Calvin, *Commentaries*, 15:343 (Hag. 1:12).
58. See Calvin, *Institutes*, 4.1.5.
59. Calvin, *Commentaries*, 15:630 (Mal. 4:6).
60. Calvin, *Commentaries*, 8:9 (Isa. 49:2).
61. Calvin, *Commentaries*, 6:316 (Ps. 149:9).

to coerce, and ought not to seek it (I am speaking of civil coercion), it is the duty of godly kings and princes to sustain religion by laws, edicts, and judgments."[62]

If Christ's sword is the preaching of the Word and his scepter the gospel, it should be no surprise that the church's preaching was at the center of Calvin's life in Geneva. As a preacher, Calvin had a long and arduous relationship with both the temporal government (city council) and the spiritual government (church consistory), and his relationship with both serves as a model for how the church ought to wield the spiritual sword. We gain some insight from Theodore Beza, Calvin's successor in Geneva: "Besides preaching every day from week to week, usually as often as he could he preached twice every Sunday; he lectured three times a week on theology; he gave remonstrances in the consistory, and delivered as it were an entire lesson in the conference on Scripture that we call a congregation; and he so closely followed this program without interruption until his death that he never failed once during extreme illness."[63] Throughout Calvin's tenure as pastor in Geneva, he faced a power struggle between the council and the consistory over the right to discipline and ban members from the communion. The consistory would ban someone from the sacrament of the Lord's Supper (in an effort to discipline said member of the church to help them in their spiritual growth), then send them to the council for civil punishment. After the person paid a fine, the council assumed they would be readmitted to the communion. Calvin and the other pastors disagreed, insisting that those who had been banned must reappear before the consistory before being readmitted, regardless of the decision reached by the civil court.

Calvin faced great opposition over many matters, from public funding of schools, to the building of a new sewage system during an outbreak of the plague, to the public care of refugees and the poor. And he was often called before the city council over what he preached from the pulpit: "With great choler [he] preached that the magistracy permits many insolences. Ordered that he should be called before the Council in order to know why he has so preached, and that if there is some insolence in the city, the lieutenant should be commanded to look into it and to do

62. Calvin, *Institutes*, 4.11.16.
63. T. Beza, *L'historie de la vie et mort de Calvin* (1565), OC 21, col. 33, quoted in Bernard Cottret, *Calvin: A Biography* (London: Bloomsbury, 2003), 288–89.

justice concerning it."[64] Calvin's struggle to establish the church's independence from the state provides a glimpse into how preaching becomes a means of advocating social reform, even as Calvin concedes the church has certain obligations vis-à-vis the state. First, Christians are encouraged to pray for the civil government and must submit to its *legitimate* authority. Second, the church has a duty to make sure the state defends the poor and powerless against the rich and powerful. Third, the church has a duty to admonish the state when it has failed in its duties or when it acts unjustly.

Calvin never sanctioned open rebellion against the state, although, as has been demonstrated, he outlined a process for the removal of a tyrannical government. One of the things that marks an illegitimate and abusive government, according to Calvin, is its inability to provide for the welfare of its citizens, especially the most vulnerable of its people. The church in Geneva battled usury, unemployment, disease, and economic injustice, often in conflict with the city council. It did so secure in the knowledge that elected officials in public office were members of the body of Christ. As such, they were subject to the teaching and discipline of the church, so in sixteenth-century Geneva there was an expectation that public policies would be scrutinized and criticized from the pulpit: "Oppression utters a sufficiently loud cry of itself; and if the judge, sitting on a high watchtower, seems to take no notice of it, he is here plainly warned, that such connivance shall not escape with impunity."[65]

The prophet Amos's warning to rulers, "Hear this, you who trample on the needy, and bring to ruin the poor of the land. . . . The LORD has sworn by the pride of Jacob: Surely I will never forget any of their deeds" (Amos 8:4, 7),[66] inspires Calvin to write, "But as more guilt belongs always to leaders, this is the reason why the Prophets treated them with more sharpness and severity: for many of the common people go astray through thoughtlessness or ignorances or are led on by others, but they who govern, pervert what is just and right, and then become the originators of all kinds of licentiousness. It is no wonder then that the Lord by

64. John Calvin, "Draft Ecclesiastical Ordinance (1541)," in *John Calvin: Selections from His Writings*, ed. John Dillenberger (Missoula, MT: Scholars Press, 1975), 242n21 (citing the *Registres du Conseil*, May 21, 1548).

65. Calvin, *Commentaries*, 6:332 (Ps. 82:3).

66. This is also a favorite text among Latin American liberation theologians.

his Prophets inveighed so sharply against them."[67] The preacher, as the "mouth of God," is duty bound to speak out publicly against all injustice and to exhort civic leaders to perform their God-ordained tasks with equity and compassion. Calvin demonstrates why he wanted a church free from the control of the state—not to establish and expand ecclesial power but to maintain the purity of doctrine (teaching) needed to preach the Word of God in prophetic criticism of the state. Calvin wielded the spiritual sword with great care, persuading political opponents by the truth and righteousness of God's Word, acting with certainty and assurance that both the state and the church are under the lordship of Christ.

Here, once again, we find much in common with the church reforms taking place in Latin America during the 1960s and 1970s, led by grassroots lay movements and nurtured by the teaching of liberation theologians like Gustavo Gutiérrez. While Calvin does not explicitly speak about liberation in the same way as Gutiérrez, his emphasis on the political rights of the poor and powerless leads to a struggle for equity in all human relations. Both movements—the Protestant Reformation in sixteenth-century Geneva and Latin American liberation theology in the late twentieth century—sought to bring about massive social transformation through the application of pastoral care and catechetical instruction. For both Calvin and Gutiérrez, the local congregation is the nexus of social change by modeling an alternative communal lifestyle that begins locally and then reaches out into the larger society, seeking to transform the world in the image of God.

In a sermon on 2 Samuel 8:9–18, Calvin burdens all believers—not just the people's duly appointed leaders—to "take as strong a stand against evil as we can. This command is given to everyone not only to princes, magistrates, and officers of justice, but to all private persons as well."[68] Calvin reads the prophets through the same lens as Archbishop Romero, understanding the Christian life as a call to suffer persecution for the sake of righteousness even to the point of martyrdom. For Calvin, this suffering even becomes a source of joy, "for we are too ungrateful if we do not willingly and cheerfully undergo these things at the Lord's hand."[69] As we

---

67. Calvin, *Commentaries*, 14:363–64 (Amos 8:4).

68. John Calvin, *Sermons on 2 Samuel: Chapters 1–13*, trans. Douglas Kelly (Carlisle, PA: Banner of Truth, 1992), 419.

69. Calvin, *Institutes*, 3.8.8.

will see in the following chapter, Geneva in the sixteenth century presented Calvin with many opportunities to suffer for the sake of righteousness.

For Further Reading

Calvin, John. "Commentaries on the Epistle of Paul the Apostle to the Romans." In vol. 19 of *Calvin's Commentaries*, translated by Calvin Translation Society, 23 vols., 500th anniversary ed. Grand Rapids: Baker Books, 2009.

——. *God and the Civil Government: Magistrates, Elections, and the Duties of Citizens and Rulers*. Edited and translated by R. A. Sheats. Independently published, 2020.

——. *Sermons on Deuteronomy*. Translated by Arthur Golding. 16th–17th Century Facsimile Editions. London: Banner of Truth, 1987.

——. *Sermons on 2 Samuel: Chapters 1–13*. Translated by Douglas Kelly. Carlisle, PA: Banner of Truth, 1992.

The Undocumented Calvin

Therefore, we have no reason to refuse any who come before us needing our help. If we say that he is a stranger, the Lord has stamped on him a sign that we know [the image of God]. . . . If we allege that he is contemptible and worthless, the Lord responds by showing us that he has honored him by making his own image to shine in him.

—John Calvin[1]

Immigration was a defining feature of the early Reformation.[2] Whether fleeing political persecution, seeking religious freedom, sending missionaries, or welcoming refugees into their midst, sixteenth-century reformers

An earlier version of this chapter was previously published as "Immigrants, Refugees, and Asylum Seekers: The Migratory Beginnings of Reformed Public Theology," in *Reformed Public Theology: A Global Vision for Life in the World*, ed. Matthew Kaemingk, 23–34 (Grand Rapids: Baker Academic, 2021). Used with permission of Baker Academic, a division of Baker Publishing Group.

1. John Calvin, *Calvin's New Testament Commentaries*, vol. 12, *The Epistle of Paul the Apostle to the Hebrews and the First and Second Epistles of St. Peter*, ed. T. F. Torrance (Grand Rapid: Eerdmans, 1994), 204–5.

2. See Mack P. Holt, "International Calvinism," in *John Calvin in Context*, ed. R. Ward Holder (Cambridge: Cambridge University Press, 2020), 375–82.

and their followers were people on the move, constantly interacting with different languages and cultures, crossing political borders, planting churches in new soil, and wrestling with biblical injunctions to provide justice and hospitality for foreigners.

John Calvin's Geneva offers a fascinating case study of a community of faith struggling to make space for newcomers, all the while resisting the temptations of xenophobia and nativist protectionism. The Genevan community was intimately familiar with both ends of the immigrant experience. The city not only welcomed thousands of dislocated refugees from cultures and kingdoms all over Europe; it also sent forth settlers, missionaries, and pastors to nations all over the continent. In reforming the church in Geneva, Calvin sought to build a church that was ecumenical and transnational in scope. Consequently, "Geneva not only welcomed refugees, it created them."[3] The migratory experiences of the early reformers would have a profound impact on the movement's self-understanding. Their spiritual and political responses to these profound experiences of dislocation have a lot to offer twenty-first-century Christians wrestling with the enduring problem of immigration.

Calvin, himself a French political exile, had fled to Basel, then Geneva, then Strasbourg before finally settling in Geneva, where he established a church order that by design enabled the city to become a haven for Protestant refugees fleeing persecution from all over Europe. Throughout his life, Calvin worked tirelessly on behalf of persecuted Protestants, particularly those from his native France (the Huguenots). Their persecution in France would send a massive wave of refugees to Geneva between 1545 and 1555. During this time, the city's cramped geographic borders and limited resources prevented its citizens from permanently welcoming all refugees. The lack of space, combined with a passion for global mission, would inspire several Protestant resettlement missions throughout Europe and beyond. Through it all, Calvin and his fellow reformers fostered a diverse and complex international movement that was migratory, hospitable, transnational, and ecumenical. An enduring message within sixteenth-century Geneva was, quite simply, offer hospitality when you can do so, for soon enough you may find yourself in the role of the migrant in need of hospitality.[4]

3. Carter Lindberg, *The European Reformations* (Oxford: Blackwell, 1996), 249.
4. See Karin Maag, *Seminary or University? The Genevan Academy and Reformed Higher Education, 1560–1620* (Aldershot, UK: Scolar, 1995). Under Calvin, Geneva was heavily involved

Ironically, today in the United States many self-identified Calvinists willingly support anti-immigrant (and often racist) political leaders and cruel immigration policies. These Calvinists will even attempt to use their faith as a tool by which they calmly turn refugees away and ignore the moral horrors being perpetrated on the southern border, justifying their moral and political quietism through a reading of Romans 13:1 that commends submissive acceptance to the laws and leaders whom God has placed in authority. When the Trump administration's zero-tolerance border enforcement policies created holding facilities that became de facto concentration camps, squandered innocent lives,[5] separated children from their parents, and subjected the most vulnerable detainees (women and children) to physical and sexual abuse at the hands of their jailers,[6] Christian silence in the face of such cruelty gave tacit approval to these policies and contributed to the rise in nativist anti-immigrant violence.[7]

This chapter will demonstrate how Christians' moral and political quietism is a tragic betrayal of a long Calvinist legacy of welcoming strangers, resisting tyrants, establishing justice, and reaching across borders and cultures in vulnerability and faith. It will also seek to discredit the common misconception that Calvin was a cold stickler for the rule of law. Instead, the chapter offers a more accurate presentation of Calvin as a humanistic reformer whose ecclesiastical and civil polity wanted "every resident of Geneva integrated into a caring community" and whose church-led ministries were designed to be "real networks of caring."[8] Scottish reformer

---

in mission work—most of it in France—with many of the French pastors serving repatriated Huguenot churches after being trained in Geneva.

5. Cynthia Pompa, "Immigrant Kids Keep Dying in CBP Detention Centers, and DHS Won't Take Accountability," ACLU, June 24, 2019, https://www.aclu.org/blog/immigrants-rights/immigrants-rights-and-detention/immigrant-kids-keep-dying-cbp-detention.

6. See Richard Gonzales, "Sexual Assault of Detained Migrant Children Reported in the Thousands since 2015," NPR, February 26, 2019, https://www.npr.org/2019/02/26/698397631/sexual-assault-of-detained-migrant-children-reported-in-the-thousands-since-2015; see also "Sexual Abuse in Immigration Detention—Raquel's Story," ACLU, October 16, 2011, https://www.aclu.org/other/sexual-abuse-immigration-detention-raquels-story.

7. Tyler Anbinder, "Trump Has Spread More Hatred of Immigrants Than Any American in History," *Washington Post*, November 7, 2019, https://www.washingtonpost.com/outlook/trump-has-spread-more-hatred-of-immigrants-than-any-american-in-history/2019/11/07/7e253236-ff54-11e9-8bab-0fc209e065a8_story.html.

8. Robert M. Kingdon, "Calvinist Discipline in the Old World and the New," in *The Reformation in Germany and Europe: Interpretations and Issues* (special volume of the *Archive for Reformation History*), ed. Hans R. Guggisberg and Gottfried Krodel (Gütersloh: Gütersloher Verlagshaus, 1993), 665–79.

John Knox had ample reason, after his sojourn in Geneva, to describe the city as "the most perfect school of Christ that ever was in the earth since the days of the apostles."[9] John Bale, a contemporary of John Knox also fleeing Mary Tudor's persecution of Protestants, wrote, "Geneva seems to me to be the wonderful miracle of the whole world. . . . Is it not wonderful that Spaniards, Italians, Scots, Englishmen, Frenchmen, Germans, disagreeing on manners, speech, and apparel . . . being coupled with only the yoke of Christ, should live so lovingly . . . like a spiritual and Christian congregation."[10] When balancing the biblical demand for the rule of law (Rom. 13) with Peter's exhortation that "we must obey God rather than any human authority" (Acts 5:29), Calvin erred on the side of compassion for the immigrant.[11] He was firmly convinced that as citizens and as Christians we are called to "take as strong a stand against evil as we can."[12]

Refugees in Geneva

During Calvin's pastoral tenure in Geneva (1538–64), the Protestant Reformation was fighting for its very life. The movement encountered Catholic persecution across the whole of Europe, leading to substantial dislocation and migration of various populations. Between 1545 and 1555, a flood of French refugees overwhelmed Geneva. Historians estimate that, in this single decade, the population of Geneva grew from 13,100 to as high as 21,400.[13] Needless to say, this crushing influx of refugees challenged Geneva's already strained social welfare infrastructure. In a normal year, about 5 percent of the native population (about five hundred people) depended on regular assistance from the general hospital. Add to that the massive flow of refugees, and the social welfare agencies would likely have had

9. John Knox, "Letter XIII (To Mr. Locke)," in *Writings of the Rev. John Knox: Minister of God's Word in Scotland* (London: Religious Tract Society, 1842), 454.

10. Quoted in John T. McNeill, *The History and Character of Calvinism* (New York: Oxford University Press, 1967), 178.

11. See David M. Whitford, "Robbing Paul to Pay Peter: The Reception of Paul in Sixteenth Century Political Theology," in *A Companion to Paul in the Reformation*, ed. R. Ward Holder (Leiden: Brill, 2009), 573–606. Whitford argues that Calvin prioritized Peter's Acts statement over Paul's in Rom. 13.

12. John Calvin, *Sermons on 2 Samuel: Chapters 1–13*, trans. Douglas Kelly (Carlisle, PA: Banner of Truth, 1992), 419.

13. Robert M. Kingdon, "Calvinism and Social Welfare," *Calvin Theological Journal* 17 (1982): 223.

to serve up to an additional ten thousand strangers per year.[14] Sixteenth-century Geneva was a modest-size city with a small area of surrounding farmland (converted from existing suburbs after the break with the Roman Catholic Church and the surrounding Catholic cantons), often besieged by political enemies with standing armies. Given these limitations, the city was ill-equipped to handle such a large influx of political refugees, so even the most charitable Genevans hoped most refugees were not planning to settle permanently. Thankfully, many would merely pass through to other Reformed settlements and sanctuaries. This pressing need to resettle refugees directly affected and informed Geneva's later missionary efforts.

Protestant refugees were attracted to Geneva during Calvin's tenure owing to the popularity of his preaching and the success of his church reforms. They were also attracted to the civil reforms he had helped foster. While many of Geneva's charitable institutions predated Calvin's arrival in Geneva, their long-term success and impact benefited from Calvin's astute reorganization of church and civil governance. Consequently, one of the causes of friction between Calvin and the native Genevans was his constant spiritual and political insistence on providing hospitality to exiles. This was no inconsequential matter, for what had been a trickle of refugees in 1523 became a flood by 1555, when there were more immigrants than native citizens in the city. Not surprisingly, the natives had several legitimate grievances, complaining that refugees were taking jobs and straining resources, that wealthy exiled French nobles were exercising an undue influence over the city, and that the distinctive culture of the city was being destroyed.

One can understand the economic concerns of the native Genevans. One can even understand their resentment. By midcentury, every single one of their local pastors was foreign born. In claiming their city's independence years earlier, the Genevans had liberated themselves from the local nobility. Now they had to watch as nobles fleeing from France and Italy entered their gates and wielded a disproportionate amount of influence in economic matters.[15] Anti-immigrant sentiment reached its peak in

14. William Naphy, "Calvin's Church in Geneva: Constructed or Gathered? Local or Foreign? French or Swiss?," in *Calvin and His Influence, 1509–2009*, ed. Irena Backus and Philip Benedict (Oxford: Oxford University Press, 2011), 114–15.

15. See William C. Innes, *Social Concern in Calvin's Geneva* (Eugene, OR: Wipf & Stock, 1983), 205–36. Despite the artisan and peasant Huguenot populations' tendency to migrate

1555 under the leadership of Ami Perrin, who called himself a Genevan patriot. Perrin goaded a street mob to threaten foreign-owned businesses in the city. The mob gathered outside the city council in an attempt to intimidate the magistrates. Calvin himself stepped into the fray. He stood in the midst of the angry crowd that was chanting "Kill the French!" and proclaimed, "If you must shed blood, let mine be first."[16] Perrin later sought to oust Calvin by force but was defeated and exiled from the city. Calvin's public victory allowed him to consolidate his authority as pastor and use his political influence to better provide for the needs of refugees.

In the context of providing pastoral care to the dispossessed, the diaconate came to differentiate the care of native Genevans through the General Hospital from the care of Geneva's burgeoning refugee population through a special fund. Many of the refugees arriving in Geneva were affluent, and to address the crisis caused by immigration, wealthy French refugees established the *Bourse des pauvres étrangers français*, commonly called the French Fund, around 1545, during a period of intensified persecution of evangelicals in France. Calvin himself quietly supported the work of the fund for many years from his own modest income. Records indicate that by 1549 the deacons were managing this fund as part of the church's comprehensive poor relief, just prior to the greatest wave of French political and religious immigration.[17] Apart from emergency relief and medical services, the deacons used this fund to obtain housing for refugee families and to help refugees secure employment in the city. The fund provided tools for the refugees to use so that they could work for themselves. It even paid for vocational training to ensure that the refugees did not depend on charity for their long-term subsistence. Early on, any

---

back and forth between Geneva and France, demographic analysis reveals that very few of the wealthy exiled French nobles returned to their native land. Nobles like Laurent de Normandie and Jean Crespin, who had served in government positions before their exile, could not serve in government as resident aliens of Geneva, so they redirected their talents and resources in different industries, with foreigners making "the greatest contributions to the city's budget, for they amassed the largest fortunes in sixteenth century Geneva. Their purchases and renewals of rights of bourgeoisie put money annually in the city's treasury. Later in the century, they made the largest private loans to the city and paid more personal revenue to the Councils via a new, graduated income tax" (213).

16. Lindberg, *European Reformations*, 251.

17. For the most comprehensive archival study of the activities of the French Fund, see Jeannine E. Olson, *Calvin and Social Welfare: Deacons and the Bourse française* (London: Associated University Press, 1989).

refugee from any nation who was in genuine need received assistance from the French Fund. However, as persecution spread across Europe, similar funds were established in Geneva by and for the various ethnic communities seeking refuge (Italian, Spanish, Polish, etc.). Eventually, some of these resources were also allocated toward establishing Reformed congregations in France, thus addressing some of the problems caused by the influx of immigrants through the repatriation of French refugees.

A Theology of Exile

As demonstrated in chapter 1, Calvin argues in the *Institutes* that God establishes civil governments to maintain the social order,[18] and he views magistrates as the divinely appointed protectors and guardians of the public well-being.[19] Temporal governments exist "to cherish and protect the outward worship of God, to defend sound doctrine of piety, and the position of the church, to adjust our life to the society of men, to form our social behavior to civil righteousness, to reconcile us with one another, and to promote general peace and tranquility."[20] It follows that for Calvin there are preferable forms of government. Despite believing in a division of labor between spiritual (church) and temporal (state) governments, Calvin argues that the temporal establishment of a stable social order is grounded in and springs from "that spiritual and inward Kingdom of Christ . . . initiating in us upon earth certain beginnings of the Heavenly Kingdom."[21] By this understanding, neither the church nor the state represents a perfect and holy community, but both are mixed societies of saints and sinners, elect and reprobate, making it necessary to acknowledge certain ambiguities and tensions within both spiritual and temporal governance.

Even when advocating some separation of church and state as Calvin did, he did not separate theology from politics. One reason theology needs to engage public life is to ensure that the fundamental Christian obligation of compassion toward those in need is properly carried out. For Calvin, and those traditions influenced by Calvin, the establishment of a just social

18. See John Calvin, *Institutes of the Christian Religion*, ed. John T. McNeill, trans. Ford Lewis Battles, 2 vols. (Louisville: Westminster John Knox, 1960), 4.20.3.
19. See Calvin, *Institutes*, 4.20.6.
20. Calvin, *Institutes*, 4.20.2.
21. Calvin, *Institutes*, 4.20.2.

order is central to the Christian life. The call to minister to the poor, the sick, the widow, the orphan, the refugee, and the prisoner (Matt. 25:34–40) is a matter of concern for both the church and the state because it is first and foremost a spiritual concern for all Christians—as Calvin preached.

The defeat of Perrin in 1555 was a great setback for the anti-immigration party in Geneva. Previously, the city had not encouraged immigrants to become citizens, but now the policy began to change, and by 1560 laws had been passed allowing some immigrants to become citizens. Calvin himself had officially become a Genevan citizen only a year earlier. Still, the resistance to the influence of immigrants and their descendants continued, particularly in the realm of politics and government. It was not until 1559 that the first son of an immigrant was allowed to sit in the Council of Two Hundred, and it was thirty-five years later, in 1594—long after Calvin's death—that the first son of an immigrant sat in the Small Council, which was the real seat of political power. Calvin disagreed with the anti-immigration party on the basis of simple Christian duty. Commenting on the passage in Hebrews about those who entertained angels unawares, he says,

> He is not only speaking about the right of hospitality which used to be practised among the rich, but rather he is giving orders that the poor and the needy are to be received since at that time many were refugees from their homes for the Name of Christ. To add additional commendation for this kind of duty, he says that angels have sometimes been entertained by those who thought they were receiving men. I have no doubt that he is thinking of Abraham and Lot. . . . If anyone objects that this was an unusual occurrence, I have a ready answer in the fact that we receive not only angels but Christ himself when we receive the poor in His Name.[22]

In the *Institutes*, Calvin connects the hospitality and support that are to be given to the foreigner and the poor with the doctrines of God's grace and of the divine image in humankind, and he appears to be speaking about religious refugees when he argues that within them the divine image "is most carefully to be noted." On this basis, he concludes, "Therefore, we have no reason to refuse any who come before us needing our help."[23]

22. Calvin, *New Testament Commentaries*, 12:204–5.
23. Calvin, *Institutes*, 3.7.6.

But it is not enough to say that Calvin, himself an exile, defended others who were exiles.

During these turbulent years, Calvin began to lecture on the Psalms to an audience increasingly composed of refugees, and he completed his *Commentary on the Psalms* in 1557, at the height of Protestant migration to Geneva. Therefore, it is not unrealistic to assume that the plight of persecuted Protestants throughout Europe—but especially in his native France—informed Calvin's exegesis of the Psalms. Herman J. Selderhuis characterizes Calvin as a refugee ministering to other refugees and is not surprised to find within his commentary on the Psalms repeated references to the themes of exile and asylum.[24] While Calvin's autobiographical sensitivity to the plight of persecuted and displaced Protestants resonates throughout his exegesis of the Psalms, it is always placed within the explicit theological framework of the Christian life as a pilgrimage on this earth. In comparing the Protestant churches to Israel, Calvin reminds persecuted Protestants that the children of God in David's psalms are distinguished

> for the trial of their faith; for he speaks of them, not as *righteous* or *godly*, but as those that *wait upon the Lord*. What purpose would this waiting serve, unless they groaned under the burden of the cross? Moreover, the possession of the earth which he promises to the children of God is not always realised to them; because it is the will of the Lord that they should live as strangers and pilgrims in it; neither does he permit them to have any fixed abode in it, but rather tries them with frequent troubles, that they may desire with greater alacrity the everlasting dwelling-place of heaven.[25]

Calvinist Missionaries in Sixteenth-Century Brazil

In telling the story of the conquest and settlement of the "New World" by Europeans, certain false narratives still dominate—for example, the assumption that Latin America was evangelized exclusively by the Roman Catholic Church, or the North American nation-building myth that Protestants crossed the ocean solely in search of religious freedom. The brief

---

24. See Herman J. Selderhuis, *John Calvin: A Pilgrim's Life*, trans. Albert Gootjes (Downers Grove, IL: IVP Academic, 2009), 85–109.

25. John Calvin, *Calvin's Commentaries*, trans. Calvin Translation Society, 23 vols., 500th anniversary ed. (Grand Rapids: Baker Books, 2009), 5:25–26 (Ps. 37:9).

history of Fort Coligny, a sixteenth-century French island fortress built in the vicinity of present-day Rio de Janeiro, challenges and undermines both of these prevailing assumptions. It also provides a glimpse into the cosmopolitan vision of a global church espoused by Calvin in Geneva.

In 1555, the Reformed Church in Geneva became the first Protestant communion to establish missions in the New World, and contrary to the dominant narrative about the dearth of Protestantism in Latin America, this effort did not take place in the North American English-speaking colonies. The first Protestant mission in the New World was a French colony intended as a refuge for persecuted Huguenots in what was then called Antarctic France (modern-day Brazil). Many Protestants came to Latin America despite the fact that it was under Spanish and Portuguese rule and was considered the exclusive mission field of the Roman Catholic Church via the papal bull *Inter caetera* (1493), which granted to the Catholic sovereigns Ferdinand and Isabella of Spain all lands to the "west and south" of a pole-to-pole line one hundred leagues west and south of any of the islands of the Azores or the Cape Verde islands. The price for granting the Spanish and Portuguese crowns sovereignty over these lands was the accompanying duty to evangelize the New World, so that "in our times especially the Catholic faith and the Christian religion be exalted and be everywhere increased and spread, that the health of souls be cared for and that barbarous nations be overthrown and brought to the faith itself."[26] Not surprisingly, the fate of Protestants in Latin America was very often the same: "They were promptly detected, captured and tried by the Inquisition. Under the ordeal, a majority recanted, mainly in order to avoid punishment, but some, who remained loyal to the end, were burnt at the stake."[27] The migratory experience of these early Calvinists was one of danger, fragility, and dislocation.

Despite this interdiction against Protestant evangelization in the New World, the French crown gave permission for the construction of an island fortress sheltering six hundred French citizens as part of an exploratory venture in the New World in 1555 at Fort Coligny, named after

26. Pope Alexander VI, *Inter Caetera: Division of the Undiscovered World between Spain and Portugal* (May 4, 1493), Papal Encyclicals Online, https://www.papalencyclicals.net/Alex06/alex06inter.htm.

27. Gonzalo Báez-Camargo, "The Earliest Protestant Missionary Venture in Latin America," *Church History* 21, no. 2 (June 1952): 135.

the French admiral Gaspard de Coligny (1519–72). The fort was under the command of Vice Admiral Nicolas Durand de Villegagnon, himself briefly a convert to Protestantism, who had suggested to Admiral Coligny that they staff the venture by providing refuge to Huguenots, a persecuted Protestant minority in France who held to the Reformed, or Calvinist, tradition of Protestantism. Coligny is remembered as one of the leaders of the Huguenots during the French Wars of Religion (1562–98) who had a close relationship with King Charles IX of France, a friendship greatly opposed by Charles's mother, Catherine de' Medici, who conspired to assassinate Coligny on August 22, 1572, triggering the St. Bartholomew's Day Massacre (August 24, 1572), which resulted in the deaths of over ten thousand Huguenots in Paris and the outlying provinces.[28] Yet, in 1555, by emphasizing the political and economic advantages of establishing a colony in the New World, Coligny was able to gain the support of King Henry II of France to establish a colony in Brazil that would serve as a refuge for Huguenots—though even with this incentive, Villegagnon still had to scour the Parisian prisons in order "to get enough men . . . to add to his Huguenot contingent."[29]

Very little is known about this colonial venture since the two extant eyewitness accounts were written by Huguenots who were killed when Fort Coligny was overrun by the Portuguese in 1560. These memoirs were published in Foxe's *Book of Martyrs* (1564) and were used by Protestants in their polemical arguments with Catholics during the Wars of Religion, so they are largely discredited as reliable sources by historians.[30] The support that Admiral Coligny had been able to garner from the crown for the expedition to establish Fort Coligny amounted to "three vessels and 10,000 livres."[31] The original settlement effort overcame many difficulties, and in a letter to Admiral Coligny, Vice Admiral Villegagnon narrates that when the colonists faced a shortage of food, both his soldiers and the Huguenot refugees struggled to survive. But it was the Huguenots—whom he described as "a race, fearing God, patient and kind"—who

---

28. See R. J. Knecht, *The French Civil Wars, 1562–1598* (London: Routledge, 2014), 157–70.

29. James I. Good, "Calvin and the New World," *Journal of the Presbyterian Historical Society* 5, no. 4 (December 1909): 179.

30. See John McGrath, "Polemic and History in French Brazil, 1555–1560," *Sixteenth Century Journal* 27, no. 2 (Summer 1996): 385–97.

31. Good, "Calvin and the New World," 179.

performed the bulk of the labor and became his "best workmen [who] would exert a good influence on the others."[32] Consequently, Villegagnon wrote to King Henry II, Admiral Coligny, and the magistrates of Geneva requesting that more artisans, as well as Protestant ministers, be sent to Fort Coligny from Geneva.

While these letters are not extant, according to the consistory minutes the Genevan church sent two ministers, Peter Richier and William Chartier, bearing letters from Calvin to Villegagnon. They arrived in Brazil on March 7, 1557. So, while Coligny desired to create a Huguenot haven in Brazil for his own religious reasons, the primary and official motivation for the establishment of Fort Coligny was financial profit and the expansion of France's global sphere of influence. Still, Fort Coligny became a refuge for Huguenots fleeing persecution in France, and in 1557 Richier conducted the first Reformed worship in the New World according to the Genevan Church Order.[33] A letter from Villegagnon to Calvin and two letters from the two ministers to Calvin and the Genevan consistory were sent on the returning ship in April 1557. In his letter, Villegagnon expresses joy at the arrival of the ministers, personal concerns about threats from the Indigenous population and the physical hardships of surviving in the region, and lamentations that those "who had out of friendship followed him had gone back to France on account of the hardships they had endured, and he himself had been somewhat discouraged at the difficulties. But when he remembered that the object of the voyage was to promote Christ's kingdom, he felt he would dishonor His [Christ's] name if he should be deterred by the perils."[34] Villegagnon's letter demonstrated tolerance for the Huguenot settlers and closed with language supportive of the Calvinist missionary effort: "Our Lord Jesus Christ preserve you and your colleagues from all evil, strengthen you with His Spirit and prolong your life for the Church's Work."[35]

Unfortunately, Villegagnon's support was rooted in pragmatism and proved lukewarm at best. When the Lutheran colonist Jean Cointat raised objections to the Genevan celebration of the Lord's Supper and baptism,

32. Quoted in Good, "Calvin and the New World," 180.
33. See R. Pierce Beaver, "The Geneva Mission to Brazil," *Reformed Journal* 17 (July/August 1967): 14–20.
34. Good, "Calvin and the New World," 181.
35. Quoted in Good, "Calvin and the New World," 181.

Villegagnon sided with Cointat and eventually forbade the Genevan order of worship despite his promise and assurances to Calvin that they would adhere to the Genevan Church Order. In their April letter to Calvin, Richier and Chartier assured him that they had presided over the proper celebration of the Lord's Supper, and they even mentioned that Vice Admiral Villegagnon had made a public profession of faith. Two months later, in June 1557, Villegagnon placed Chartier on a ship to Geneva to consult with Calvin on how to resolve the dispute over the sacraments, while Richier was allowed to continue preaching and leading worship so long as he did not celebrate the sacraments.[36]

Whatever Admiral Coligny's original intentions in support of Huguenot missions in the New World, Villegagnon's Protestant profession of faith proved insincere, for he later declared transubstantiation, mandated Roman Catholic doctrine at Fort Coligny, forbade Reformed worship (though it continued for a time in secret), and eventually drove the Huguenots off the island. Ironically, it was during their exile on the Brazilian mainland that the Huguenots began their true missionary efforts, evangelizing the Topinambu tribe, who had welcomed them. Jean de Léry, one of the Huguenot colonists, even developed a dictionary of their tribal language for the benefit of future missionaries.[37] Sadly, their efforts were short-lived, as Villegagnon conspired to return them to France, charged as heretics with a death sentence awaiting them on arrival. For unknown reasons, the captain of the ship allowed five of the Genevan settlers to return, but upon their return, Villegagnon had them arrested as spies and sentenced to death. One recanted, but three were executed—Peter Bourdon, John Bortel, and Matthew Vernuil—the first martyrs to die for the sake of Protestant missions in the New World. The fifth, John Boles, settled on the mainland south of Fort Coligny and became such a successful preacher among the Indigenous tribes that he aroused the ire of the Jesuits, who had him arrested and imprisoned for eight years before burning him at the stake in Rio de Janeiro in 1567, "the first Protestant *auto-da-fé* [burning of a heretic] in America."[38]

36. See Charles E. Nowell, "The French in Sixteenth-Century Brazil," *The Americas* 5, no. 4 (April 1949): 388–91.

37. For a translation of Léry's brief account of his missionary adventure, see Francis Parkman, *Pioneers of France in the New World* (Boston: Little, Brown, 1865), 16–27.

38. Good, "Calvin and the New World," 185.

Villegagnon's fickleness had undermined the stability of the French colony. And in 1560, shortly after his persecution of the Huguenots, he returned to France and spent his last years conducting a polemical attack against Calvin, his missionary efforts in the New World, and the Protestant heresy. Ironically, Portuguese accounts of the strength of Fort Coligny suggest that had Villegagnon managed to maintain the peace among the settlers (Huguenot, Lutheran, and Catholic), they might have easily resisted and survived the Portuguese siege in March 1560. These accounts describe how "a Portuguese fleet of twelve ships took three weeks to be able to land on the island, using up almost all of their ammunition in doing so. In fact, the attackers had suffered so many casualties that they were on the verge of departing when untimely panic among the French civilian defenders enabled a Portuguese victory."[39]

The Reformed Tradition's Migratory Identity

Even though Calvin's experience as an exile and his struggles in defense of other exiles evoke clear echoes of present-day experiences and struggles, from our perspective as Christians, the more important question is, What does God demand of Christ's followers concerning the least of our brothers and sisters (Matt. 25)? The hospitality of Reformed hosts in Geneva and the fragility, danger, and suffering of Reformed migrants at Fort Coligny ought to inform our present-day experiences and struggles around the issue of global migration.

Following Christ faithfully in the world involves movement—it's a journey, a pilgrimage. For Calvin, bearing one's cross will always involve suffering. Our faithful movement, he argues, is possible when we accept that life "is troubled, turbulent, unhappy in countless ways, and in no respect clearly happy. . . . From this, at the same time, we conclude that in this life we are to seek and hope for nothing but struggle."[40] But there is hope. Because of Christ's cross—because of his sacrifice for us—we followers of Christ can bear the cross for others as they move and migrate through this world. Christ's gracious gift to us demands a public and even political response. For Calvin, standing by while the poor, the immigrant, and the

39. McGrath, "Polemic and History," 394–95.
40. Calvin, *Institutes*, 3.9.1.

political refugee are suffering and exploited is a sinful act, a violation of the image of God.[41] It is our Christian duty not only to alleviate this suffering through ministries of compassion but also to order our political life in faithfulness to God to eliminate such suffering.

Idolatry and Calvinism are supposed to be antithetical to each other—absolutely inimical. For the Calvinist, God alone is sovereign. Nothing can be allowed to compete with or diminish God's image, God's law, or God's sovereign power. When Reformed Christians in the United States ignore the suffering of refugees (the image of God in their midst), when they quietly hide behind an unjust rule of law (placing the nation's laws above God's laws), when they passively submit to an unjust leader (placing the leader's sovereignty above God's sovereignty), not only do they risk committing injustice against their neighbor, but they are also in danger of committing idolatry against their God. The twenty-first century is already marked by massive global migration. Religious persecution, economic distress, racial hatred, and political conflict are all driving enormous movements of souls and bodies created in the image of God. As we Reformed Christians around the globe wrestle with how to respond, we would do well to learn from our own migratory past.

For Further Reading

Calvin, John. "Advocacy for Justice and Pastoral Care for the Afflicted." In *John Calvin: Writings on Pastoral Piety*, edited and translated by Elsie Anne McKee, 315–32. New York: Paulist Press, 2001.

———. "Counsel and Mutual Encouragement." In *John Calvin: Writings on Pastoral Piety*, 305–14.

———. "The Genevan Confession (1536)." In *Calvin: Theological Treatises*, edited and translated by J. K. S. Reid, 25–33. Philadelphia: Westminster, 1954.

———. "Prefatory Address." In *Institutes of the Christian Religion, 1536 Edition*, translated by Ford Lewis Battles, 1–14. Grand Rapids: Eerdmans, 1975.

———. "Psalm 82." In vol. 5 of *Calvin's Commentaries*, translated by Calvin Translation Society, 23 vols., 500th anniversary ed. Grand Rapids: Baker Books, 2009.

———. "Psalm 137." In vol. 6 of *Calvin's Commentaries*.

---

41. Calvin, *Institutes*, 3.7.6.

4

Calvin's Vision for an Ecumenical and Transnational Church

First, then, the question is not whether the Church suffers from many and grievous diseases, for this is admitted even by all moderate judges; but whether the diseases are of a kind whose cure admits of no longer delay, so that it is neither useful nor proper to wait upon too slow remedies.

—John Calvin[1]

Looking to the future with an eye toward the past reminds us that our inherited doctrinal formulations—especially our ecclesiologies—prove inadequate in the face of secularization, globalization, and religious pluralism.

This chapter draws on, revises, and greatly expands material from two of my previously published works: "Calvin's Legacy of Compassion: A Reformed Theological Perspective on Immigration," in *Immigrant Neighbors among Us: Immigration across Theological Traditions*, ed. Leopoldo A. Sánchez M. and M. Daniel Carroll R., 44–62 (Eugene, OR: Wipf & Stock, 2015), used with permission of Wipf & Stock Publishers, www.wipfandstock.com; and "Calvin and 'Communion Ecclesiology': An Ecumenical Conversation," *Theology Today* 66, no. 2 (July 2009): 154–69, used with permission of the editors.
    1. John Calvin, "The Necessity of Reforming the Church," in *Calvin: Theological Treatises*, ed. and trans. J. K. S. Reid (Philadelphia: Westminster, 1954), 185.

Yet the plurality of perspectives characterizing contemporary Christianity need not threaten the unity and catholicity of the church but arguably embodies the fullness of the Christian tradition. In *Poetics of the Flesh* (2015), Latina theologian Mayra Rivera writes, "The Christian body has never been one."[2] On one level, her comment speaks to the historical reality that the church is a broken communion—split along denominational and ideological lines. On a more visceral level, Rivera is not just concerned about institutional unity but is offering critical insight into the clashing cultural imaginaries about flesh and embodied existence hindering Christian thought. She diagnoses a persistent contradiction in contemporary forms of Christianity that embrace Christ's bodily incarnation as salvific even as they demand a flesh-denying sexual purity, all while deeply entangled in the material world and all its comforts and pleasures. As a result of this enduring confusion, Christians have tolerated and allowed untold violence, exploitation, and even enslavement of human flesh to go unchallenged. Accordingly, when talking about the brokenness of the one body of Christ, we need to address both institutional unity and sociopolitical strife.

This chapter evaluates John Calvin's ecclesiology—especially its emphasis on plural ministries—as a model for articulating a contemporary ecumenical ecclesiology in conversation with post–Vatican II Roman Catholic communion ecclesiology. Several questions immediately come to mind when considering adapting Calvin's doctrine of the church for contemporary ecumenical discourse. First, can we speak of Calvin as a genuinely catholic conversation partner given the highly polemical character of his disagreements with sixteenth-century Roman Catholicism? Second, given the visible and persistent divisions within Christianity, is it even possible to speak of an ecumenical ecclesiology today? In addressing these concerns, this chapter (1) defends Calvin's "high" ecclesiology under the ecumenical Nicene marks of the church (one, holy, catholic, and apostolic) even as he offers a critique of the Church of Rome; (2) engages post–Vatican II communion ecclesiology as a promising paradigm for ecumenical conversations; and (3) explores Calvin's ecclesiology as independent of the state in order to advocate for a transnational church under the Word of God rather than subservient to any human word.

2. Mayra Rivera, *Poetics of the Flesh* (Durham, NC: Duke University Press, 2015), 17.

Calvin's "High" Ecclesiology and the Idolatry of Rome

Calvin never abandoned his anti-Roman polemical stance. In fact, with each succeeding edition of the *Institutes*, he added more vitriol to his polemic against the Church of Rome. Therefore, it is legitimate to question whether Calvin can be viewed as a catholic theologian who can contribute meaningfully to the contemporary ecumenical conversation on ecclesiology. Thankfully, numerous Catholic-Reformed exchanges over the centuries, such as the Calvin Studies Colloquium held in April 2007 at the University of Notre Dame,[3] enable modern readers to see Calvin's theology through Catholic eyes and thereby kindle the flame of rapprochement.[4] This chapter argues it is important to revisit Calvin's contributions to ecclesiology since we are dealing with a thinker who simultaneously embraced Saint Cyprian (who taught that the church is "Mother" of all believers and apart from her there is no salvation) and described the Roman Catholic Church as "a perverse government compounded of lies" whose "public assemblies have become schools of idolatry and ungodliness."[5] Also, throughout his struggles with the Church of Rome, Calvin consistently decried the sin of schism and worked to maintain ecclesial unity.[6] A second-generation Protestant reformer, Calvin followed Martin Luther in his treatment of most doctrines but distinguished himself from previous reformers—and is arguably at his most innovative—in book 4 of the *Institutes*, on the external means of grace. In the final 1559 edition of the *Institutes*, this last and longest of the four books is devoted primarily to the subject of the church.

All sixteenth-century Protestant reformers rejected the late-medieval Roman Catholic notion that the church, solely defined by its priesthood and the accompanying sacramental system they controlled, is necessary

3. The proceedings of this colloquium have been published as Randall C. Zachman, ed., *John Calvin and Roman Catholicism: Critique and Engagement, Then and Now* (Grand Rapids: Baker Academic, 2008).

4. See Alexandre Ganoczy, *Calvin et Vatican II: L'église servante* (Paris: Cerf, 1968); Alexandre Ganoczy, *Calvin, théologien de l'église et du ministère* (Paris: Cerf, 1964); George H. Tavard, *Starting Point of Calvin's Theology* (Grand Rapids: Eerdmans, 2000); Tavard, *The Church, Community of Salvation: An Ecumenical Ecclesiology* (Collegeville, MN: Liturgical Press, 1992); and Kilian McDonnell, *John Calvin, the Church, and the Eucharist* (Princeton: Princeton University Press, 1967).

5. John Calvin, *Institutes of the Christian Religion*, ed. John T. McNeill, trans. Ford Lewis Battles, 2 vols. (Louisville: Westminster John Knox, 1960), 4.2.2.

6. Calvin, *Institutes*, 4.1.10–16; 4.2.9–12.

for mediating God's grace. Grounded in the scriptural exhortation that the church is a royal priesthood encompassing all believers (1 Pet. 2:9), this revisioning of the doctrine of the church entails a redefinition of Christian ministry and religious vocation. No longer is ordained ministry the sole mediator of grace, since justification by grace alone implies that access to salvation is available to all believers. This turns the concept of religious vocation on its head by denying priests privileged access to the divine, by severing the efficacy of the sacraments from ecclesial authority, and by no longer viewing the religious realm as inherently more "holy" than the secular. Given this reading of the priesthood of all believers, the sixteenth-century Protestant conception of religious vocation is necessarily more inclusive in scope than its Roman Catholic adversary since any task done for the glory of God and in service to the neighbor is now understood as a Christian ministry.

Calvin sought to liberate Christian spirituality—the religious life—from the confines of the cloister by locating it within the everyday lives of believers, encompassing all aspects of human existence. Since "no task will be so sordid and base, provided you obey your calling in it, that it will not shine and be reckoned very precious in God's sight,"[7] the church and the clergy are no longer the sole depositories of holiness. As members of the priesthood of all believers, lay Christians occupy as important a place in the life of the church as its clergy. Nevertheless, while all vocations can be considered religious and all Christians are called to ministry, not all ministries are necessary for governing the church and not all ministers are placed in positions of leadership. Thus, while no single person within the priesthood of all believers possesses a special "holy" character, some individuals are called to fill specific offices (as pastors, doctors, elders, and deacons) within the body of Christ. Accordingly, while Protestants reject any special status granted via ordination, they retain a very high view of ordained ministry to preach the Word of God and administer the sacraments of the Lord's Supper and baptism.[8] Unlike its sixteenth-century Roman Catholic counterpart, the Calvinist wing of the Protestant Reformation recognized plural ministries—both lay and ordained—as necessary for the life of the church because they are so instituted by God.

7. Calvin, *Institutes*, 3.10.6.
8. See John Calvin, "Draft Ecclesiastical Ordinances (1541)," in Reid, *Theological Treatises*, 59–66.

The two fundamental ecclesial offices recognized by Calvin are those of presbyter and deacon. Departing from the Roman Catholic reading of New Testament terminology in which *episkopos* (bishop) and *presbyteros* (elder) are different offices, Calvin argues that according to scriptural usage the various terms for those who govern the church—bishop, presbyter, pastor, and minister—are interchangeable and refer to the same office.[9] Furthermore, he contends that the New Testament identifies only two permanent offices in the church: church governors (*presbyteroi*)—among whom are the teaching elders, whose primary duty is to preach the Word of God and administer the sacraments, and the ruling (lay) elders, who oversee the communal life of the congregation—and deacons (*diakonoi*), who are charged with care of the poor. By this reading, church governance (the ministry of the Word and administration of the sacraments, instruction in the faith, and moral guidance and discipline) is shared by ordained clergy and lay church leaders (elders chosen from the people) who work with the pastors in the day-to-day governance of congregations, especially in resolving conflicts and disciplining believers. The care of the poor is also subdivided into two kinds of deacons (*diakonoi*)—namely, those who manage and distribute the alms (procurators) and those who minister physically to the sick and the poor (hospitallers).[10] In the Ecclesiastical Ordinances, Calvin explains the division of labor within the diaconate: "There were always two kinds in the ancient Church, the one deputed to receive, dispense, and hold goods for the poor, not only daily alms, but also possessions, rents, and pensions; the other to tend and care for the sick and administer allowances to the poor."[11] The result is an ecclesiology characterized by shared governance rather than the centralized authority of the clergy.

While eventually breaking with Rome, Calvin (like all sixteenth-century Protestant reformers) did not set out to establish a new communion but was attempting to reform the one, holy, catholic, and apostolic church. By framing his discussion in terms of the Nicene marks of the church,[12] yet articulating a distinctly Reformed understanding of these *notae ecclesiae* (marks of the church),[13] Calvin at once identifies that which divides him

9. See Calvin, *Institutes*, 4.3.8.
10. See Calvin, *Institutes*, 4.3.9.
11. Calvin, "Draft Ecclesiastical Ordinances (1541)," 64.
12. See Calvin, *Institutes*, 4.1.2.
13. See Calvin, *Institutes*, 4.1.9.

from Rome and what must change for reconciliation with Rome to take place. Even though he affirms that the church is defined in terms of God's election, throughout book 4 of the *Institutes* he is very clearly speaking about the visible church as a historical reality,[14] which can be known by concrete marks. By distinguishing between the visible and the invisible church (categories derived from Augustine of Hippo), Calvin wants readers to understand that our historical communions are *not* the pure embodiment of God's elect but a thoroughly human and sinful historical reality always in need of reform, one that includes "many hypocrites who have nothing of Christ but the name and outward appearance."[15]

Nevertheless, while the visible church may harbor hypocrisy, scandal, and corruption, there is no excuse for "capricious separation" so long as the means of grace survive within this tainted communion—for "knowing how necessary it is to our salvation,"[16] any "separation from the church is denial of God and Christ."[17] In other words, while external to the inner workings of the Holy Spirit by which believers participate in mystical union with Christ and partake in salvation, the church and its ministries remain necessary for salvation insofar as God has instituted them in response to our weakness, "in his wonderful providence accommodating himself to our capacity."[18] Furthermore, influenced by Martin Bucer's Reformed ecclesiology, Calvin identifies the disciplining of believers as one of the visible manifestations of the Holy Spirit in the life of the church. Given this "high" view of the church—in which the church is the means God has chosen for communicating salvation to humankind—Calvin reaffirms the two criteria, first identified by Luther, by which the visible church can be recognized as the true church (in spite of its impurity): "Wherever we see the Word of God purely preached and heard, and the sacraments administered according to Christ's institution, there, it is not to be doubted, a church of God exists."[19] By this standard, Calvin and the other Protestant reformers were never guilty of schism; rather, it was the Roman Church's rejection of the Word of God and usurping of Christ's role as

14. See Calvin, *Institutes*, 4.1.4.
15. Calvin, *Institutes*, 4.1.7.
16. Calvin, *Institutes*, 4.1.8.
17. Calvin, *Institutes*, 4.1.10.
18. Calvin, *Institutes*, 4.1.1.
19. Calvin, *Institutes*, 4.1.9.

the head of the church that created scandal and division.[20] It is at this point that Calvin appeals to Cyprian's *On the Unity of the Catholic Church*, a third-century patristic text, to argue that the Roman Catholic Church replaced Christ with the papacy and its episcopate. Therefore, the break with Rome was not an act of schism but necessary to bring believers to Christ.[21]

Calvin's anti-Roman polemics were motivated by two overarching fears—the "divinization" of the institutional church into a false idol that supplanted Christ as head of the church and the imposition of a rigid religious authoritarianism that defined the church solely in terms of its magisterium. While the sixteenth-century debate ended in schism, Kilian McDonnell, a Benedictine monk writing just after Vatican II, contended that the Roman Church's new constitution "allays Calvin's fears and fulfills Calvin's hopes" for reconciliation with Roman Catholic ecclesiology.[22] Roman Catholic ecclesiology after Vatican II recognizes the primacy of grace over hierarchical governing structures and defines its apostolic mission as incorporating both the ordained priesthood and the laity. According to McDonnell, *Lumen gentium* (1964)[23] even sets aside the "simple identification between the Mystical Body of Christ and the Roman Catholic Church" such that "the mystery of the church extends beyond the boundaries of canonical jurisdiction."[24] Without question, the reforms of Vatican II still contain much that Calvin would find objectionable, but the current conversation on ecclesiology is not between this sixteenth-century reformer and post–Vatican II theology but between contemporary Protestants and Catholics. To that end, while an encounter with the historical Calvin is vital to the discussion, it is more important that contemporary "Calvinisms" engage recent developments in Catholic ecclesiology, lest we run the risk of "divinizing" our own ecclesiology above all others.

20. See Calvin, *Institutes*, 4.2.3–4.2.6.
21. See Calvin, *Institutes*, 4.2.6.
22. Kilian McDonnell, OSB, "The Ecclesiology of John Calvin and Vatican II," *Religion in Life* 36 (1967): 547.
23. *Lumen gentium*, the Dogmatic Constitution on the Church, is one of the principal documents of the Second Vatican Council. See Pope Paul VI, "Dogmatic Constitution on the Church, *Lumen gentium*," The Holy See (November 21, 1964), https://www.vatican.va/archive/hist_councils/ii_vatican_council/documents/vat-ii_const_19641121_lumen-gentium_en.html.
24. McDonnell, "Ecclesiology," 550–51.

The Promise of Communion Ecclesiology

By grounding his doctrine of the church in the "communion of saints,"[25] Calvin offers a point of commonality with post–Vatican II Roman Catholic theology. Catholic theologian Susan K. Wood identifies communion ecclesiology as the dominant approach for conceptualizing church within Roman Catholic circles today and suggests it is the best paradigm for future ecumenical dialogue and cooperation.[26] Building on biblical images of the church and the documents of Vatican II reaffirmed in the June 1992 letter issued by the Congregation for the Doctrine of the Faith to the bishops of the Catholic Church, "Some Aspects of the Church Understood as Communion," communion ecclesiology draws on the image of the church as the body of Christ (Rom. 12:4–8; 1 Cor 12; Eph. 2:11–3:6; Col. 1:18, 24) in order to confirm all believers' participation in the life of Christ via mystical union.[27] Throughout these documents, the use of Pauline texts to affirm that the institutional church always remains subordinate to Christ as the sole head of the church aims to dispel Protestant fears.

At the same time, however, Catholic communion ecclesiology emphasizes Paul's discussion of the community as the body of Christ in the context of the Lord's Supper (1 Cor. 10:16–22; 11:17–34), which leads Wood to conclude, "Where the Eucharist is, there is church."[28] The resulting ecclesiology, building on a trinitarian understanding of God as a divine communion (*perichoresis*), affirms the sacramental real presence of Christ without reducing the church to the Eucharist, yet it understands the very possibility of human communion with Christ and with one another as inseparable from the "elements of grace and sacrament that ultimately identify ecclesial communities in terms of their relationship to Christ."[29] One of the most important efforts at reaching ecumenical consensus on ecclesiology, *Baptism, Eucharist, and Ministry* (BEM), issued in 1982 by the Commission on Faith and Order of the World Council of Churches,

25. Calvin, *Institutes*, 4.1.3.

26. Susan K. Wood, "Communion Ecclesiology: Source of Hope, Source of Controversy," *Pro Ecclesia* 2, no. 4 (Fall 1993): 424–32.

27. See Joseph Cardinal Ratzinger and Alberto Bovone, "Letter to the Bishops of the Catholic Church on Some Aspects of the Church Understood as Communion," The Holy See (May 28, 1992), https://www.vatican.va/roman_curia/congregations/cfaith/documents/rc_con_cfaith_doc_28051992_communionis-notio_en.html.

28. Wood, "Communion Ecclesiology," 425.

29. Wood, "Communion Ecclesiology," 426.

brings together insights from various Christian traditions to affirm the predominance of the sacraments in the life of the church.[30]

BEM stands as a historical landmark in ecumenical rapprochement, underscoring the appeal of and obstacles to communion ecclesiology for the contemporary situation. Protestant criticism of BEM centers on the document's assertion that the Lord's Supper is "the central act of the Church's worship," preferring the Protestant reformers' principle that the central act of God's self-revelation in Jesus Christ is manifest through both Word and sacrament. Equally objectionable is BEM's insistence that episcopal succession is a necessary mark of apostolicity—though by no means the only mark—required for achieving full Christian unity. Many Protestant traditions contend that apostolic succession is preserved by fidelity to the proclamation and practice of the apostles rather than by means of a monarchical episcopate. While this criticism by some Protestant bodies, that BEM leans in a more "catholic" direction by emphasizing the sacrament of communion, could be seen as an impediment to genuine dialogue between Protestants and Catholics, Catholic theologians continue to assert communion ecclesiology as a vital resource for ecumenical reconciliation, even while acknowledging the difficulty of achieving "full ecclesiastical communion."[31]

One objection that is immediately raised to the use of communion ecclesiology as a bridge for ecumenical understanding is its use of the term *sacrament*. In Western Christianity, the focus on community-defining sacraments as "authorized" means of grace—that is, officially recognized media of divine self-communication—has worked to undermine tolerance, pluralism, and cooperation in ecumenical relations. No better example exists than the five-hundred-year schism between Roman Catholic and Protestant Christianity over the number and efficacy of the sacraments. Specifically, disagreements over the sacrament of Communion, or the Eucharist (from the Greek *eucharistia*, meaning "thanksgiving")—which for

---

30. See *Baptism, Eucharist, and Ministry* (Geneva: World Council of Churches, 1982). Also see Max Thurian, ed., *Churches Respond to BEM* (Geneva: World Council of Churches, 1986); and *Baptism, Eucharist, and Ministry 1982–1990: Report on the Process and Responses* (Geneva: World Council of Churches, 1990).

31. Joseph Cardinal Ratzinger and Tarcisio Bertone, SDB, "Declaration '*Dominus Iesus*' on the Unicity and Salvific Universality of Jesus Christ and the Church," The Holy See (August 6, 2000), 4.17, https://www.vatican.va/roman_curia/congregations/cfaith/documents/rc_con_cfaith_doc_20000806_dominus-iesus_en.html.

Roman Catholicism is the focal point of the Mass but in most Protestant traditions is celebrated infrequently—have perpetuated and escalated confessional strife. Admittedly, there has been increased cooperation between Protestant and Roman Catholic governing bodies since the Second Vatican Council (1962–65), as evidenced by BEM and the more recent *Joint Declaration on the Doctrine of Justification* (1999), issued by the Lutheran World Federation and the Roman Catholic Church.[32] Still, ecumenical reconciliation remains a distant hope given the statement in *Dominus Iesus* (2000) that describes Protestant communions as "not Churches in the proper sense."[33]

Whether or not communion ecclesiology succeeds as a paradigm for articulating an ecumenical ecclesiology, however, depends in great part on how well it attends to Protestant objections to BEM. As interpreted by some Catholic theologians, communion ecclesiology focuses almost exclusively on the church's sacramental life—particularly participation in the Eucharist—and consequently creates a doctrinal barrier with those churches that do not affirm the same understanding of sacramental practice. One strand of Roman Catholic theology—Latin American liberation theology—embodies a model of communion ecclesiology that holds much promise for articulating a genuinely ecumenical doctrine of the church; and, as discussed in chapter 2, it is a movement that has much in common with Calvin's political theology. Liberation theologians challenge the church to look beyond its liturgical celebrations to recognize the sacramental dimension of the work of political liberation as a means of extending Christ's redemptive work to all humankind. The vision of Christian community arising from the apostle Paul's reflections on the body of Christ embraced at Vatican II and reaffirmed at the Second General Conference of the Latin American Episcopate in 1968 in Medellín, Colombia, upholds a plurality of ministries that challenge traditional ecclesiologies to move beyond clericalism, recognizes the need to transcend existing boundaries (such as the ordination of women) that limit the full expression of spiritual gifts, and encourages the church to work toward

---

32. The Lutheran World Federation and the Catholic Church, *Joint Declaration on the Doctrine of Justification* (Geneva: Lutheran World Federation, 1999), https://www.lutheranworld.org/sites/default/files/Joint%20Declaration%20on%20the%20Doctrine%20of%20Justification.pdf.

33. Ratzinger and Bertone, "*Dominus Iesus*," 4.17.

full eucharistic unity as members of the one body: "For in the one Spirit we were all baptized into one body—Jews or Greeks, slaves or free—and we were all made to drink of one Spirit" (1 Cor. 12:13).

By conceptualizing the church as a living sacrament of God's salvific work—with an emphasis on human political liberation—theologians like Gustavo Gutiérrez and Leonardo Boff built on Vatican II's "body of Christ" ecclesiology while transcending traditional understandings of the church as a sacramental community.[34] By linking the church's liturgical practice to its social ethics, liberation theologies also broaden the Catholic view of church as mystical communion to include concrete action without compromising sacramental realism (a primary Catholic concern), while embodying an alternative model of communion that does not privilege one particular organizational model (a chief Protestant objection to many Catholic ecclesiologies), since the "notion of sacrament enables us to think of the Church within the horizon of the salvific work and in terms radically different from those of the ecclesiocentric emphasis."[35] In other words, while drawing inspiration from the new, more inclusive ecclesiological perspective of Vatican II, Latin American liberation theology has articulated one of the strongest criticisms of the hierarchical Roman Church, thus providing contemporary theology with a paradigm for evaluating the inherited ecclesiologies of both Roman Catholic and Protestant traditions.

Susan Wood identifies this latter aspect of communion ecclesiology—the concept of communion of saints as providing a more inclusive structure for church governance—as the most promising direction for advancing the contemporary ecumenical conversation. She draws particular attention to Leonardo Boff's work with base Christian communities in Brazil to make the point that ministries arise to meet the needs of the community, affirming that the church as "communion" exists prior to any concrete historical church order because "the risen Christ and the Spirit are immanently present in the community."[36] Reformed theologian Philip Butin identifies an analogous conceptualization of church in Calvin's fourth book of the

---

34. See Gustavo Gutiérrez, *A Theology of Liberation: History, Politics, and Salvation*, trans. and ed. Sister Caridad Inda and John Eagleson, rev. ed. (Maryknoll, NY: Orbis Books, 1988); and Leonardo Boff, *Ecclesiogenesis: The Base Communities Reinvent the Church* (Maryknoll, NY: Orbis Books, 1986).

35. Gutiérrez, *Theology of Liberation*, 146.

36. Wood, "Communion Ecclesiology," 428.

Institutes, in which the church is defined as the visible embodiment of God's trinitarian grace: "All that Calvin had previously said in Books I–III of the 1559 *Institutes* about the trinitarian basis, pattern, and dynamic of God's relationship with human beings becomes incarnate on a human level for us only insofar as by the Spirit, we live in and are nurtured by that triune God as members (in the corporeal sense) of Christ, in the womb of the church."[37] Granted, Calvin's discussion of the mystical body of Christ differs from the late-medieval Roman Catholic conception that dominated the sixteenth century, yet in both cases the trinitarian action of God "for us" enables Christian community. While Calvin never employs the term *perichoresis*, Butin argues that Calvin's thoughts on the divine unity are conceptually similar, as evidenced by his understanding of the church as a communion in which the divine gifts are shared: "So powerful is participation in the church that it keeps us in the society of God."[38]

Demonstrative of yet another point of harmony with liberation theology, Butin concludes that the practical consequence of Calvin's trinitarian vision of the church as a visible "means of grace" is a conception of Christian ministry that not only is plural but also embodies God's grace through acts of political and cultural transformation. Communion ecclesiology holds great promise as a means of attaining confessional convergence in great part because it forces participants in ecumenical dialogue to address those doctrinal differences that continue to divide Christians by centering the conversation on the transcendent communion that is also historically concrete and politically engaged when it is mediated sacramentally.

Plural Ministries in Calvin's Ecclesiology

Allusions to the church as the body of Christ are scattered throughout the New Testament (Mark 14:22 and parallels; John 2:19–21; Heb. 10:5, 10; 13:3, 11–12; 1 Pet. 2:24), but only the Pauline letters use the image explicitly to describe the church community and its members. Without minimizing existing doctrinal divisions, by revisiting these complex biblical images at the heart of communion ecclesiology, with guidance from the emancipatory concerns of liberation theology, we can delineate the level of

37. Philip W. Butin, "Reformed Ecclesiology: Trinitarian Grace according to Calvin," *Studies in Reformed Theology and History* 2, no. 1 (Winter 1994): 15–16.
38. Calvin, *Institutes*, 4.1.3.

ecumenical consensus that can be achieved. While there are many images for the church in the New Testament, communion ecclesiology—especially as articulated by Latin American liberation theologians—employs the Pauline phrase "body of Christ" to highlight universal participation in the triune life of Christ while acknowledging that human community is not possible without the spiritual transformation effected by Jesus Christ.

Sadly, this more inclusive view of ecclesial communion is not universally accepted by Roman Catholics, as evidenced by "Some Aspects of the Church Understood as Communion," the letter from the Congregation for the Doctrine of the Faith, in which Cardinal Ratzinger raises concerns about Latin American liberation theology's narrow focus on grassroots organizing: "The Church, some say, would arise 'from base level.' These and other similar errors do not take sufficiently into account that it is precisely the Eucharist that renders all self-sufficiency on the part of the particular Churches impossible. Indeed, the unicity and indivisibility of the eucharistic Body of the Lord implies the unicity of his mystical Body, which is the one and indivisible Church."[39] In practical terms, Ratzinger's concern is that Christian base communities locate authority at the local church level to such a degree that they undermine the unity and catholicity of the church. Ironically, the letter seeks to preserve the universality of the church by reasserting a Tridentine conception of church grounded exclusively in the episcopate and the papal office, undermining many of the gains for plural lay ministries made by the Second Vatican Council. In calling for "a new conversion to the Lord, [that] all may be enabled to recognise the continuity of the Primacy of Peter in his successors, the Bishops of Rome, and to see the Petrine ministry fulfilled, in the manner intended by the Lord,"[40] Ratzinger subverts Vatican II's promise of ecclesial reconciliation. Most disheartening from an ecumenical perspective is the language describing those churches that do not acknowledge the primacy of the See of Rome as wounded: "The wound is even deeper in those ecclesial communities which have not retained the apostolic succession and a valid Eucharist."[41]

Methodologically, Calvin viewed his *Institutes* (along with his commentaries) as a rigorous effort to construct a biblical theology that addresses

39. Ratzinger and Bovone, "Church Understood as Communion," 3.11.
40. Ratzinger and Bovone, "Church Understood as Communion," 5.18.
41. Ratzinger and Bovone, "Church Understood as Communion," 5.17.

the whole of Scripture without meandering down paths of theological speculation. For Calvin, doctrine is simply the interpretation of Scripture. Accordingly, to address the major issues dividing Protestants and Catholics on the doctrine of the church, it is vital that we understand what the Scriptures have to say about the sacrament of Communion and ecclesial ministry. In the Letter to the Romans, Paul develops an argument about redemption from the "body of death" through the body of Christ in which a bifurcation exists between death and life, and life becomes possible only through mystical union with Christ:

> For if we have been united with him in a death like his, we will certainly be united with him in a resurrection like his. We know that our old self was crucified with him so that the body of sin might be destroyed, and we might no longer be enslaved to sin. For whoever has died is freed from sin. But if we have died with Christ, we believe that we will also live with him. We know that Christ, being raised from the dead, will never die again; death no longer has dominion over him. The death he died, he died to sin, once for all; but the life he lives, he lives to God. So you also must consider yourselves dead to sin and alive to God in Christ Jesus. (Rom. 6:5–11)

Throughout the letter, Paul is addressing the church—defined as the spiritual community of believers who have died with Christ through faith and been raised to new life in Christ. Much is now expected of them: "You have died to the law through the body of Christ, so that you may belong to another, to him who has been raised from the dead in order that we may bear fruit for God" (7:4). While life in the Spirit is described as a form of bondage—slavery to Christ as opposed to slavery to sin (8:15)—we are slaves "in the new life of the Spirit" (7:6), which brings freedom. According to Paul, all of humanity is subject to the law of sin and death; the only other option available to humanity is life in Christ. One way of understanding the church as a spiritual community in Christ is through this mystical participation in the death and resurrection of Christ.

The community of believers (the "saints") is made up of individuals who belong to Christ and to one another. By employing this image of a body composed of many members with Christ as its head (1 Cor. 12:12), Paul underscores the importance of individual moral responsibility for the preservation of community: "For you were bought with a price; therefore glorify God in your body" (1 Cor. 6:20). Accordingly, enforcing community discipline is one of the Pauline (and therefore Calvinist) marks of the new spiritual community in Christ, since our bodies belong to Christ as members of his body and that which we do with our bodies either profanes or glorifies Christ. But who is included as "members" of the "body of Christ"? Those who through faith have received grace and have been incorporated into the new spiritual community inaugurated by Christ's death on the cross.

While Paul divides the world into those who are enslaved to sin and those who have taken on the yoke of discipleship, he does not envision the church as an exclusionary community. In fact, in the Pauline literature the very notion of Christ as our "head" (*kephalē*) stresses the vastness of Christ's self-sacrifice: "For in him the whole fullness of deity dwells bodily, and you have come to fullness in him, who is the head of every ruler and authority" (Col. 2:9–10). In other words, Christ is the "head" of each and every human being whether or not they acknowledge him as such. Consequently, since Christ is the ruler of all, his reconciliation extends to all: "For in him all the fullness of God was pleased to dwell, and through him God was pleased to reconcile to himself all things, whether on earth or in heaven, by making peace through the blood of his cross" (Col. 1:19–20). That Christ seeks to reconcile with all of humanity (and all of creation), not just with those who self-identify as "members" of the one body, resonates with the liberationist understanding of spiritual community located concretely in God's emancipatory work and undermines the exclusionary tendencies of many traditional ecclesiologies.

Despite the universal scope of Christ's lordship, unity remains one of the desired characteristics of the new spiritual community described by Paul. Corinth was a community divided over the eucharistic meal, and Paul's words to that community provide a strong challenge to those confessional traditions that do not affirm a real sacramental presence in the celebration of the Lord's Supper *and* to all who persist in accepting doctrinal divisions without working toward a historical unity: "The cup of blessing that we bless, is it not a sharing in the blood of Christ? The bread that we break, is it not a sharing in the body of Christ? Because there is one bread, we who are many are one body, for we all partake of the one bread" (1 Cor. 10:16–17). Paul distinguishes between a shared common meal and the eucharistic fellowship, arguing that for a meal to be the

Lord's Supper, an embodied unity of Spirit—characterized by the sharing of common resources for the well-being of all—*must* exist. This dying of self-interest and living for others—"Do not seek your own advantage, but that of the other" (10:24)—is essential for a genuine celebration of the eucharistic meal in which the many become one in Spirit with the risen Christ. Consequently, Paul warns, "Whoever, therefore, eats the bread or drinks the cup of the Lord in an unworthy manner will be answerable for the body and blood of the Lord. Examine yourselves, and only then eat of the bread and drink of the cup" (11:27–28).

Martin Bucer's Influence on Calvin's Ecclesiology

Historian Heiko Oberman makes this observation about Calvin's understanding of the reforming church as a transcultural, transnational entity in sixteenth-century Europe: "Calvin discovered the ecumenical church at his conversion. . . . But in Strasbourg he discovered a new mark of the church (*nota ecclesiae*): the authentic church of Christ, like the people of the Jews, is persecuted and dispersed."[42] While Calvin the theologian did not rank autobiography and personal experience high on his list of theological sources, the fact remains that his life and thought were indelibly marked by the experience of political persecution and displacement and that an understanding of his time in Strasbourg working alongside the German reformer Martin Bucer is crucial for understanding the development of his ecclesiology. As demonstrated in an earlier chapter, Calvin's Geneva became a haven for Protestant refugees fleeing persecution throughout Catholic Europe. Carter Lindberg contends that Geneva was not merely a port in the storm for the victims of persecution; rather, Geneva's highly successful example of a Christian society built on Protestant principles encouraged further migration: "Geneva not only welcomed refugees, it created them. At the center of all the praise and blame that swirled through and around Geneva stood John Calvin, himself a displaced person from France."[43] Consequently, Geneva under Calvin's pastoral care became a refuge for persecuted Protestants as well as a beacon for reformers throughout Europe, who came to Geneva to

---

42. Heiko Oberman, *The Two Reformations* (New Haven: Yale University Press, 2003), 148.
43. Carter Lindberg, *The European Reformations* (Oxford: Blackwell, 1996), 249.

learn under Calvin to replicate his successes back home, as evidenced by John Knox's brief stay from 1555 to 1558.

One of the lessons Calvin learned during his three years in Strasbourg (1538–41) as the minister of a French refugee congregation was the importance of having a well-organized and unified church structure. It is not surprising, then, that when he returned to Geneva from Strasbourg, Calvin was tasked with writing the rules of church governance for the Genevan church (the Ecclesiastical Ordinances of 1541) as well as with "leading the committee to write what would become Geneva's first, postrevolutionary constitution."[44] Thus, in 1541 he was given oversight for reforming both the Genevan church and Geneva's civil government. While in Strasbourg, Calvin benefited from contact with Bucer, an advocate of Protestant unity, and many of the reforms Calvin later implemented in Geneva—especially those concerning ecclesiology and church governance—were first articulated in Strasbourg.[45] T. H. L. Parker's biography of Calvin identifies this sojourn in Strasbourg as particularly positive and influential: "A happy situation for him; a Frenchman among Frenchman, a refugee among refugees, a poor man among generally poor men."[46] Ironically, while he was never fully welcomed as one of their own, it was Calvin's experience as a refugee—first in Geneva, briefly in Strasbourg, then again in Geneva until his death—that most informed the church order he implemented in Geneva.

However, given the political tensions that led to Calvin's expulsion from Geneva in 1538 before his eventual return in 1541, the ecclesiology encapsulated in the Ecclesiastical Ordinances cannot be understood without reference to Geneva's first postrevolutionary constitution, also drafted by Calvin. Not surprisingly, Calvin's constitution is a conservative document, providing stability and order to a city that had been ripped apart by revolution, infighting, and internecine strife. In William Naphy's analysis, "Calvin offered stability and the expertise necessary to construct not only an enduring ecclesiastical structure but also a system to institutionalise and

44. William Naphy, "Calvin's Church in Geneva: Constructed or Gathered? Local or Foreign? French or Swiss?," in *Calvin and His Influence, 1509–2009*, ed. Irena Backus and Philip Benedict (Oxford: Oxford University Press, 2011), 102.

45. Willem van 't Spijker, "Bucer's Influence on Calvin: Church and Community," in *Martin Bucer: Reforming Church and Community*, ed. D. F. Wright (Cambridge: Cambridge University Press, 1994), 37–41.

46. T. H. L. Parker, *John Calvin: A Biography* (Louisville: Westminster John Knox, 2007), 68.

constitutionalise Geneva's revolutionary governmental and bureaucratic structure. One might justifiably argue that Calvin was recalled as much for his legal training as for his theological prowess."[47] At its core, Calvin's constitution simply took the powers granted the bishops, nobles, and canons under the old monarchical government and reallocated them to the new elected representative bodies while creating some new offices, "most notably the city's investigating magistrate (the Lieutenant)."[48] While Geneva was not as true a democracy as the New England townships of colonial America would be a century later, the move to transfer the executive and judicial powers away from inherited offices and ecclesiastical appointments (the nobility and Catholic bishops) into the hands of elected local officials was—for Europe in the sixteenth century—quite radical. Thus, while far from a modern democracy, sixteenth-century Geneva stands as a crucial step in the development of modern democracy. In fact, as much as 90 percent of the adult male population of Geneva was politically enfranchised. Granted, the degree of enfranchisement was relative to birthright: native-born Genevans (*citoyen*) had full political enfranchisement, foreign-born long-term residents could purchase *bourgeois* status, and those unable to afford *bourgeois* status lived in Geneva as resident aliens (*habitants*).[49] Resident aliens had the right to sue in legal cases and were subject to the same laws as full citizens, but they "had no right to carry swords, to participate in elections, or to hold any public post, except pastor or lecturer at the school."[50] Ironically, Calvin, who drafted the Genevan constitution, was himself a *habitant* until 1559, a few years before his death, which meant that "until 1559 he was liable to summary expulsions."[51]

Admittedly, even if he did not initiate them, Geneva's more oligarchical tendencies existed with Calvin's tacit approval, but he was instrumental in the transfer of power from a medieval feudal system to a more egalitarian constitutional republican form of government. Thus, despite Calvin's

47. William G. Naphy, "Church and State in Calvin's Geneva," in *Calvin and the Church: Papers Presented at the 13th Colloquium of the Calvin Studies Society, May 24–26, 2001*, ed. David Foxgrover (Grand Rapids: Published for the Calvin Studies Society by CRC Product Services, 2002), 14.

48. Naphy, "Church and State," 15.

49. Harro Höpfl, *The Christian Polity of John Calvin* (Cambridge: Cambridge University Press, 1982), 132–34.

50. Höpfl, *Christian Polity*, 133.

51. Höpfl, *Christian Polity*, 134.

authoritarian and dogmatic reputation, Jean-Jacques Rousseau rightly praises Calvin in *The Social Contract* (1762): "Those who know Calvin only as a theologian much under-estimate the extent of his genius. The codification of our wise edicts, in which he played a large part, does him no less honour than his *Institute*. Whatever revolution time may bring in our religion, so long as the spirit of patriotism and liberty still lives among us, the memory of this great man will be for ever blessed."[52] Both Bucer and Calvin were magisterial reformers who welcomed the state's assistance in implementing ecclesiastical reforms, but "magistrates and laity, having at the invitation of evangelicals eliminated clerical autonomy and power, were now quite unprepared to relinquish any part of their new-found independence to an evangelical clergy."[53] In practical terms, the anticlericalism that had fueled many of the Protestant reforms prevented a new clerical hierarchy from replacing the old one, even as fears of the Anabaptist and peasant revolts pushed for Christian obedience to the secular state (with Rom. 13:1 cited as justification for this position). Therefore, even though Bucer and Calvin both viewed the state as a partner in the spiritual care of believers, neither granted the state final say in matters of doctrine and discipline. This is yet another example of how Calvin's thought is both conservative—demanding believers obey the governing authorities—and surprisingly progressive, laying the groundwork for the separation of church and state that now defines the modern secular state.

As discussed in chapter 2, while demanding obedience to the state, Calvin also argues for and defends legitimate resistance to tyrannical rulers in instances where the state usurps the Word of God. This is a point of commonality with Bucer, who also argued that rulers must submit themselves to the lordship of Jesus Christ: "As the Kingdom of Christ subjects itself to the kingdoms and powers of this world, so in turn every true kingdom of the world (I say kingdom, not tyranny) subjects itself to the Kingdom of Christ, and the kings themselves are among the first to do this, for they are eager to develop piety not for themselves alone, but they also seek to lead their subjects to it."[54] These comments, written in

52. Jean-Jacques Rousseau, *The Social Contract & Discourses*, trans. G. D. H. Cole (London: J. M. Dent & Sons, 1920), 36n1.

53. Höpfl, *Christian Polity*, 31.

54. Martin Bucer, *De Regno Christi*, in *Melanchthon and Bucer*, ed. and trans. Wilhelm Pauck (Philadelphia: Westminster, 1969), 186–87.

1533 amid Bucer's efforts to implement ecclesiastical and civil reforms in Strasbourg, show how the idea that the state confers legal authority on the church's governance was well established by the time Calvin settled in Strasbourg between stays in Geneva. Calvin, like Bucer, assumed that the church and the state were coworkers in ministry, each with distinct jurisdictions but working in tandem to build the common good. Crucial to both Bucer's and Calvin's ecclesiologies is the caveat that the legitimate governing authority (whatever form it takes) draws its authority from its obedience to the Word of God, as illustrated by Bucer's distinction between "kingdom" and "tyranny."

In Romans 13:1, the Christian is expected to obey the established authorities and all prevailing laws as if instituted by God, which is why those ordained to pastoral ministry in Geneva were expected to take an oath that stated, "I promise and swear to be subject to the polity and constitution of the City, to show a good example of obedience to all others, being for my part subject to the laws and the magistracy."[55] Yet the significant proviso for understanding both Bucer's and Calvin's conceptions of church-state relations is the clause immediately following: "so far as my office allows."[56] *If* the state is obedient to the Word of God and embraces its role in the proclamation of the gospel, *then* it is deserving of obedience; if the state usurps God's authority and implements unjust laws, then pastors, as well as legally appointed magistrates, have a duty to resist the tyranny of the state (Acts 5:29)—"that is to say without prejudice to the liberty which we must have to teach according to what God commands us and to do the things which pertain to our office."[57]

The ensuing vision of church and civil community resounds throughout Calvin's works; the church's responsibility of spiritual governance works harmoniously with the state's responsibility for maintaining peace, order, and the common good—all grounded in the biblical mandate that the faithful become the body of Christ in the priesthood of all believers (1 Pet. 2:9). The theme of plural ministries within an egalitarian governing structure proceeds from Calvin's project to liberate spirituality from the cloister and relocate it within every dimension of the secular world, and the consequence is a view of ministry that involves all believers—the

---

55. Calvin, "Draft Ecclesiastical Ordinances (1541)," 72.
56. Calvin, "Draft Ecclesiastical Ordinances (1541)," 72.
57. Calvin, "Draft Ecclesiastical Ordinances (1541)," 72.

believer in the pew, the pastor in the pulpit, and the politician in public office—such that "each individual has his own kind of living assigned to him by the Lord as a sort of sentry post so that he may not heedlessly wander about throughout life."[58] These ideas, also woven throughout Bucer's ecclesiology, had a profound influence on the direction of the Protestant Reformation and the rise of the modern nation-state, as evidenced in this passage from Bucer's *De Regno Christi* (1533): "Everyone, a private person as well as one appointed to public service, has his watchman, inspector, and observer who will urge him to do his duty if he should fail it in some manner or if he should sin in any way."[59] Since every Christian is subject to Christ's lordship, from the lowliest laborer to the highest-ruling monarch, the communion of saints (*communio sanctorum*) is ultimately an egalitarian fellowship (*koinōnia*), a shared life together in which all believers are responsible for and accountable to one another. This, above all else, is the basis on which ecclesiastical and civil polity are founded.

The most important consequence of this kind of egalitarian communal structure is the rejection of any kind of authoritarian absolutism in either the church or the state. Ultimately, these ideas—whether in rejection of papal absolutism or absolute monarchy—became part of the cultural milieu that gave rise to the new nation-states of Europe. At the same time, the multinational character of the Reformation can be seen in Calvin's commitment to the social and economic practices of the diaconal ministry in Geneva and was also embodied in the founding of the Genevan Academy, an international school designed to educate clergy and doctors to serve in nascent Protestant communities throughout the diverse nations and cultures of Europe and later the world. It is no surprise, then, that within this international and migratory reforming movement, Calvin's vision for church order and ecclesial communion across borders evinced a certain level of what we might today call "multicultural tolerance." Reformed catechisms and local confessional statements were one way for different churches across political and cultural boundaries to mutually recognize one another and form a unified-yet-diverse community. Rather than adopting the top-down universalism of Rome, Calvin took steps to bring together diverse congregations into a "network of churches, geographically

58. Calvin, *Institutes*, 3.10.6.
59. Bucer, *De Regno Christi*, 368.

separate, each possessing its own confession."[60] This international and multicultural network "was intended to be both mutually supportive and mutually correcting, a family in which there was room for some diversity in common communion."[61]

For Further Reading

Calvin, John. "The Doctors and Ministers of the Church, Their Election and Office." In *Institutes of the Christian Religion*, vol. 2, edited by John T. McNeill, translated by Ford Lewis Battles, bk. 4, chap. 3, 1053–68. Philadelphia: Westminster John Knox, 1960.

———. "Draft Ecclesiastical Ordinances (1541)." In *Calvin: Theological Treatises*, edited and translated by J. K. S. Reid, 56–72. Philadelphia: Westminster, 1954.

———. "The Necessity of Reforming the Church." In *Calvin: Theological Treatises*, 183–216.

———. "The True Church with Which as Mother of All the Godly We Must Keep Unity." In *Institutes of the Christian Religion*, vol. 2, bk. 4, chap. 1, 1011–41.

60. Elsie Anne McKee, "The Character and Significance of John Calvin's Teaching on Social and Economic Issues," in *John Calvin Rediscovered: The Impact of His Social and Economic Thought*, ed. Edward Dommen and James D. Bratt (Louisville: Westminster John Knox, 2007), 19.
61. McKee, "John Calvin's Teaching," 19.

The Cosmopolitan Calvin and Religious Intolerance

Consequently, though ecclesiastical discipline does not permit us to live familiarly or have intimate contact with excommunicated persons, we ought nevertheless to strive by whatever means we can, whether by exhortation and teaching or by mercy and gentleness, or by our own prayers to God, that they may turn to a more virtuous life and may return to the society and unity of the church. And not only those are to be so treated, but also Turks and Saracens, and other enemies of religion. Far be it from us to approve those methods by which many until now have tried to force them to our faith, when they forbid them the use of fire and water and the common elements, when they deny to them all offices of humanity, when they pursue them with sword and arms.

—John Calvin[1]

This chapter expands and develops an idea that first appeared in my previously published article "*De orilla a orilla*: The Ecumenical Theology of Luis Rivera-Pagán," *Journal of Hispanic/ Latino Theology* 18, no. 1 (November 2012): 26–34. Used with permission.

1. John Calvin, *Institutes of the Christian Religion, 1536 Edition*, trans. Ford Lewis Battles, rev. ed. (Grand Rapids: Eerdmans, 1986), 62. For the Latin text, see Joannis Calvini, *Opera*

John Calvin's reforms aimed to create uniformity of belief and liturgical practice among the residents of Geneva and its immediate rural environs, shifting the focus of corporate worship away from the Mass and onto the reading and interpretation of God's written Word. The twofold role of church presbyters—pastors and ruling elders—was to educate believers in the Reformed faith and maintain proper discipline among the faithful, guided by a careful reading of Sacred Scripture. Accordingly, when reading Calvin's *Institutes*, one ought to take seriously his admonition that it is a text written *for believers*—those desiring to better understand God's loving mercy—and not intended to provide a thorough refutation of blasphemous or heretical views, let alone an attempt to convert the infidel: "Because my intention here is to lead teachable persons by the hand, not to fight hand to hand with contentious, rebellious men, I will not now combat them with troops in battle array."[2] Therefore, the primary goal of the Genevan consistory was "to educate residents in the Reformed faith and to wean them of a wide range of Catholic and popular practices they deemed unacceptable."[3] Given this desire for confessional unity, a brief but rich passage unique to the 1536 edition of the *Institutes* hints at a more cosmopolitan attitude toward other religions that might help us better understand Calvin's views on religious toleration.

The passage, quoted in its entirety as the epigraph for this chapter, presents an irenic vision of Christian coexistence with Turks and Saracens (and, by extension, Jews), but its removal from subsequent editions of the *Institutes* undermines the argument that Calvin advocated for tolerance of the non-Christian other. In fact, the argument can be made—and was made by the humanist scholar and Reformed theologian Sebastian Castellio (1515–63)—that its omission in later editions is proof of Calvin's intolerance.[4] Outraged by Calvin's involvement in the execution of Michael Servetus in 1553, Castellio included two short passages from Calvin's theological oeuvre (including this passage from chapter 2 of the 1536 *Institutes*) in a

selecta, ed. P. Barth (Munich: Keiser, 1926), 1:91. When citing the 1536 edition, if a passage is found also in the final 1559 edition, its location there will be provided parenthetically.

2. Calvin, *Institutes, 1536 Edition*, 44.

3. Jeffrey R. Watt, *The Consistory and Social Discipline in Calvin's Geneva* (Rochester, NY: University of Rochester Press, 2020), 40.

4. For an overview of Castellio's polemical argument over against Calvin's Genevan reforms, see Ronald H. Bainton, *Studies in the Reformation* (Boston: Beacon, 1963), 139–81; and Steven E. Ozment, *Mysticism and Dissent: Religious Ideology and Social Protest in the Sixteenth Century* (New Haven: Yale University Press, 1973), 168–202.

published anthology of patristic and contemporary theological texts arguing for religious toleration. Castellio's intent was to expose Calvin's hypocrisy: the man who defended Turks and Saracens in 1536 was complicit in burning Servetus at the stake in 1553. While Castellio's polemical attack should be read with some degree of skepticism given it was crafted to discredit Calvin, Castellio's argument does raise a genuine problem for interpreters of Calvin's work: "Three years after its first appearance, a text which seemingly argues for the rights of Turks, Saracens, and others vanishes without trace. No remotely equivalent phrase replaces it. What factors determined its inclusion in the first *Institutio*, and what its exclusion in the second?"[5]

This chapter begins by exegeting this controversial passage within the context of the larger argument Calvin makes in chapter 2 of the 1536 *Institutes*, compares this passage to similar (if scant) texts in the rest of Calvin's oeuvre that advocate for religious tolerance, and argues for a more forgiving take on Calvin's involvement in the execution of Michael Servetus. The chapter concludes by comparing Calvin's humanistic impulse for tolerance to that of another highly influential sixteenth-century theological figure, the Dominican friar Bartolomé de Las Casas (1484–1566).

The Question of Religious Toleration

The passage under investigation, present only in the 1536 edition of Calvin's *Institutes*, should be read not as part of a structured argument for religious tolerance—though, as this chapter will demonstrate, one can find traces of a humanistic call for greater tolerance in Calvin's theology—but as part of Calvin's defense of a Reformed understanding of church governance and discipline. Specifically, the passage in question is located in the middle of an extensive argument about the proper use of excommunication in the life of the church, which is to bring the errant Christian into full communion: "In this sense are to be taken excommunications, not those by which persons who have (before men) separated from the church's flock, are cast outside the hope of salvation; but only those by which they are chastised until they return to the path from the filth of their previous life."[6] In other words, unlike the ban or excommunication in the Anabaptist and

5. Robert White, "Castellio against Calvin: The Turk in the Toleration Controversy of the Sixteenth Century," *Bibliothèque d'Humanisme et Renaissance* 46, no. 3 (1984): 575.
6. Calvin, *Institutes, 1536 Edition*, 62 (4.12.5).

Roman Catholic churches, excommunication in the Reformed churches is neither permanent nor reflective of the sinner's eternal state, for only God knows who is saved and who is damned: "The elect cannot be recognized by us with assurance of faith."[7] While it is God's singular prerogative to know the elect, God still provides the church with some concrete criteria by which to identify its members and maintain them on the Christian path: "Scripture describes certain sure marks to us, as has previously been said, by which we may distinguish the elect and the children of God from the reprobate and the alien, insofar as He wills us so to recognize them."[8]

Christ has instituted the church as a beacon for the elect, gathering them together in fellowship, united by confession of faith, with the understanding that in this world the elect and the reprobate live side by side and many a hypocrite remains ensconced in the visible church. The clearest marks of election are the believer's acceptance of God's Word for living their (moral) life and participation in the sacraments (properly administered). Accordingly, the church recognizes no believer is perfect, so it exercises the ban as a way of instructing and nurturing believers to keep them on the narrow path (Matt. 7:13–14). Thus, those who stray from the example set by Christ "ought by some sort of judgment of love to be deemed elect and members of the church. They should so be considered, even if some imperfection resides in their morals (as no one here shows himself to be perfect), provided they do not too much acquiesce and flatter themselves in their vices. And it must be hoped concerning them that they are going to advance by God's leading ever into better ways, until, shed of all imperfection, they attain the eternal blessedness of the elect."[9] In other words, God provides these external marks of the faithful (*notae fidelium*) to distinguish the Christian from the unrepentant sinner, as well as from the heretic, the infidel, and the pagan. Excommunication exists to preserve the integrity of the church, to protect it from heresy and moral hypocrisy. While moral perfection is unattainable in this life, and some common vices are tolerated in the congregation (even as church discipline is employed to move believers closer to perfection), the unity of the church is maintained by excommunicating those who profess heretical beliefs or whose hypocritical recidivism reveals a persistent pattern of unrepentance. Nevertheless, upon confession of sin

7. Calvin, *Institutes, 1536 Edition*, 61 (4.1.8).
8. Calvin, *Institutes, 1536 Edition*, 61 (4.1.8).
9. Calvin, *Institutes, 1536 Edition*, 61 (4.1.8).

and proper penance (usually an act of public contrition and a statement of faith), such persons should be welcomed back into the communion.

The proper use of excommunication is not to punish but to reform the believer, motivated by a "judgment of love" on the part of the pastors and ruling elders, who seek to reunite the errant sinner with the people of God. Accordingly, Calvin warns church leaders against abusing their power to discipline believers: "Let us not claim for ourselves more license in judgment, unless we wish to limit God's power and confine his mercy by law. For God, whenever it pleases him, changes the worst men into the best, engrafts the alien, and adopts the stranger into the church. And He does this to frustrate men's opinion and restrain their harshness— which venture to assume for themselves a greater right of judgment than is fitting."[10] It is in this context, after having made it clear that through excommunication one is never "cast outside the hope of salvation" but is only "chastised until they return to the path," that Calvin introduces the Turks and the Saracens among a list of the "enemies of religion" in order to illustrate proper Christian comportment toward those currently outside the communion. While the faithful are exhorted not to live among or have "intimate contact with" the excommunicated, this does not justify cruel or abusive treatment of the excommunicated.[11] Far from it. Instead, Calvin chastises past Christian behavior toward the non-Christian other, from trying "to force them to our faith," to denying "them all offices of humanity," to pursuing them "with sword and arms," implying that we ought to treat the infidel (Turks, Saracens, Jews) and heretics (Catholic and Anabaptist Christians) the same way we treat the excommunicated Christian—with love, mercy, and compassion in the hope that through our Christlike praxis we might bring them into union with the church.[12]

Calvin's advice focuses on the Christian's actions toward the religious other, specifically those who through their words and deeds undermine Christian faith, be it the moral hypocrite, the religious heretic, or the religious infidel, in order to commend a distinctly Christian attitude toward those who oppose Christian faith and virtue. By accepting "the acts done

10. Calvin, *Institutes, 1536 Edition*, 62 (4.12.9).
11. Calvin, *Institutes, 1536 Edition*, 61 (4.12.10).
12. Calvin, *Institutes, 1536 Edition*, 61 (4.12.10). While the first part of this paragraph is found in all subsequent editions, the second part, in which Calvin mentions Turks and Saracens explicitly in a plea for Christian tolerance, appears in no other edition of the *Institutes*.

to one another in the best part," and "not twist[ing] them deviously and sinisterly as suspicious persons are accustomed to do [Matt. 7:1–5; Rom. 12:9–10; 14:13, 19; 1 Thess. 5:15; Heb. 12:4]," the Christian is then encouraged to "commit them [those who oppose us] to God's hand, commend them to his goodness, hoping for better things from them than we now see. For thus it will come to pass that as we bear with one another in mutual equity and patience and nourish peace and love, not stupidly bursting into God's more secret judgments, we will not entangle ourselves in the darkness of error."[13]

Calvin's vision of the church is both local and transnational, confessional and ecumenical, to the degree that he "does not exclude members of other churches from the true church" and "leaves the determination of the true Christians up to God."[14] Calvin never authorizes the church to overstep its limits; it has been empowered to employ discipline to make sure that in its confessions and its actions the church is as faithful as humanly possible in this life, but it has also been warned that the power to discipline members is to be used in love to build up the body of Christ (Eph. 4:12). It is a sinful act of idolatry for the visible, historical church to set itself up as gatekeeper of eternal judgment, yet it does have a responsibility to make sure the church in the world reflects the two Reformed marks of the church: "Wherever we see the Word of God purely preached and heard, and the sacraments administered according to Christ's institution, there, it is not to be doubted, a church of God exists [cf. Eph. 2:20]."[15] Under this overarching rubric, it is entirely possible for a believer to be a member of the true church even if they worship in an errant congregation or belong to a heretical sect, because "we recognize as members of the church those who, by confession of faith, by example of life, and by partaking of the sacraments, profess the same God and Christ with us."[16] Consequently, while Calvin continued his attack on what he perceived to be the Roman Catholic Church's idolatrous practices in every edition of the *Institutes*,

13. Calvin, *Institutes, 1536 Edition*, 61 (4.12.9).
14. Jeannine E. Olson, "Church and Society: Calvin's Theology and Its Early Reception," in *Calvin's Theology and Its Reception: Disputes, Developments, and New Possibilities*, ed. J. Todd Billings and I. John Hesselink (Louisville: Westminster John Knox, 2012), 197.
15. John Calvin, *Institutes of the Christian Religion*, ed. John T. McNeill, trans. Ford Lewis Battles, 2 vols. (Louisville: Westminster John Knox, 1960), 4.1.9. Assume the 1559 *Institutes* is being cited unless otherwise noted.
16. Calvin, *Institutes*, 4.1.8.

he nevertheless acknowledged that "individual Catholics were not necessarily excluded from the true church."[17]

As noted in the previous chapter, Calvin opposed schism in the church[18] and worked to maintain ecclesial unity through his participation in ecumenical colloquies, both with Rome and with other Protestant bodies.[19] Thus, while Calvin and the Genevan consistory desired creedal and liturgical uniformity in Geneva, Calvin tolerated a level of doctrinal dissensus in his dialogue with other confessional bodies, often for diplomatic reasons, as evidenced by the actions of his associate and successor, Theodore of Beza (1519–1605), at the Colloquy of Poissy in 1561. There Beza rejected aspects of the Lutheran Augsburg Confession to appease the Roman Catholic contingent in an effort to effect some degree of reconciliation between the Roman Catholic rulers of France and the persecuted Huguenot minority.[20] As Calvin argues in book 4 of the *Institutes*, "The church universal is a multitude gathered from all nations; it is divided and dispersed in separate places, but agrees on the one truth of divine doctrine."[21] Accordingly, every local church, and those in positions to discipline members within those bodies, must proceed in humility to treat those with whom they disagree—even those who threaten the unity and well-being of the local church—with a spirit of reconciliation and a gentleness of conduct in the hope that, through their Christlike compassion and moral example, these "enemies" might become reunited with the church, since "we are not to despair of them as though they were cast outside God's hand."[22]

Without question, Calvin is arguing for increased patience and tolerance from Christians toward all those outside the church, whether excluded via excommunication, national origin, or religious identity. Therefore, even though this passage from the 1536 edition was excised from all later editions, the gist of Calvin's argument remains, since limiting God's ability to

17. Olson, "Church and Society," 197.
18. Calvin, *Institutes*, 4.1.10–16; 4.2.9–12.
19. See Randall C. Zachman, "Revising the Reform: What Calvin Learned from Dialogue with the Roman Catholics," in *John Calvin and Roman Catholicism: Critique and Engagement, Then and Now*, ed. Randall C. Zachman (Grand Rapids: Baker Academic, 2008), 165–92; and Eva-Maria Faber, "Mutual Connectedness as a Gift and a Task: On John Calvin's Understanding of the Church," in *John Calvin's Impact on Church and Society, 1509–2009*, ed. Martin Ernst Hirzel and Martin Sallmann (Grand Rapids: Eerdmans, 2009), 122–44.
20. See Carter Lindberg, *The European Reformations* (Oxford: Blackwell, 1996), 271–73.
21. Calvin, *Institutes*, 4.1.9.
22. Calvin, *Institutes, 1536 Edition*, 61 (4.12.5).

redeem even the most hostile infidel is itself an act of rebellion and idolatry by the church. Admittedly, Calvin stands with the early church fathers, citing Saint Cyprian, in naming the church the "Mother" of all believers, declaring, "Away from her [the church], one cannot hope for any forgiveness of sins or any salvation."[23] Yet we need to recall that these admonitions were written for believers, specifically church leaders, as guidance for disciplining members and maintaining church unity. Therefore, when Calvin says that "it is always disastrous to leave the church,"[24] it is not a call for excluding non-Christians who have never heard the gospel but a nurturing act of pastoral care toward those who have turned away from the church.

Ultimately, the goal of the church's proclamation—whether aimed at the censured believer or the religious outsider—is to persuade the sinner to repent. Thus, while the doctrinal instruction and pastoral discipline that maintain the purity and unity of the church are provided primarily for the Christian believer, Calvin is convinced that the church stands as a beacon and example for the entire world, the external means by which the Holy Spirit acts in the world to invite humanity into and maintain relationship with Christ. Unlike the Anabaptists, who sought to maintain the purity of the church by excommunicating all who dissented from their understanding of doctrinal unity, Calvin strove for a church that was as pure as possible *while* working to reform the whole of society (rather than withdraw from it) by having the church work in complement with the state. Thus, *if* believers are commanded to encourage reconciliation with the excommunicated and the unchurched through their prayers, compassionate acts, and moral toleration without undue recrimination, *then* the state is tasked with maintaining a just social order in which virtuous behavior is encouraged through the enactment of just laws. As Calvin makes clear when delineating the separate jurisdictions of church and state, "The church does not have the right of the sword to punish or compel, not the authority to force; not imprisonment, nor the other punishments which the magistrate commonly inflicts."[25] Furthermore, the church's discipline, unlike the use of coercion by the state, is not designed to force obedience through punishment but aims at an interior change of heart.

Therefore, while Calvin's plea for religious tolerance in the 1536 *Institutes* is secondary and peripheral to his central argument about church

23. Calvin, *Institutes*, 4.1.4.
24. Calvin, *Institutes*, 4.1.4.
25. Calvin, *Institutes*, 4.11.3.

governance, structure, and discipline, the adequate treatment of the religious other remains a concern. In the 1539 edition, the passage explicitly naming Turks and Saracens is replaced by a quotation from the apostle Paul exhorting the Christian believer to clemency when dealing with the religious enemy: "Do not regard them as enemies, but warn them as believers" (2 Thess. 3:15). Again, while this teaching is primarily intended to instruct the church on how to treat those members it has excommunicated, Christians are encouraged to always act with mercy and compassion because in doing so they might encourage genuine repentance—an admonition that includes not only the chastised Christian but *anyone* outside the walls of the church. Once again citing the apostle Paul, Calvin writes that the church ought to balance severity with mildness in exercising church discipline: "But we ought not to pass over the fact that such severity as is joined with a 'spirit of gentleness' [Gal. 6:1] befits the church. For we must always, as Paul bids us, take particular care that he who is punished be not overwhelmed with sorrow [2 Cor. 2:7]. Thus a remedy would become destruction."[26] Without explicit reference to Turks or Saracens, Calvin's theology preserves the core humanist principles of toleration and nonviolence while concentrating on the primarily pastoral and ecclesiological concerns stemming from the church's use of excommunication. There is no evidence that Calvin ever recanted the idea of religious tolerance articulated in the 1536 edition. A brief overview of how Calvin treated Jews and Muslims in his theological and polemical works will confirm Calvin's more cosmopolitan direction, especially when compared to the medieval church and Calvin's theological precursor, Martin Luther.

Jews and Muslims in the Protestant Reformation

Though Calvin often employed Jews and Muslims (the latter he usually referred to as Turks) as convenient tropes in his sermons and commentaries, he had little to no direct knowledge of Muslims and likely did not meet any Jews until he lived in Strasbourg (1538–41), since all Jews had been expelled from France in 1394 and Geneva in 1491.[27] Therefore, when evaluating Calvin's attitudes toward Jews and Muslims, readers

26. Calvin, *Institutes*, 4.12.8.
27. See William W. Emilsen, "Calvin on Islam," *Uniting Church Studies* 17, no. 1 (June 2011): 69–86; and Mary Potter Engel, "Calvin and the Jews: A Textual Puzzle," *Princeton Seminary Bulletin*, Supplementary Issue 1 (1990): 106–23.

deal mostly with rhetorical categories far removed from the historical realities of sixteenth-century Jews and Muslims. Like that of almost all his Christian contemporaries, Calvin's general attitude toward Judaism is supersessionist insofar as he reads the Old Testament through a christological lens and faults the Jews for not recognizing Christ (Messiah) in their Scriptures: "God willed that the Jews should be so instructed by these prophecies that they might turn their eyes directly to Christ in order to seek deliverance."[28] Yet, unlike that of many of his sixteenth-century contemporaries, Calvin's exegesis of the Old Testament led him to conclude that, despite there being a distinction between the Old and New Testaments, "there has always been only a single covenant of grace embracing Israel and the church."[29] Therefore, Calvin's comments about Judaism tend to focus on biblical Judaism in ancient Israel and during the time of Christ; they have very little to say about Judaism in sixteenth-century Europe.

Similarly, his comments about Muslims tend to focus on the denial of trinitarian belief in the Qur'an rather than on the political and military realities of the Ottoman Empire under Suleiman I in the sixteenth century. Unlike his contemporaries Martin Luther (1483–1546), Martin Bucer (1491–1551), and Philip Melanchthon (1497–1560),[30] Calvin never wrote a treatise on the Turkish problem and did not enter the debate over whether Christians ought to engage in holy war against the Turks. Arguably, Calvin's geographic location in Western Europe shielded him from the direct effects of the Turkish threat since he was not a citizen of the Holy Roman Empire—in fact, Francis I of France was a political enemy of the Hapsburgs and enlisted the Ottoman Empire in his machinations against the Hapsburg dynasty—though it has been theorized that Calvin removed the passage about Turks and Saracens from the second edition of the *Institutes* in protest of King Francis's alliance with the Turks.[31]

28. Calvin, *Institutes*, 2.6.4.
29. Paul E. Capetz, "The Old Testament and the Question of Judaism in Reformed Theology: Calvin, Schleiermacher, and Barth," *Journal of Reformed Theology* 8 (2014): 140.
30. Martin Luther published several treatises on the Turkish threat, including *On War against the Turk* (1529), *Army Sermon against the Turks* (1529), and *Admonition to Prayer against the Turk* (1541). For a thorough study of Luther's writings and engagement of Islam in the sixteenth century, see Adam S. Francisco, *Martin Luther and Islam: A Study in Sixteenth-Century Polemics and Apologetics* (Leiden: Brill, 2007).
31. White, "Castellio against Calvin," 579. See Noel Malcolm, *Useful Enemies: Islam and the Ottoman Empire in Western Political Thought, 1450–1750* (Oxford: Oxford University Press, 2019), 57–103.

Regardless, there are few references to the Qur'an in Calvin's oeuvre, and he does not quote a single passage from it despite having access to a Latin translation. What emerges from a survey of Calvin's references to Turks and Islam in his published works is the sense that Calvin is mostly concerned with the threat Islamic faith poses to Christian orthodoxy, since he focuses on those aspects of Islamic belief that repeat and condone past Christian heresies like Arianism and Nestorianism.

Even though Calvin considered Jews and Muslims infidels, primarily because both religions denied the divinity of Christ and rejected the trinitarian God, there is much in Calvin's humanistic outlook that distinguishes him on this issue from the mainstream of late-medieval Christianity (which commonly employed torture and holy war in its efforts to convert Jews and Muslims) as well as from his Protestant contemporaries, who argued for holy war against the Ottoman Empire. Calvin had a more tolerant and cosmopolitan Christian attitude toward the non-Christian other. In fact, his approach to the study of Jewish sources when interpreting the Old and New Testaments led to accusations of "Judaizing." In keeping with his humanist training, Calvin sought to better understand the New Testament by returning to the original sources (*ad fontes*) in their original languages, Koine Greek and ancient Hebrew. The Protestant reformers' efforts to translate the Bible into the vernacular (for example, Luther's German New Testament) necessitated detailed study of the Septuagint (the Greek translation of the Old Testament used by the New Testament authors), which in turn led the reformers to study the Old Testament in Hebrew and to adopt the Masoretic text and canon of the Old Testament preserved by rabbinic Judaism. Here Protestant reformers distinguished themselves from Roman Catholic and Eastern Orthodox traditions by accepting as canonical *only* those Old Testament texts accepted as canonical by rabbinic Judaism in the Tanakh and placing those other texts found in the Catholic and Orthodox Old Testaments in a separate "Apocrypha."[32] The charges of "Judaizing" leveled against many Protestant reformers, Calvin included, stemmed from their appeal to Jewish exegetes of the Old Testament in efforts to better understand the grammatical and historical meaning of the Hebrew source materials.

32. Capetz, "Old Testament," 125–30.

In Calvin's exegesis of the Old Testament, this "Judaizing" tendency becomes most apparent in his defense of divine inspiration in the authorship of both Testaments, in distinction from Luther, thereby affirming one covenant with humanity that necessitated a reading of the Bible as one unified text: "Therefore, inasmuch as all divinely uttered revelations are correctly designated by the term 'word of God,' so this substantial Word is properly placed at the highest level, as the wellspring of all oracles."[33] Consequently, Calvin did not believe that Jesus taught a new or different law than Moses; rather, he believed that Jesus in the Sermon on the Mount provided the correct interpretation of the law first given to Moses, restoring "it to its integrity, in that he freed and cleansed it when it had been obscured by the falsehoods and defiled by the leaven of the Pharisees."[34] Thus, unlike Luther, who opposed the law to the gospel, Calvin embraced the law as the same revelation from God, only now that we are under Christ's forgiveness it becomes possible for the law to lead us on the path of righteousness: "Where the entire law is concerned, the gospel differs from it only in respect to its clear manifestation."[35] This is evident in Calvin's "third" use of the law: "The third and principal use, which pertains more closely to the proper purpose of the law, finds its place among believers in whose hearts the Spirit of God already lives and reigns."[36] Accordingly, despite ultimately falling in the supersessionist camp, Calvin differentiated himself from many of his sixteenth-century contemporaries by valuing the Jews and Israel as exemplars of faithful discipleship and not just rebellious disobedience. He also rejected the dominant trope that labeled and rejected Jews as "Christ killers," even as he concluded that Jews had cut themselves off from God by rejecting Christ, cautioning Christian believers in his commentary on Romans 9–11 not to boast of their status as God's elect in place of the Jews, since God can just as easily graft the Jews back in again: "It should be enough for us that God threatens the Gentiles with the same punishment as He had inflicted on the Jews, if they become like them."[37]

33. Calvin, *Institutes*, 1.13.7.
34. Calvin, *Institutes*, 2.8.7.
35. Calvin, *Institutes*, 2.9.4.
36. Calvin, *Institutes*, 2.7.12.
37. John Calvin, *Calvin's New Testament Commentaries*, vol. 8, *The Epistles of Paul the Apostle to the Romans and to the Thessalonians*, trans. Ross MacKenzie, ed. David W. Torrance and Thomas F. Torrance (Grand Rapids: Eerdmans, 1995), 253.

While Calvin had less knowledge of Islam than he did of Judaism, there are multiple references to Turks and Saracens in the *Institutes*, and his letters, sermons, and biblical commentaries often mention Turks, who in sixteenth-century Christian literature had become representative of all of Islam. As Anthony Lane has noted, "There are thirty-three mentions of Muhammad in the fifty-nine volumes of the *Calvini Opera*, more than any other medieval author, including Gregory I and Calvin's beloved Bernard of Clairvaux."[38] As with Judaism, Calvin's comments on Islam reveal little about Islam itself—especially the faith of his sixteenth-century Muslim contemporaries—and serve mostly as convenient polemical tropes in some larger argument. As William W. Emilsen contends, "Islam becomes a kind of rhetorical device, a 'whipping boy,' and not every anti-Islamic statement is primarily directed against Islam."[39] Thus, while Calvin does state in a sermon on Deuteronomy 18:15 that the prophet is one of "the two horns of antichrist,"[40] and in his commentary on Daniel 11:37 he contends that "Mohammed allowed full scope to various lusts, by permitting a man to have a number of wives,"[41] these texts appear amid polemical attacks on the hypocrisy of the Church of Rome and the papacy, which "shall pay no respect to any other god, for he shall consider himself greater than all" (Dan. 11:37). Like Rome, Islam tolerates no other gods yet is oblivious to its own idolatry. In this regard, Islam is no more or less deluded than Roman Catholicism and is thus no further from salvation than Rome is. In fact, in an apologetic treatise addressed to Emperor Charles V and the princes of Europe, Calvin pleads with them to prioritize reforming the church despite the potential of invasion by the Turks:

> The Turkish war now occupies the minds of all, and fills them with alarm. It may well. Consultations are held to prepare the means of resistance. This, too, is prudently and necessarily done. All exclaim that there is need of no ordinary dispatch. I admit that there cannot be too much dispatch, provided

---

38. Emilsen, "Calvin on Islam," 73. See Anthony S. Lane, *John Calvin: Student of the Church Fathers* (Edinburgh: T&T Clark, 1999) and *Calvin and Bernard of Clairvaux*, Studies in Reformed Theology and History (Princeton: Princeton Theological Seminary, 1996).

39. Emilsen, "Calvin on Islam," 73–74.

40. See John Calvin, *Sermons on Deuteronomy*, trans. Arthur Golding, 16th–17th Century Facsimile Editions (London: Banner of Truth, 1987), quoted in Theodore Bowers, *What You Should Know about Islam* (Bloomington, IN: iUniverse, 2019), chap. 11 (ebook).

41. John Calvin, *Calvin's Commentaries*, trans. Calvin Translation Society, 23 vols., 500th anniversary ed. (Grand Rapids: Baker Books, 2009), 13:188.

in the meantime, the consultation which ought to be first, the consultation
how to restore the Church to its proper state is neither neglected nor re-
tarded. . . . The fuel of the Turkish war is within, shut up in our bowels, and
must first be removed, if we would successfully drive back the war itself.[42]

Calvin, like Erasmus and Luther before him, interpreted the rise of the
Ottoman Empire as divine judgment against a faithless Christendom, in
the same way God had used the ancient Assyrian and Babylonian Em-
pires to punish the nation of Israel for its apostasy. Thus, the ever-present
threat of Turkish invasion was not evidence of God's impotence against
the rising tide of Islam but the unfolding of a divine providence that had
"allowed him [the Turk] greater freedom, for the purpose of punishing
the ungodliness and wickedness of men."[43]

Despite the military threat posed by the Turks, Calvin considered the
papacy a bigger threat, and in his mind all three—the Roman Church,
Jews, and Turks—represented variations of the same sinful idolatry: "The
Turks, the Jews, and the papists will confess that there is one God, Creator of heaven and earth, but they nonetheless overflow with thousands
of superstitions, and instead of worshipping the living God, they have
idols upon idols."[44] In fact, it could be argued that Calvin directed the
worst of his polemical rhetoric at the Roman Church because at least the
idolatry of the Turks originated in their ignorance of the gospel: "They
[Roman Catholics] know no more than a pagan or Turk who has lived
his entire life in barbarism, and who has never heard of God, the Father
of the Lord Jesus Christ."[45] Yes, Calvin employs the Turks as a warning
motif in his argument against Rome, and in doing so often demonizes
Muslims, but ultimately he does not present them as wholly outside the
scope of God's salvation: "This much is certain. When God comes to
judge the world, Turks, gentiles, papists, and other unbelievers will be

42. John Calvin, "The Necessity of Reforming the Church," in *John Calvin: Tracts and
Letters* (London: Banner of Truth, 2009), 1:233.

43. John Calvin, *Commentary on the Book of the Prophet Isaiah*, trans. William Pringle
(Ingersoll, ON: Devoted Publishing, 2019), 3:66.

44. John Calvin, "Release from Fear in God's Mercy (26 October 1550), Sermon 34," in
*Sermons on the Acts of the Apostles Chapters 1–7: Forty-Four Sermons Delivered in Geneva
between 25 August 1549 and 11 January 1551*, trans. Rob Roy McGregor (Edinburgh: Banner
of Truth, 2008), 475.

45. John Calvin, *Sermons on Galatians*, trans. Kathy Childress (Edinburgh: Banner of Truth,
1977), 486.

treated much more gently than we, unless we take better advantage than we usually do of the kindness and benefits God provides for us daily."[46] Yes, if Jews, Muslims, and even papists persist in their idolatry, they will be judged accordingly—in the *Institutes* Calvin unequivocally states, "God is comprehended in Christ alone"[47]—but Protestant Christians who have received the Word of God in the Holy Spirit and yet turned away in disobedience will be judged more harshly.

The Case of Michael Servetus

Calvin has been singled out and rebuked for his involvement in the execution by burning at the stake of Michael Servetus in 1553 in Geneva, as if any of his Christian contemporaries would have acted any differently. As Alister McGrath argues, if anyone is to blame, it is the whole of sixteenth-century Christendom, since "every major Christian body which traces its history back to the sixteenth century has blood liberally scattered over its credentials. Roman Catholic, Lutheran, Reformed and Anglican: all have condemned and executed their Servetuses."[48] In fact, McGrath suggests Calvin's Geneva ought to be noted for its restraint and toleration, given that "Servetus was the *only* individual put to death for his religious opinions in Geneva during Calvin's lifetime, at a time when executions of this nature were a commonplace elsewhere."[49] There is no better example of the sectarian violence motivated by religious hatred that defined the Reformation era than the St. Bartholomew's Day Massacre of 1572, where a targeted series of assassinations of Huguenot leaders gave rise to a wave of Catholic mob violence that resulted in three thousand deaths in Paris alone and over thirty thousand deaths across all of France.[50] This heinous act of religious intolerance was then commemorated by Pope Gregory XIII, who commissioned the artist Giorgio Vasari to paint three frescos in the Sala Regia, the state hall of the Apostolic Palace in Vatican

46. John Calvin, "To Whom the Promise Belongs (18 January 1550), Sermon 4," in *Sermons on the Acts of the Apostles Chapters 1–7*, 47.
47. Calvin, *Institutes*, 2.6.4.
48. Alister McGrath, *A Life of John Calvin: A Study in the Shaping of Western Culture* (Oxford: Blackwell, 1993), 120.
49. McGrath, *Life of John Calvin*, 116.
50. See Barbara B. Diefendorf, *Beneath the Cross: Catholics and Huguenots in Sixteenth-Century Paris* (Oxford: Oxford University Press, 1991), 93–106.

City, depicting the wounding and death of Admiral Coligny, whose assassination triggered the mob violence, to go along with a set of frescos
commemorating the defeat of the Turks at the Battle of Lepanto (1571).[51]

Yet Calvin is singled out and reviled as the repressive theocrat of Geneva
intent on imposing Reformed orthodoxy on the world. As Calvin biographer Bruce Gordon states in his chapter on the Servetus affair, "The execution of Michael Servetus in Geneva has defined John Calvin's posthumous
reputation. From the sixteenth century to this day detractors have seized this
moment as confirmation of his tyrannical, intolerant character."[52] Needless
to say, Calvin's own personality and fiery rhetoric contributed to this perception, as Reformation historian Ronald H. Bainton observes, since maintaining doctrinal purity was the driving force behind having Servetus executed.
It was done "to vindicate the honor of God by silencing those who sully
His holy name."[53] To be fair to Bainton, Calvin's published statements on
heresy from his commentary on Deuteronomy 13:5 are decidedly hardline:

> It must then be remembered, that the crime of impiety would not otherwise
> merit punishment, unless the religion had not only been received by public
> consent and the suffrages of the people, but, being supported also by sure
> and indisputable proofs, should place its truth above the reach of doubt.
> Thus, whilst their severity is preposterous who defend superstitions with the
> sword, so also in a well constituted polity, profane men are by no means to
> be tolerated, by whom religion is subverted. . . . God commands the false
> prophets to be put to death, who pluck up the foundations of religion, and
> are the authors and leaders of rebellion. Some scoundrel or other gainsays
> this, and sets himself against the author of life and death. What insolence
> is this! . . . And what wonder if God should command magistrates to be
> the avengers of His glory, when He neither wills nor suffers that thefts, for-
> nications, and drunkenness should be exempt from punishment. In minor
> offenses it shall not be lawful for the judge to hesitate; and when the wor-
> ship of God and the whole of religion is violated, shall so great a crime be
> fostered by his dissimulation? Capital punishment shall be decreed against
> adulterers; but shall the despisers of God be permitted with impunity to

51. E. Howe, "Architecture in Vasari's 'Massacre of the Huguenots,'" *Journal of the Warburg
and Courtauld Institutes* 39 (1976): 258–61.

52. Bruce Gordon, *Calvin* (New Haven: Yale University Press, 2009), 217.

53. Roland H. Bainton, *Hunted Heretic: The Life and Death of Michael Servetus, 1511–1553*
(Providence: Blackstone Editions, 2005), 116.

adulterate the doctrines of salvation, and to draw away wretched souls from the faith? Pardon shall never be extended to poisoners, by whom the body alone is injured; and shall it be sport to deliver souls to eternal destruction? Finally, the magistracy, if its own authority be assailed, shall take severe vengeance upon that contempt; and shall it suffer the profanation of God's holy name to be unavenged? What can be more monstrous! But it is superfluous to contend by argument, when God has once pronounced what is His will, for we must needs abide by His inviolable decree.[54]

Yet Bainton does not adequately acknowledge that Servetus's actions were considered heretical by all the magisterial reformers—including those of the Lutheran, Reformed, and Anglican traditions—as well as by the Roman Catholic Church and that the civil authorities of every nation in Europe recognized heresy as a capital criminal offense.

Meanwhile, Renaissance humanism influenced Reformation thought and contributed to the rise of religious tolerance as both a civic virtue and a doctrinal problem. Sir Thomas More, best known for his fictional *Utopia* (1516), arguably stands as the first humanist to advocate for complete legal recognition of religious tolerance in the sixteenth century. *Utopia* presents an ideal society affirming religious pluralism whose king "decreed first of all that everyone could practice the religion of his choice and could also strive to convert others to it, but only so long as he advocated it calmly and moderately with rational arguments," while anyone who "quarrels insolently about religion is punished with exile or enslavement."[55] In a later philosophical treatise, *A Dialogue concerning Heresies and Matters of Religion* (1528), More questions the logic of punishing heresy with the death penalty and reflects on the possibility of toleration and clemency, even to the point of abolishing capital punishment, while recognizing the civil government's duty to maintain order and restrain sectarian violence: "Princes are bound to see that they shall not suffer their people to be reduced and

---

54. Calvin, *Commentaries*, 2:76.

55. Thomas More, *Utopia*, trans. Clarence H. Miller, 2nd ed. (New Haven: Yale University Press, 2014), 118. Like Calvin, Thomas More is a product of his day and age. Therefore, we must contextualize his humanistic cosmopolitanism within the Catholic-Protestant conflicts of the sixteenth-century reformations and acknowledge his unfair treatment of evangelicals and his persecution of William Tyndale. See Carl S. Meyer, "Thomas More and the Wittenberg Lutherans," *Concordia Theological Monthly* 39, art. 23 (1968): 246–56. According to biographer Peter Ackroyd, in rooting out the Protestant heresy More broke into Lutherans' homes and sent men to the stake. Peter Ackroyd, *The Life of Thomas More* (New York: Anchor Books, 1999), 224–34.

corrupted by heretics, since the peril shall in short while grow to as great, both with men's souls withdrawn from God and their goods lost and their bodies destroyed by common sedition, insurrection and open war, within the bowels of their own land."[56] Although advocating for religious toleration, More also recognizes that the state will not surrender the power of the sword so long as sectarian voices continue to employ seditious violence.

Calvin lived and breathed the same humanist oxygen as Thomas More, as did Calvin's critic Sebastian Castellio, who exploited the "toleration controversy" over the paragraph in the 1536 *Institutes*, encouraging tolerance of Turks and Saracens, as part of his spirited defense of Michael Servetus. Not only did Castellio present Calvin as an opportunist and hypocrite who backpedaled on religious tolerance for political gain, but he also presented Servetus as a paradigm of humanist thought and religious toleration by noting his profound engagement with Islam and the Qur'an in his controversial book *Christianismi Restitutio* (1553). In the end, one of the charges brought against Michael Servetus was his familiarity with the teachings of the Qur'an in defending his anti-trinitarian views. However, to then blame Calvin for Servetus's execution, even as every nation in Europe would have prosecuted him for his published heretical works, seems unwarranted and indicative of an anti-Calvin prejudice.

Michael Servetus (1511–53), a Spanish humanist, theologian, physician, and cartographer, published his first heretical text, *On the Errors of the Trinity* (1531), in his youth, ostensibly an attack on traditional Christology and trinitarian dogma, which "necessitated his withdrawal from Catholic lands"; and his insistence on articulating an anti-trinitarian theology later made "his residence untenable also on Protestant soil."[57] After being prosecuted by the Inquisition, Servetus assumed the name Michel de Villeneuve while living in France and established his reputation as a cartographer, medical doctor, and pharmacologist. After concluding his medical studies in Paris, he took a position as court physician for the archbishop of Vienne, and in 1545 Servetus (having gained French citizenship under the name Villeneuve) began a lengthy correspondence

---

56. Thomas More, *A Dialogue concerning Heresies and Matters of Religion*, in *The Dialogue concerning Tyndale by Sir Thomas More: Reproduced in Black Letter Facsimile from the Collected Edition (1557) of More's English Works*, ed. William Edward Campbell (London: Eyre and Spottiswoode, 1927), 279.

57. Bainton, *Hunted Heretic*, 13.

with Calvin in Geneva, who, given the heretical nature of the topics discussed in their correspondence, adopted the pen name Charles d'Espeville. The pattern of their exchange is consistent: Servetus would present his objections to trinitarian orthodoxy to Calvin, Calvin would defend the orthodox position, and Servetus would dispute Calvin's arguments. Calvin responded to Servetus's arguments and eventually sent him a copy of his *Institutes* to provide a fuller presentation of the orthodox position, which Servetus returned with handwritten commentary along with a copy of his unfinished and yet unpublished *Christianismi Restitutio* (Restoration of Christianity) and suggested he come visit Calvin in Geneva. Calvin, convinced only God could change Servetus's rebellious heart, warned Servetus not to come to Geneva. When Servetus published his book and sent Calvin a copy, Calvin judged it to be filled with errors and "prodigious blasphemies against God," so when on August 13, 1553, Michael Servetus was recognized while attending Sunday worship in Calvin's church, Calvin contacted the civil magistrate to arrest him.

Calvin, as pastor of Geneva, acted to protect his congregation and Geneva's church reforms from the stain of heresy and political sedition at a time when he had yet to solidify his position in Geneva and was involved in a struggle with the Libertine party. Furthermore, at the time Calvin did not even have citizenship in Geneva, much less any governmental authority of his own, so all he could do was appeal to the civil authorities as pastor. Ultimately, Servetus's fate rested entirely in the hands of the duly elected magistrates. By 1553, Michael Servetus had lived most of his adult life as a fugitive. He had been tried and convicted to be burned at the stake in Spain, after which he was forced to live under a false identity in France. Yet he continued to publish heretical texts, knowing that the religious and spiritual authorities of every nation in Europe agreed that tolerating views as openly defiant of religious orthodoxy as those he espoused threatened the social order.

The prosecution of Servetus in Geneva, ironically led by Claude Rigot, a member of the Libertine party and a political enemy of Calvin, was noted for its careful adherence to procedure. The Genevan rulers even sought the advice and opinions of leaders in neighboring sovereign states, including those in Zurich, who affirmed that they too would enforce capital punishment in the case of Servetus. This encouraged the magistrates of Geneva, in the words of Rigot, to "work against him with great faith and diligence especially as our churches have an ill repute abroad as heretics and patrons of heretics. God's holy providence has now indeed provided this occasion whereby you may at once purge yourselves and us from this fearful suspicion of evil."[58] Thus, Servetus's trial, conviction, and execution did not arise from any animosity harbored by Calvin, and beyond serving as a theological expert witness in Servetus's trial, Calvin had no direct impact on the outcome of the trial. In fact, Calvin appealed to the city council for a more humanitarian means of execution but was ignored. Yes, the burning at the stake of Servetus stands as a stain on Reformed Christianity—actually, a black mark against all sixteenth-century Christendom—but "it is improper to single out Calvin as if he were somehow the initiator of this vicious trend, or a particularly vigorous and detestable supporter of the practice, where the majority of his enlightened contemporaries wished it to be abolished."[59] At worst, Calvin's crime was that he was too much a man of his time.

Christianity and the Problem of Other Religions

The encounter between European Christianity and the autochthonous cultures of the "New World," beginning in 1492, is an event like few others in human history. As Father Virgilio Elizondo, one of the pioneering voices of North American Latinx theology, points out, never before has such a massive biological mixture, clash, and confluence of human cultures occurred.[60] The conquest of the Americas—taking place at the same time the Protestant Reformation was challenging Catholic hegemony in Europe—is instructive when wrestling with the theological problems that arise when Christianity encounters and engages other religions and cultures. There is a tendency to look to one of the central figures during the discovery, conquest, and evangelization of the Americas, Bartolomé de Las Casas (1484–1566), when articulating a theology of religious tolerance. In this regard, Luis Rivera-Pagán's body of work has provided an invaluable service to both theological and historical scholarship on Las Casas, taking great pains to portray the uniqueness of Las Casas's views on the emancipation and evangelization of Native and African peoples in the Americas in historical context, while

58. Quoted in Bainton, *Hunted Heretic*, 138.
59. McGrath, *Life of John Calvin*, 120.
60. Virgilio Elizondo, *Galilean Journey: The Mexican-American Promise*, 2nd ed. (Maryknoll, NY: Orbis Books, 2000), 5.

simultaneously cautioning modern readers against projecting anachronistic theological agendas onto the sixteenth-century Dominican friar.

Whether one frames the problem in the language of evangelism and missiology or approaches it from a philosophical argument that seeks to examine the competing claims of different faith perspectives, contemporary Christian thought—in exploring the relationship of Christianity to other faiths—must try understanding the role of religion in motivating and justifying the violent conquest of the Americas. To this end, Las Casas stands as something of a proto-liberationist. Still, as Rivera-Pagán has artfully argued in his monumental work *A Violent Evangelism* (1992), Las Casas also embodied many cultural and theological attitudes incongruent with twenty-first-century emancipatory theologies. Nonetheless, we cannot minimize the importance of Las Casas's chief thesis—that as creatures made in the image and likeness of God, the Native peoples of the New World are endowed with reason and are thus the equals of European Christians in the eyes of God.

To my mind, there are similarities between the sixteenth-century Catholic perspective of Bartolomé de Las Casas and the sixteenth-century Reformed perspective of Calvin. Granted, the stereotypically theocratic Calvin bears little resemblance to the more cosmopolitan and tolerant Las Casas, yet both exhibit a similar narrow-mindedness toward other religions that makes them unlikely paradigms for articulating a contemporary theology of religious pluralism. Nevertheless, both sixteenth-century theologians fully embrace the non-Christian other as the image of God and call for more compassionate treatment of the other; even "when it is someone who not only is worthless, but also has insulted and injured us, this is not reason enough for us to cease loving, pleasing, and serving him."[61]

At best, Calvin's and Las Casas's views of other religions are paternalistic. At worst, they embody a bigoted intolerance in their push for religious uniformity. From a twenty-first-century perspective, their views are exclusivist and rooted in an ideology of Christian exceptionalism. Make no mistake, Las Casas's prophetic defense of Native cultures against Spanish dehumanization and exploitation is remarkable for its time and establishes Las Casas as one of the giants of the Christian faith. At the same time, however, it is evident that for Las Casas there is only one true

61. Calvin, *Institutes*, 3.7.6.

faith, and that is Catholic Christianity. In his worldview, Protestants are heretics, Muslims and Jews are infidels, and unbaptized Native people are pagans. Granted, as pagans the people of the Americas do not merit burning at the stake like unrepentant heretics, nor can the Spanish conquest of the New World be considered a "just war" in the same way Christians wage wars against Muslim "enemies of the faith," but their status as idolaters seems to preclude the possibility of engaging Indigenous religions in mutually enriching dialogue. As seen above, Calvin shares the same rigid categorizations when engaging and describing the non-Christian other, albeit with Roman Catholicism labeled heretical, yet there are glimpses of a more cosmopolitan outlook in his theological thought that may push against the religious intolerance that characterized the European Middle Ages, as evidenced by the passage calling for toleration of Turks and Saracens in the first edition of the *Institutes*. What makes both thinkers stand out from the rest of sixteenth-century Christendom is how they develop similar arguments about the universal human tendency to seek to know and worship God: "There is within the human mind, and indeed by natural instinct, an awareness of divinity."[62]

As we study the past, Rivera-Pagán calls us to be sensitive to historical context and to respect the particularity of our subjects. It is recognition of Las Casas's particularity as a Catholic Christian of the sixteenth century that allows us to see how unique and noteworthy his views on the emancipation and empowerment of the Native peoples are, even while he remains an uncomfortable conversation partner for contemporary interreligious discourse. As Rivera-Pagán writes, "Las Casas cannot free himself from his orthodox Catholic vision," for he "agreed with his missionary colleagues that idolatry should be completely eliminated, but exclusively through persuasive and reasonable preaching and the patient example of a genuine Christian life, excluding violence."[63] Las Casas distinguishes himself from his peers not only through his commitment to a nonviolent evangelism (though he was not a pacifist and left room in his worldview for just war) but also through his subtle analysis of Indian "idolatry." For Las Casas, those arguments made by Juan Ginés de Sepúlveda and others justifying the political domination, forced servitude, and coerced conversion

---

62. Calvin, *Institutes*, 1.3.1.

63. Luis N. Rivera, *A Violent Evangelism: The Political and Religious Conquest of the Americas* (Louisville: Westminster John Knox, 1992), 156.

to Christianity of Indigenous populations are rendered illegitimate and in certain cases, such as in the appeal to the Augustinian notion of just war, are redefined as mortal sins. While Las Casas's idealization of Native cultures has contributed to the modern myth of the "noble savage," Rivera-Pagán locates this forgivable loss of objectivity in its proper context: defending "the full humanity of the natives."[64] In light of this cosmopolitan and humanist argument, Rivera-Pagán names the *Apologética historia sumaria* (1542) by Las Casas "the most impressive effort on the part of a white and Christian European to demonstrate the rational integrity and full humanity of non-European, non-white and non-Christian nations."[65]

There is in Las Casas's works a framework for addressing the challenge of interfaith dialogue and interaction in our day and age. Guided by the axiom that "all nations of the world are human,"[66] and stressing the full equality of Europeans and Native peoples, Las Casas attempted a peaceful evangelization of the Native populations that sought to respect the political autonomy of their cultures: "Our Christian religion is the same and can be adapted to all the nations of the world and from all it equally receives, and it does not take from any of them their lordships nor does it subjugate them."[67] Despite this enlightened cosmopolitanism, Rivera-Pagán uncovers in Bartolomé de Las Casas a man very much bound by many of the biases and prejudices of sixteenth-century Iberian Catholicism in spite of his profound—and deeply theological—struggle on behalf of the defenseless and powerless Indigenous peoples. The Spanish Catholic view of the Native people of the New World was that they were unbaptized, idolatrous savages in desperate need of conversion, even forced conversion, for the sake of their eternal salvation. Thus, even Las Casas, who defended the Native cultures and civilizations of the Americas, viewed them as idolatrous and described their religions as demonic. Accordingly, such a profound lack of cultural diversity in this one sphere—religion— undermines Las Casas's applicability to the contemporary problem of religious pluralism and the relationship of Christianity to other religions.

64. Rivera, *Violent Evangelism*, 142.
65. Rivera, *Violent Evangelism*, 142.
66. Bartolomé de Las Casas, *Apologética historia sumaria*, quoted in Rivera, *Violent Evangelism*, 143.
67. Bartolomé de Las Casas, *Historia de las Indias*, quoted in Rivera, *Violent Evangelism*, 144.

Along with his argument about the inherent rationality of Native peoples, Las Casas developed an argument justifying the Spanish Catholic missionary efforts in the New World by appealing to the universal human inclination to worship God. Las Casas contended that idolatry, that "universal plague of the human race," arises when the innate human desire for communion with the divine is corrupted by devils and becomes a "parody of authentic worship."[68] Here Rivera-Pagán highlights an undeveloped but theologically weighty comment by Las Casas. Las Casas says that the Indigenous Americans "had a special knowledge of the true God."[69] Although he never expanded this particular insight further, Las Casas did defend Native religious practices, even human sacrifice, which he viewed as proof of the Native peoples' profound reverence for the divine: "I held and justified many conclusions that no one before me dared touch on or write about, and one of them was that to offer humans to a false or true God (taking the false one to be true) . . . is not against natural law or reason."[70] Yet, in spite of this high degree of tolerance toward Native spirituality, in the end Las Casas shared the Spanish Catholic belief that divine providence was utilizing the Spanish Empire as the instrument for bringing about the conversion, and thereby eternal salvation, of the Native peoples of the Americas.

For Las Casas, as for Calvin, there is no salvation outside the church—*extra ecclesiam nulla salus*. Accordingly, the same Catholic fervor that drove and motivated Las Casas's more emancipatory actions—such as his use of the sacraments of baptism and penance in his political battle to protect the rights and freedoms of the Native people—also fueled his intolerance toward Indigenous religions. His ultimate motivation was the same: both the ignorant pagans (Native peoples) and the violent oppressors (Spanish conquistadores) stood on the brink of eternal damnation. If anything, the plight of the Catholic conquerors was worse, for the sin of the Native peoples arose from ignorance while the sin of the Spanish arose from an avarice incompatible with their baptism. (It is an argument quite like Calvin's for clemency toward the Turks.) Thus, Las Casas could label the Iberian oppressors of the Indians "supporters of the reign of

68. Rivera, *Violent Evangelism*, 156.
69. Rivera, *Violent Evangelism*, 156.
70. Bartolomé de Las Casas, *De regia potestate*, quoted in Rivera, *Violent Evangelism*, 159.

Satan and opponents of the holy church of Christ . . . precursors not of Christ but of the anti-Christ."[71]

Without question, there are similarities between the sixteenth-century Catholic perspective of Las Casas and the sixteenth-century Protestant perspective of Calvin. While Las Casas points to demonic agency to explain the corruption of the natural human instinct to worship God into idolatry, and Calvin appeals to the reprobate state of fallen humanity, both conclude that whether out of ignorance or willful malice, all people "degenerate from the true knowledge of [God]" and fall into idolatry.[72] Furthermore, both agree that Christ has instituted the church and the sacraments as the means by which salvation is mediated to humanity. Thus, despite Calvin's affirmation that salvation is by grace through faith, he nevertheless argues for the necessity of the church, since "in our ignorance and sloth (to which I add fickleness of disposition) we need outward helps to beget and increase faith within us. . . . [God] instituted 'pastors and teachers' [Eph. 4:11] through whose lips he might teach his own; . . . [and] he instituted sacraments, which we who have experienced them feel to be highly useful aids to foster and strengthen faith."[73] Like Las Casas—though with a much different nuance—Calvin also proclaims that there is no salvation outside the church.

While both sixteenth-century figures reflect the religious intolerance of their age, both also preserve within their theological visions an opening, however small, that allows us to explore and engage different theological perspectives. There is only one God, and that God is Lord over all creation, which means that on the basis of our shared humanity—as creatures made in the image and likeness of God—we are created to seek communion and fellowship with that God and with one another. Therefore, despite theological and confessional differences, a central Christian belief underlies Las Casas's assertions that "all the nations of the world are human" and all people are equally "endowed with reason." Recalling Rivera-Pagán's thesis that evangelization became a secondary concern to the domination and exploitation of Native peoples, we ought to recognize that the encounter between Europeans and Indigenous peoples in the New World should not

71. Bartolomé de Las Casas, *Del único modo de atraer a todos los pueblos a la verdadera religion*, quoted in Rivera, *Violent Evangelism*, 244.

72. Calvin, *Institutes*, 1.4.1.

73. Calvin, *Institutes*, 4.1.1.

be cast as an encounter between "the one true religion" and "the idolatrous Indigenous religions." Rather, it should be cast as an encounter between competing idolatries: the conquerors' religion, which was tainted by greed and lust, and the Native religions, which perpetuated highly hierarchical caste systems that denied large segments of the populations full humanity and political freedom. Both of these were forms of false religion.

This, of course, raises the theological question of how to distinguish true from false religion, which brings us to the final theme in Rivera-Pagán's analysis of Las Casas: the Dominican friar's unyielding commitment to the liberation of all people. Las Casas and his Catholic contemporaries shared a general worldview and saw their mission in the New World in the same light, as a divine call to bring salvation to the Indigenous peoples of the Americas, but they differed on how this evangelization ought to be carried out. This difference, as Rivera-Pagán has argued, is the hermeneutical key for distinguishing between a theology that justifies the enslavement, oppression, and genocide of entire populations and a theology that struggles for the full humanity and holistic liberation of all people as the image and likeness of God. Looking back at Las Casas's sixteenth-century context, we can distinguish between false religion and true religion by considering the actions of the different parties: "What moves them: the liberation of captives . . . or the skinning of bodies?"[74]

What I am suggesting in comparing the theological defense of Indigenous peoples by Las Casas to the plea for clemency and nonviolence in Calvin's treatment of excommunicated Christians, heretics, and infidels is neither new nor particularly profound, but it bears repeating, especially when we undertake our vocation as theologians to read and interpret the Word of God for the people of God. I am arguing that all human narratives—the Bible included—are products of hermeneutical picking and choosing. I am not denying that the Bible is the revealed Word of God—far from it. But our access to this revelation is mediated through human means. And in the process of that mediation, revelation becomes distorted, whether through ignorance or deliberate deception. Therefore, the principles embodied in Luis Rivera-Pagán's study of Bartolomé de Las Casas can guide our process of discerning the spirits so that we will take care (as much as is humanly possible) when reading a text to understand

74. Rivera, *Violent Evangelism*, 268.

that text's original context, to become more aware of how our autobiography and our tradition color our reading, to intentionally engage in meaningful conversation with those who have different readings, and to ultimately judge our reading by the standard of whether or not it leads to greater liberation and human fulfillment. Narratives are products of the human imagination. Thus, the ability to create, transmit, and reshape theological narratives arises from our being created in the likeness and image of God. Rather than viewing the role of human creation in the formation of the biblical canon with suspicion, we can learn much from literary criticism about how texts are communally created and interpreted and, in that process, accept responsibility for those texts we hold most sacred. If we believe that God is love and that God commands us not to take human life, then we must accept *our role* in granting and preserving the authority of those texts that have been used to justify oppression and violence. In other words, we must take care not to make false gods—that is, idols—out of our most sacred texts. Surely, Calvin would agree.

For Further Reading

Calvin, John. "Brief Reply in Refutation of the Calumnies of a Certain Worthless Person." In *Calvin: Theological Treatises*, edited and translated by J. K. S. Reid, 331–43. Philadelphia: Westminster, 1954.

———. "The Difference Between the Two Testaments." In *Institutes of the Christian Religion*, vol. 1, edited by John T. McNeill, translated by Ford Lewis Battles, bk. 2, chap. 11, 449–64. Philadelphia: Westminster John Knox, 1960.

———. "Faith: Containing an Explanation of the Creed." In *Institutes of the Christian Religion, 1536 Edition*, translated by Ford Lewis Battles, chap. 2, 42–67. Grand Rapids: Eerdmans, 1975.

———. "Fallen Man Ought to Seek Redemption in Christ." In *Institutes of the Christian Religion*, vol. 1, bk. 2, chap. 6, 340–48.

———. *Sermons on Galatians*. Translated by Kathy Childress. Edinburgh: Banner of Truth, 1977.

———. *Sermons on the Acts of the Apostles Chapters 1–7: Forty-Four Sermons Delivered in Geneva between 25 August 1549 and 11 January 1551*. Translated by Rob Roy McGregor. Edinburgh: Banner of Truth, 2008.

6

A Scattered Inheritance—Calvin's Reception in Latin America

We have Paul's general statement that in the churches all things are to be done decently and in order. Accordingly, civil observances, by which bonds as it were order and decorum are kept in the assembly of Christians, are by no means to be classed among human traditions, but are rather to be referred to that rule of the apostle, provided they are not believed to be necessary for salvation, or bind consciences by religion, or are related to the worship of God. . . . For they not only overturn the freedom which Christ won for us but also obscure true religion and violate God's majesty, who alone wills to reign in our consciences through his Word. Let it therefore be an established principle that all things are ours, but we are Christ's. It is vain indeed to worship God where the doctrines and commandments of men are taught.

—John Calvin[1]

Ostensibly, this chapter serves as an introduction to the reception of John Calvin's theology in Latin America. The main questions guiding this research

---

An earlier version of this chapter was previously published as "Calvin's Influence in Latin America: A Scattered Inheritance," *Ciências da religião: História e sociedade* 4, no. 4 (2006): 136–48. Used with permission.

1. John Calvin, "1538 Catechism," in *Calvin's First Catechism: A Commentary*, ed. I. John Hesselink, trans. Ford Lewis Battles (Louisville: Westminster John Knox, 1997), 36–37.

are these: How is Calvin's theology understood in Latin America? What is the impact and legacy of Calvin's theology in the Latin American context? As a theologian shaped by both the Reformed/Calvinist tradition and Latin American liberation theology, I bring these two perspectives together in my work—as evidenced by the preceding chapters—in order to recover valuable and vital, though often neglected, resources within the Reformed tradition for articulating a socially transformative ethic. However, documenting the reception history and cultural influence of Calvin's theological corpus in Latin America is like putting together a jigsaw puzzle without knowing what the finished picture is supposed to look like and with several key pieces missing.

For example, although Calvin's *Institutes of the Christian Religion* (1559 edition) was translated into Spanish as early as 1597,[2] most recent Spanish-language studies on Calvin cite either the English translation of Calvin's commentaries or the original Latin texts, which suggests that the nonspecialist or layperson in Latin America has had limited access to Calvin's theology. Still, it is possible to draw some general conclusions about Calvin—or at least Calvinism—in Latin America by analyzing Protestantism's transformative role in the broader culture. There is some consensus among Latin American missiologists and church historians that Latin America never received an unmediated "Calvinist" interpretation of Christianity. Nonetheless, historian Florencio Galindo argues that the evangelical/mainstream form of Protestantism imported to Latin America and the Caribbean by nineteenth-century Protestant missionaries was greatly influenced by a Calvinist ethos, which, while not necessarily identifiable with any single confessional tradition, filters through most forms of contemporary Protestantism.[3] There is, without question, a Calvinist presence in Latin America. Just how influential Calvin himself has been on the formation of Latin American Protestantism remains an open question.

Understanding the Latin American Context

Until recently, Protestantism has not garnered serious historical analysis in Latin America, with most studies either demonstrating a Roman Catholic

2. This translation was undertaken by Cipriano de Valera, best known for his revised edition of Casiodoro de Reyna's Spanish translation of the Bible (1602).

3. Florencio Galindo, *El protestantismo fundamentalista: Una experiencia ambigua para América Latina* (Navarra: Editorial Verbo Divino, 1992), 7.

bias dismissive of Protestant sects as religious heterodoxy or reflective of the confessional interests of a specific Protestant group. Sociologist Jean-Pierre Bastian suggests analyzing Latin American Protestantism "from the angle of social political history, and in so doing to stress appropriately the actual part which Protestants played in specific political and social events."[4] This chapter adopts Bastian's methodological direction by exploring Calvinism's role in the development of the modern democratic state in Latin America to gain a tangible baseline for evaluating Calvin's influence on Latin American religion and culture.[5] By providing a very brief introduction to a broad and complex social phenomenon—the explosion of Protestantism in Latin America over the last forty years—I aim to demonstrate how the specifically religious goals of Protestant evangelistic efforts have contributed to and nurtured the development of democratic values in Latin American culture.

Protestantism did not exceed 1 percent of the Latin American population until the 1940s and 1950s. Nonetheless, Protestantism has been a force for cultural change in Latin America, even if only as a marginalized minority, since the earliest period of European conquest and colonization.[6] In the sixteenth century, Calvin and other church leaders in Geneva focused their evangelistic efforts close to home, establishing churches in the rural environs near Geneva and supporting the persecuted Protestant churches in France and, to a lesser extent, the rest of Europe. But in the 1550s, Calvin also lent his support to the establishment of a French Huguenot colony in the "New World" (see chap. 3 above). The ministry of Word and sacrament according to the Genevan rite was celebrated regularly in Brazil for a period of about five years in a region dominated by Catholic conquest, until the colony was attacked and destroyed by the Portuguese navy. Later, in the early seventeenth century, the Calvinist/Reformed presence in Latin

---

4. Jean-Pierre Bastian, "Protestantism in Latin America," in *The Church in Latin America: 1492–1992*, ed. Enrique Dussel (Maryknoll, NY: Orbis Books, 1992), 313.

5. See Aristómeno Porras, "Calvino y la cultura Occidental," in *Calvino vivo: Libro commemorativo del 450 aniversario de la Reforma en Ginebra* (Mexico City: Publicaciones El Faro, 1987), 149–57; Carlos Mondragón, "Valores de la democracia. La herencia religiosa," in *Nuevas interpretaciones de la democracia en América Latina*, ed. Horacio Cerutti and Carlos Mondragón (Coyoacán: Editorial Praxis, 1999), 143–69; and Mondragón, "Minorías sociales y el proceso de democratización en Latinoamérica," in *Democracia, cultura y desarrollo*, ed. Carlos Mondragón and Alfredo Echegollen (Coyoacán: Editorial Praxis, 1998), 179–205.

6. See Jean-Pierre Bastian, *Historia del protestantismo en América Latina* (Mexico City: Casa Unida de Publicaciones SA, 1990).

America was geographically limited to the Dutch colony of Pernambuco in northeastern Brazil, a community distinguished by its religious tolerance of Judaism and Catholicism, in marked contrast to the Portuguese-Spanish Catholic intolerance that labeled Protestantism heretical and enforced ideological and political homogeneity by means of the Inquisition.[7] Yet not until the nineteenth and twentieth centuries did North American and European missionary efforts establish a lasting Reformed theological presence in Latin America, mostly in the English-speaking Caribbean but also in Brazil, Mexico, Uruguay, and Guatemala.[8] Still, we must resist the temptation to view Latin American Protestantism as merely the result of foreign missionary efforts. Protestant ideals arrived in Latin America long before the established Protestant churches, and while it is impossible to generalize a single path of Protestant development, a country-by-country survey of Protestantism reveals a gradual diffusion of Protestant ideas that provided fertile ground for later missionary efforts.[9]

The Protestant Reformation in Europe and the Iberian conquest of Latin America were contemporaneous events. While Spain become the symbol of the Catholic Reformation in Europe, the New World became the laboratory for the systematic eradication of the Protestant heresy as the Portuguese-Spanish colonial territories established sociopolitical dominance through the marriage of church and state. In Spain, the Inquisition sought to eradicate the "Lutheran" heresy (1520–70), a policy exported to the New World with the establishment of Inquisitorial tribunals in Peru (1568) and Mexico (1571) that lasted until Latin American independence in the nineteenth century. Not surprisingly, Protestantism was viewed as both heretical and politically subversive, since Protestantism was the religion of England and the Netherlands, Spain's maritime enemies, and the colonial governments feared supporters of independence might also adopt it.

Accordingly, one method of evaluating the presence and influence of Protestantism during the three centuries of Spanish colonial rule is by

7. Bastian, *Historia del protestantismo*, 314–15.
8. See Jean-Jacques Bauswein and Lukas Vischer, eds., *The Reformed Family Worldwide: A Survey of Reformed Churches, Theological Schools, and International Organizations* (Grand Rapids: Eerdmans, 1999), 12–19.
9. See Carlos Mondragón, "Protestantes y protestantismo en América Latina: Reflexiones en torno a la variedad de experiencia en su introducción," *Espacio de diálogo* 2 (Fraternidad Theológica Latinoamericana, April 2005), http://www.cenpromex.org.mx/revista_ftl/ftl/textos/carlos_mondragon.htm.

analyzing the work of the Inquisition in the New World. The relatively few Inquisitorial cases suggest there was minimal Protestant intrusion into the political and religious hegemony of Catholic New Spain.[10] However, these cases tended to target foreign nationals who were just as likely to be targeted for differences in language and appearance as they were for heretical beliefs or criticisms of the Catholic Church. In other words, limiting study to the documented heresy trials does not account for the possibility of Native, underground Protestant movements, a possibility addressed in the Inquisition's published guidelines for identifying potential adherents of the "Lutheran" heresy.[11]

Another source for evaluating and quantifying the presence of Protestantism during the years of colonial rule comes from analyzing prosecutions for the possession, sale, and distribution of prohibited books. Not only had many of Martin Luther's works already been translated into Spanish as early as 1520 (one year prior to his excommunication), but the Roman Catholic Church in Latin America also prohibited the reading or dissemination of unauthorized Spanish translations of the Bible. In fact, possession of a Bible—even an authorized Catholic version—could lead to an Inquisitorial investigation since, in the opinion of the magisterium, an ignorant populace might stray from official orthodoxy by reading the Scriptures without proper interpretation. Bernardino de Sahagún, a prominent Franciscan, opined that "no book of Sacred Scripture, not a single chapter nor any part thereof, translated into the vulgar tongue, should be possessed by any except the [authorized] preachers in that language."[12] In 1559, five years before the official publication of the papal *Index Librorum Prohibitorum*, a list of prohibited texts appeared in Spain. This list banned translations of the Bible as well as books from heretics like Luther and Calvin and was used in Latin America by both the Inquisition and the governing authorities when inspecting trade vessels

---

10. See Gonzalo Báez-Camargo, *Protestantes enjuiciados por la Inquisición en Iberoamérica* (Mexico City: Casa Unida de Publicaciones, 1960). The author identifies 305 documented Inquisition tribunals during the three hundred years of Spanish colonial rule and another fifty-eight charged but not tried for sympathizing with the "Lutheran" heresy.

11. Báez-Camargo, *Protestantes*, 7. The author cites the relevant section of "El Edicto de Fe," titled "Secta de Lutero," providing criteria for identifying heretics. Throughout the literature of the period, the term *luterano* (Lutheran) includes *all* Protestant heretical groups.

12. Francisco Fernández del Castillo, ed., *Libros y libreros en el siglo XVI* (Mexico City: Fondo de Cultura Económica, 1982), 82 (my trans.).

arriving in the New World for subversive contraband. Yet, despite strict controls, heterodox literature entered the colony with ease, as the commercial book trade in sixteenth-century Latin America remained international and cosmopolitan in character in great part because of a thriving black market between Europe and North America. In fact, Protestant "propaganda" was not limited to texts from the European Reformation, as North American Calvinism, specifically the work of Cotton Mather (1663–1728), was disseminated in Latin America. Historian Cristina Camacho identifies Mather's Spanish-language catechism, *La Fe del Christiano*, as the first North American Protestant text written *specifically* for the promotion of Protestantism in Latin America.[13] Furthermore, prohibited literature was not limited to the Protestant heresy, as the climate of repression fostered by the Inquisition—especially fearful of the secularizing forces of modern political liberalism—sought to limit the free exchange of humanistic ideas.[14]

Protestantism and Democracy in Latin America

Eventually the independence revolutions in Latin America (1808–26) fostered a move toward modernization and secularization, and except for Brazil, the new nation-states adopted republican constitutions. Naturally, these new constitutions tended to be influenced more by the liberal Spanish constitution of Cadiz (1812) than by the more radical French and US constitutions. Thus, the greatest challenge for these new republics was reconciling Catholicism with liberal modernism. While the end of colonial rule also marked the end of the Inquisition in the New World, the spread of Protestantism in Latin America still depended on the growth of political liberalism to promote religious tolerance and eventually allow for a more permanent Protestant presence in what were still constitutionally Catholic nations. Consequently, the trade agreements between Latin American countries and Protestant countries like

13. Cristina Camacho, "La Nueva España según Cotton Mather," in *Formaciones religiosas en la América colonial*, ed. María Alba Pastor and Alicia Mayer (Mexico City: DGAPA/ UNAM, 2000), 52.

14. See Margarita Peña, *La palabra amordazada: Literatura censurada por la Inquisición* (Mexico City: UNAM, 2000); and Pablo González Casanova, *La literatura perseguida en la crisis de la Colonia* (Mexico City: Secretaría de Educación Pública, 1986).

Great Britain and the United States often hinged on clauses authorizing Protestant foreign nationals the right to worship and build churches. For example, the first draft of the Anglo-Mexican Treaty of 1825 denied religious tolerance to British subjects since the Mexican president, Guadalupe Victoria, felt such a provision violated the Mexican constitution.[15] According to Bastian, it is essential to understand the organic relationship between nascent Protestant groups and radical liberalism, "which promoted democratic and secularizing political models, if we are to distinguish the indigenous from the imported aspects of Latin American Protestantism."[16]

Countering the thesis that Protestant missions were little more than religious justification for United States colonial activity, Bastian argues that when United States imperialism expanded into Latin America after 1860, Protestantism had already been a stable presence for more than two decades. Therefore, "the raison d'etre of Protestant societies in Latin America during these decades had less to do with 'North American imperialism' than with the internal political and social struggles in the continent, which can be summed up as the confrontation between an authoritarian political culture and those minorities that desired a bourgeois modernity grounded in the individual redeemed from his/her caste origin and based on the equality of a participatory and representative democracy."[17] José Míguez Bonino, while accepting Bastian's hypothesis that the rise of Protestantism as a political and cultural force in Latin America was the consequence of many internal factors (including a populist yearning for political liberalization), warns that the marriage of convenience between North American missionaries (with their conservative and pietistic spirituality) and Latin American liberal intellectuals (with a more secularist orientation) contained within it certain irreconcilable differences: "I do not think it exaggerated to suspect that here we have a convergence of interests more than a similarity of ideas."[18]

Given Protestantism's role as a political and religious minority in Latin America, it follows that the growth of Protestantism is linked to

15. Bastian, "Protestantism in Latin America," 320.
16. Bastian, "Protestantism in Latin America," 325.
17. Bastian, *Historia del protestantismo*, 187 (my trans.).
18. José Míguez Bonino, *Faces of Latin American Protestantism: 1993 Carnahan Lectures*, trans. Eugene L. Stockwell (Grand Rapids: Eerdmans, 1997), 4.

the growth of religious freedom, respect for individual human rights, and increased constitutional protection for religious minorities. However, Latin American Protestantism has often been characterized as politically conservative and colonial in outlook for encouraging its members to avoid direct involvement in social and political struggles.[19] Such is the critique of Presbyterianism in Brazil by liberationist Rubem Alves, who argues that the characteristic feature of this brand of Protestantism is a complete and total agreement with a series of doctrinal affirmations ("right-doctrine Protestantism").[20] Most troubling for Alves is the fact that, at a time when many Protestants in Brazil were becoming involved in movements for social justice and reaching out to like-minded Roman Catholics, the Presbyterian Church of Brazil denounced such efforts as contrary to the gospel and banned from their communion pastors and laypersons involved in struggles for political liberation. In fact, when the military regime in Brazil consolidated its power through acts of political repression in the mid-1960s, Protestant churches remained silent (some even openly supported the regime). This analysis of what Alves calls the failure of liberal Protestantism's "utopian project" at the hands of "right-doctrine Protestantism" has often been applied mutatis mutandis to all Latin American Protestantism. However, more recent studies of Protestantism in Latin America contend that evangelicalism and social/political activism are not as incompatible as Alves suggests.

In the late 1960s, sociologist Christian Lalive D'Epinay, analyzing the rapid expansion of Protestantism in Latin America, argued that churches— especially the Pentecostal branch of Latin American Protestantism— encouraged members to avoid direct involvement in social and political struggles.[21] According to D'Epinay, the church became a "refuge" from the problems caused by the cultural shift from a traditional agricultural society to a more urban, industrial, and democratic one. This analysis has been called into question by Richard Shaull and Waldo Cesar, who put forth the thesis that Brazilian Pentecostals are increasingly concerned

19. See Antonio Carlos Barro, "The Identity of Protestantism in Latin America," in *Emerging Voices in Global Christian Theology*, ed. William A. Dyrness (Grand Rapids: Zondervan, 1994), 229–52.

20. See Rubem A. Alves, *Protestantism and Repression: A Brazilian Case Study*, trans. John Drury and Jaime Wright (Maryknoll, NY: Orbis Books, 1985).

21. See Christian Lalive D'Epinay, *Haven of the Masses: A Study of the Pentecostal Movement in Chile* (London: Lutterworth, 1969).

with struggles for social transformation.[22] Alongside those Protestants who rejected liberation theology there existed a movement of Protestant pastors and theologians, the Fraternidad Teológica Latinoamericana (established in 1971), that sympathized with many aspects of the liberation theology movement by emphasizing responsible social action even while remaining anti-communist. One of its members, José Míguez Bonino, argues in *Faces of Latin American Protestantism* (1997) that Protestantism in Latin America contains aspects of all three "faces"—liberal, evangelical, and Pentecostal. I contend that a yearning for political and social change exists in all branches of Latin American Protestantism and that only by ignoring those facets of the Calvinist/Reformed tradition that encourage political resistance and empowerment can Alves narrowly define Brazilian Presbyterianism—and by extension the entire evangelical "face" of Latin American Protestantism—as irredeemably repressive. The truth is that in the last thirty years, as evidenced by increased political involvement and electoral victories by evangelicals and Pentecostals in Peru, Brazil, and Mexico, there has been a resurgence of an emancipatory biblical hermeneutic within Latin American Protestantism that encourages Christians to embrace their civic responsibility. Some even see communal political action as facilitating their calling to evangelize in predominately Catholic countries.[23]

As the late Richard Shaull notes in his foreword to Alves's *Protestantism and Repression*, Alves has written an insightful and accurate description of how the Presbyterian Church of Brazil was transformed by a small number of reactionary leaders from a beacon of utopian hope to a facilitator of political repression—so much so that "the word 'Presbyterian' now calls to mind the destructiveness of religious fanaticism and repression."[24] Yet Shaull also observes that "Alves is more interested in understanding how Protestantism has functioned in the past than in showing what it can become in the future."[25] Nowhere in his analysis does Alves explain why the liberation movement within Brazilian Presbyterianism did not survive in any institutional form. So why didn't it? Shaull offers some thoughts: "Granted,

22. See Richard Shaull and Waldo Cesar, *Pentecostalism and the Future of the Christian Churches* (Grand Rapids: Eerdmans, 2000).

23. Mondragón, "Minorías sociales," 185.

24. Richard Shaull, foreword to Alves, *Protestantism and Repression*, xi.

25. Shaull, foreword to Alves, *Protestantism and Repression*, xvii.

the suppression was thorough and ruthless. Yet the leadership of the Presby-terian Church of Brazil could do no more than throw those who represented [the new, liberative spirit] out of the Church; they could not destroy the movement. In the past, many 'heretical' groups have survived and grown under severe persecution. One reason why this movement was destroyed was that its members did not expect nor were they prepared for the drastic steps that were taken against them. They had no strategy worked out for the survival of their communities."[26] The theme uniting many of my theological musings is the possibility of nurturing just such a strategy of resistance for the Latin American context by mining the rich theological resources of the Reformed tradition.

Protestants and Pentecostals in Latin America now number over forty million, still a political minority, but in some countries a powerful voting bloc. Latin American countries with substantial Protestant populations include Brazil (20 percent), Nicaragua (20 percent), Chile (12 percent), El Salvador (20 percent), and Guatemala (40 percent). Each of these has a strong Calvinist/Presbyterian presence. Even Mexico (4 percent Protestant), while still strongly Catholic, has between four and five mil-lion politically active evangelicals who have established political parties capable of affecting national elections.[27] Regardless of the numbers, the fact remains that Protestantism is a force of social and political change in Latin America, and one that can benefit from engaging the theo-logical resources of the Reformed tradition—specifically the theology and pastoral practice of Calvin—in order to empower Christian commu-nities in their political and evangelical struggles within the broader civil society.

Given all this, it is safe to conclude that the Calvin known in Latin America is a mediated Calvin—more Calvinist than Calvin—one filtered through the doctrinal orthodoxy encapsulated by the Synod of Dort (1618) and imported via Anglo-American missionary efforts. One recent study of Protestant fundamentalism in Latin America contends that Calvinism is foundational for understanding *most* forms of contemporary Latin American Protestantism:

26. Shaull, foreword to Alves, *Protestantism and Repression*, xvii.
27. See "Religion in Latin America: Widespread Change in a Historically Catholic Region," Pew Research Center, November 13, 2014, https://www.pewresearch.org/religion/2014/11/13/religion-in-latin-america/.

By *Calvinism* I refer not only to the theological system elaborated by John Calvin (1509–64) himself, but also to those streams of thought originating in his theology that today constitute the doctrinal foundation of the Reformed churches as well as the foundation of other traditions and churches (with slight variations)—like the Anglicans, Methodists, and Baptists. Accordingly, Calvinism is not identified with any single denomination or confession but with a system of thought that serves as the foundation for all Protestantism and has been an essential element in the cultural and social development of Protestant nations.[28]

Ironically, one thing both ideological extremes within Latin American Protestantism (fundamentalism and liberationism) have in common is that neither has undertaken a direct and thorough critical analysis of Calvin's theology, especially his writings on the church's transformative role in civil society.

Alfonso López Michelsen published an analysis of the Calvinist roots of Latin American political institutions in which he demonstrated, using his native Colombia as a case study for the development of Protestantism and democratic values, how the Calvinist tradition has shaped many of our modern political institutions.[29] Michelsen focused not on what Calvin said about different forms of government (monarchy, aristocracy, or democracy) but on what Calvin did in terms of organizing the civic and ecclesial life of Geneva, finding in Calvin's church order a representative system of government in which power flowed from the local to the national level and in which no one person or group wielded unilateral power. For Michelsen, the church governance implemented by the Calvinist tradition is a direct antecedent and model for the modern secular representative democracy, and in direct opposition to the top-down episcopal model of the Roman Catholic Church. Consequently, even though Calvinism has had a muted influence in Colombia (and the rest of Latin America), scholars must consider that wherever there has been a Calvinist presence, however small, it has contributed to the formation of democratic values. Carlos Mondragón argues that the Calvinist influence Michelsen has identified in Colombian political institutions ought to be expanded to the rest

---

28. Galindo, *El protestantismo fundamentalista*, 107 (my trans.).

29. See Alfonso López Michelsen, *La estirpe calvinista de nuestras instituciones políticas* (Bogotá: Ediciones Tercer Mundo, 1966).

of Latin America, especially when one considers the role of European political liberalism on the formation of independent nation-states in the nineteenth and twentieth centuries as well as the influence of the French and North American revolutions and the philosophical framework behind those revolutions—which can be traced to John Locke and Jean-Jacques Rousseau, two thinkers with links to the Calvinist tradition.

Throughout Calvin's discussion of civil government in the *Institutes*, a distinction is maintained between the spiritual and temporal realms; they are two aspects of a single "twofold government." While the spiritual "resides in the soul or inner man and pertains to eternal life," and the temporal is concerned with the "establishment of civil justice and outward morality,"[30] there is no inherent conflict between them. Thus, unlike the modern-day separation of church and state, in Calvin's theology these two realms interpenetrate each other as manifestations of the one divine will. While Protestants in France endured much at the hands of a Catholic government, Calvin did not support revolutionary activities; his theological writings reflect great care and effort to prevent social unrest and disorder. Accordingly, each realm in Calvin's twofold government has clearly demarcated jurisdictions: the temporal government makes laws that maintain the social order and build the common good, while the spiritual government oversees the formation and discipline of church members. Calvin's position is not only a contrast to Anabaptist separatism; it also opposes the sixteenth-century Roman Catholic view that the visible church represents the highest civil authority. While recognizing a distinction between the spiritual and temporal realms, Calvin calls both jurisdictions religious vocations, describing the office of "magistrate" as a sacred calling.[31] Consequently, the question for Reformed/Calvinist theology is not whether the church has the right to enter the public arena or exert political influence; the question becomes how, and to what end? Calvin's theology was conceived in exile and directly addressed many social problems, from population dislocation to urban poverty, so a critical retrieval of Calvin's theology in Latin America reinforces its character as a political theology concerned with social transformation on behalf of the poor and oppressed.

30. John Calvin, *Institutes of the Christian Religion*, ed. John T. McNeill, trans. Ford Lewis Battles, 2 vols. (Louisville: Westminster John Knox, 1960), 4.20.1.
31. See Calvin, *Institutes*, 4.20.2.

Salatiel Palomino López, Reformed theologian and leader in the National Presbyterian Church of Mexico, reminds us that a very important aspect of the Calvinist/Reformed ethos is the church's ability to continually adjust to changing historical and cultural contexts:

> It is evident that we [the church] cannot make the mistake of resting on past glories. We can neither simply repeat by rote nor crudely imitate past accomplishments. No. What we are called to do is reassess who we are, reencountering the dynamic spirit of our historical identity, in order to realize the necessary changes and readjustments pertinent to our current situation and context. . . . Or, in other words, we are faced with the demand of fulfilling this matter essential to the spirit of Calvinism: the constant reform of the church by means of obedience to the Word of God and the Holy Spirit. Which, in our case, demands many justifications, many corrections to the orientation of our ecclesiastical life, many acts of repentance, many conversions, much reflection about our sense of denominational life and the necessary changes of attitude and action.[32]

López appeals to the popular Reformed slogan *ecclesia reformata semper reformanda* (the church reformed always being reformed) to challenge narrow and exclusionary "right-doctrine Protestantism," the kind so accurately described and denounced by Rubem Alves, while also suggesting that the way forward for Latin American Presbyterianism might lie in its Calvinist past, specifically in the Christocentric theology of Calvin himself.

Presbyterian Missions in Latin America

Consistent with analyses of Latin American Protestantism made by Bastian, Michelsen, and Lopéz, Eduardo Galasso Faria asserts that "Protestant thought in Latin America since the nineteenth century has had as its matrix the Calvinist doctrinal accents of the Presbyterian churches in the United States."[33] He argues that Presbyterian missions in the second half

32. Salatiel Palomino López, "Herencia reformada y búsqueda de raíces," in *Calvino vivo: Libro conmemorativo del 450 aniversario de la Reforma en Ginebra* (Mexico City: Publicaciones El Faro, 1987), 102–3 (my trans.).

33. Eduardo Galasso Faria, "Calvin and Reformed Social Thought in Latin America," in *John Calvin Rediscovered: The Impact of His Social and Economic Thought*, ed. Edward Dommen and James D. Bratt (Louisville: Westminster John Knox, 2007), 93.

of the nineteenth century sent more pastors, established more churches and schools, and expanded more rapidly than the missionary efforts of other US denominations, reinforcing the claim that "the Protestantism that is so diverse today had Reformed Calvinist thought as its formative matrix."[34] These Presbyterian missions prospered with support from liberal Latin American politicians openly courting US political and economic favor by appealing to the ideology of Manifest Destiny, which ultimately sought to extend the sphere of US influence to the whole of the Western Hemisphere (if not the world).[35] This ideology was advanced by the Monroe Doctrine as European colonial powers like England and Spain lost their hegemonic position over Latin America to the United States, ultimately culminating in the Spanish-American War of 1898, which saw the United States position itself as an imperial power under the guise of advocating independence and democratic nation-building in Latin America and the Caribbean.[36] Accordingly, "American missionary action in the area of religion and education supported American political and economic expansionism," bringing together the more conservative and traditional ethos of missionary proselytization with the secular liberal ideal of democratization and modernization.[37]

Traces of this Presbyterian missionary nation-building remain to this day, as evidenced by the fact that the second-largest university in Puerto Rico, a territorial acquisition of the United States following the Spanish-American War, is the Universidad Interamericana de Puerto Rico (UIPR), which maintains ties with the Presbyterian Church (USA). A more insidious, if camouflaged, manifestation of the cultural force of Protestantism in Latin America is its ties to US political interests, to the degree that, for many in Latin America, Protestantism, along with bilingual education, is equated with upward social mobility and economic success. As church historian and theologian Justo L. González reflects, Protestants in the Caribbean and Latin America—as members of an often-persecuted religious minority—turned to the United States for external validation:

34. Faria, "Reformed Social Thought," 94.
35. See Anders Stephanson, *Manifest Destiny: American Expansion and the Empire of Right* (New York: Hill & Wang, 1995); and Reginald Horsman, *Race and Manifest Destiny: The Origins of American Racial Anglo-Saxonism* (Cambridge, MA: Harvard University Press, 2009).
36. See Virginia M. Bouvier, *Whose America? The War of 1898 and the Battles to Define the Nation* (London: Bloomsbury Academic, 2001).
37. Faria, "Reformed Social Thought," 95.

My fellow [Protestant] believers and I came to the conclusion that North American culture was more Christian, and more advanced, than ours. Missionaries have often been blamed for spreading such views. There is no doubt that many of them had difficulty distinguishing between the gospel and North American culture. But as I now look back at those days, I must confess that there were many reasons why we ourselves were ready to accept such a confusion of Christianity and culture. In the midst of a society built on the general assumption of an agreement between Catholicism and culture, we found it comforting to be able to point to another society where there seemed to be a similar connection between Protestantism and culture. And we found it particularly comforting when we could point to the technological, political, and economic triumphs of that society.[38]

Thankfully, González also notes the changes that have taken place in Latin American Catholicism and Protestantism since his youth and believes this "new Protestantism is more ready to enter into genuine dialogue and collaboration with the new Catholicism" to work together for a more just society.[39]

One of the major forces behind Presbyterian "mission Protestantism" in Latin America was the Princeton theology that preserved and perpetuated a Calvinist orthodoxy in forming pastors and missionaries at Princeton Theological Seminary in reaction to the rise of the social gospel in the nineteenth century. Influenced by pietism and Methodist revivalism, adherents of the social gospel "called for personal sanctification that, being multiplied, would grow into an effort to establish the kingdom of God on earth and build a better world. Social issues such as poverty, the abolition of slavery, and the moralization of society were among its themes."[40] The Presbyterian churches undertaking missionary efforts in Latin America were threatened by the social gospel's focus on justice and progress—both the Southern Presbyterian churches that defended slavery, as evidenced by the preaching of James Henley Thornwell (1812–62), and the Northern Presbyterian churches that were under the tutelage of Thornwell's rival, Charles Hodge (1797–1878) of Princeton Theological Seminary, who warned that "the social gospel denied traditional doctrines and reduced

38. Justo L. González, *Mañana: Christian Theology from a Hispanic Perspective* (Nashville: Abingdon, 1990), 23.

39. González, *Mañana*, 27.

40. Faria, "Reformed Social Thought," 96–97.

the kingdom of God to its material and worldly heretical expression."[41] The fundamentalism that arose from the split between Old School Presbyterians and New School theology in the nineteenth century played a major role in the Protestant evangelization of Latin America, emphasizing the infallibility of Scripture and the underlying supernatural foundation of the universe over against political liberalism and scientific (Darwinian) advancement.

While the Reformed churches have never formed a single confessional body—or shared a unifying official corpus of confessional writings—catholicity has always been an important locus of Reformed theology.[42] In the contemporary context, catholicity most often manifests itself in church missions since, by "responding to the challenges presented by contemporary struggles for social justice and liberation from oppression, conflicting parties within the churches find themselves in solidarity with like-minded others."[43] Latin American liberation theology, by linking the church's mission to the struggle for a just and sustainable world, challenges the Reformed tradition to move beyond its confessional walls. Arguably, liberation theology began in Latin America in the late 1960s and early 1970s, with parallel African American liberation movements in the United States, soon followed by the articulation of feminist liberation theologies and other Third World theologies. No single event led to the birth of liberation theology; however, the Second Vatican Council (which met in four separate sessions between October 1962 and December 1965) stands as an important contributing factor. The theological statements emerging from Vatican II challenged the church to integrate doctrine with pastoral practice to bring its mission to bear on the harsh realities in much of the world. This challenge was then taken up at the Second General Conference of the Latin American Episcopate in 1968 in Medellín, Colombia. The central themes of Medellín were the Latin American reality of absolute poverty, the struggle for peace and justice under regimes of institutionalized violence, and the political dimension of faith.

41. Faria, "Reformed Social Thought," 97. See Paul C. Gutjahr, *Charles Hodge: Guardian of American Orthodoxy* (New York: Oxford University Press, 2011), 135–96, 281–310, 311–46.

42. See Jan Rohls, *Reformed Confessions: Theology from Zurich to Barmen*, trans. John Hoffmeyer (Louisville: Westminster John Knox, 1998), 3–5.

43. John W. de Gruchy, "Toward a Reformed Theology of Liberation: A Retrieval of Reformed Symbols in the Struggle for Justice," in *Toward the Future of Reformed Theology: Tasks, Topics, Traditions*, ed. David Willis and Michael Welker (Grand Rapids: Eerdmans, 1999), 104.

At this point, it is important to acknowledge that liberation theology had its genesis in the pastoral practice and theological reflection of various Christian communities, most often in a context of ecumenical cooperation. In fact, Enrique Dussel credits Rubem Alves, a Brazilian Presbyterian, with naming this new theology "liberation" theology in his 1968 PhD dissertation for Princeton Theological Seminary, "Toward a Theology of Liberation," two years before Gutiérrez published *A Theology of Liberation*.[44] So while Latin American liberation theology is most often linked with post–Vatican II Roman Catholic theology, equally important Protestant sources for liberation theology cannot be ignored. These include the first three Latin American Protestant Conferences (CELA—Conferencia Evangelica Latinoamericana), of 1949, 1961, and 1965; the Union of Protestant Youth Leagues (ULAJE—Union de Ligas Juveniles Evangelicas); and the 1966 Geneva Conference of the World Council of Churches, where the Latin American delegation played an important role. Protestant theological critiques of bourgeois capitalism began to appear, voicing explicit sympathy for democratic socialism, and in 1960 the leadership of the Church and Society movement (ISAL—Iglesia y Sociedad en America Latina) called for active participation by the church in struggles for social and political liberation.

This theological development within Latin American Protestantism was influenced by leading Presbyterian missionaries like John A. Mackay (1889–1983), president of Princeton Theological Seminary, whose 1953 Carnahan Lectures, given in Buenos Aires, contributed to the proliferation of Karl Barth's theology in Latin America;[45] Richard Shaull (1919–2002), who became professor of ecumenics at Princeton Theological Seminary in 1962 after many years of missionary work in Colombia and Brazil;[46] and Paul Lehmann (1906–94), professor of systematic theology and Christian ethics at Princeton Theological Seminary, Harvard Divinity School, and Union Theological Seminary, who (along with Shaull)

44. Enrique Dussel, "Theology of Liberation and Marxism," in *Mysterium Liberationis: Fundamental Concepts of Liberation Theology*, ed. Ignacio Ellacuría and Jon Sobrino (Maryknoll, NY: Orbis Books, 1993), 87.

45. See Luis N. Rivera-Pagán, "John A. Mackay's 'The Other Spanish Christ': Theology and Culture in Latin America," *Journal of Presbyterian History* 93, no. 2 (2015): 60–69.

46. See Raimundo C. Barreto, "The Prophet and the Poet: Richard Shaull and the Shaping of Rubem Alves's Liberative Theopoetics," *Religions* 12, no. 4 (2021): 251–64.

helped disseminate the theology of Dietrich Bonhoeffer in Latin America.[47] Among their students were many important first-generation Latin American Protestant liberation theologians, including Rubem Alves, Julio de Santa Ana, and José Míguez Bonino. Therefore, while the biggest impact of US Presbyterian missions came via the importation of Calvinist fundamentalist evangelicalism, as Alves and others have demonstrated, there was also a strong mainline Presbyterian presence in Latin America more welcoming of liberal politics and secular democratic institutions, with deep roots in Calvin's theology of civil governance.

Cotton Mather's Spanish Catechism

In *Democracy in America* (1835), Alexis de Tocqueville identifies two core values that define and distinguish American democracy, the "spirit of religion" and the "spirit of liberty," motivational drives that from a purely secular perspective appear contradictory but in the American experience have complemented each other to allow religious *and* democratic freedoms to develop together. While these ideas first flourished in New England under the leadership of Puritan Calvinist clergy like Cotton Mather (1663–1728) and Jonathan Edwards (1703–58), they soon became guiding principles for all the original thirteen colonies and the new nation born from the Declaration of Independence (1776) and the American Revolution (1765–83). Echoing many of the ideas and sentiments presented in book 4, chapter 20 ("Civil Government"), in Calvin's *Institutes*, Tocqueville describes the relationship between religion and democracy as one between two distinct-but-interwoven cultural forces: "Liberty looks upon religion as its comrade in battle and victory, as the cradle of its infancy and divine source of its rights. It regards religion as the safeguard of mores, and mores as the guarantee of law and surety for its own duration."[48]

Expounding on the Puritan vision of a "city on a hill" or a "beacon on a hilltop," the New England clergy worked to make both the church and the civil government examples for others to emulate. In analyzing and describ-

47. See Beatriz Melano Couch, "The Influence of Dietrich Bonhoeffer, Paul Lehmann, and Richard Shaull in Latin America," *Princeton Seminary Bulletin* 22, no. 1 (2001): 64–84.
48. Alexis de Tocqueville, *Democracy in America*, ed. Olivier Zunz, trans. Arthur Goldhammer (New York: Library of America, 2004), 49.

ing the Puritan ethos at the heart of American democracy, Tocqueville drew on the work of Cotton Mather, whose *Magnalia Christi Americana; or, The Ecclesiastical History of New England, 1620–1698* records the history of New England from its founding, detailing the lives of its governors and other important political figures as well as recounting the ministries of the clergy whose responsibility it was to preach the gospel and tend to the souls of the Puritan settlers. Concerning Mather, Tocqueville writes, "All the ardor and all the religious passions that led to the founding of New England animate and vivify his writing. . . . He is often intolerant and still more often credulous, but one never detects signs of an intent to deceive. There are even some beautiful passages in his work and some true and profound thoughts."[49] It is noteworthy that Tocqueville places Mather's evangelistic efforts within the global context of England's European wars with Catholic France, describing the New England churches as carrying "the *Gospel* into *those* parts of the world (North America), and rais[ing] a bulwark against the kingdom of *antichrist*, which the Jesuits labor to rear up in all parts of the world."[50]

In fact, Puritan preaching in New England from the late 1680s to the 1730s was affected by the political struggles in Europe, as the Glorious Revolution in England "ended the reign of the crypto-Catholic Stuarts and brought to the throne a line of monarchs widely perceived to hold strong Protestant sympathies: William of Orange, George I, and George II."[51] Consequently, Calvinist ministers in New England, including Mather, "revered the Hanoverian monarchy," and their preaching "injected the language of providence and divine sovereignty into imperial politics. They detected the hand of God in Protestant and English triumphs over French Catholic absolutism and superstition."[52] Interestingly, Tocqueville mentions Mather's role in the infamous Salem witch trials yet does not see his involvement as detrimental to his contributions to civil liberty: "In another part of his work, he gives an extremely long account of several incidents of witchcraft that sowed terror in New England. To him, the

49. Tocqueville, *Democracy in America*, 846.
50. Tocqueville, *Democracy in America*, 847 (emphasis original).
51. Mark Valeri, "Calvin and the Social Order in Early America: Moral Ideals and Trans-atlantic Empire," in *John Calvin's American Legacy*, ed. Thomas J. Davis (Oxford: Oxford University Press, 2010), 27.
52. Valeri, "Calvin and the Social Order," 27.

visible action of the demon in the affairs of the world is clear and incontrovertible and demonstrated truth."[53] Tocqueville immediately follows
these comments by praising Mather's work, noting how the "spirit of civil
liberty and political independence that was characteristic of the author's
contemporaries is apparent at any number of places in the book," as the
Puritans labored to build up the common good; he cites as an example
the decision by the settlers of the Massachusetts Bay Colony to "set aside
400 pounds sterling to establish the university in Cambridge [Harvard]."[54]
The overarching vision to reform the church *and* the civil society in light of
the gospel superseded other concerns and often necessitated the harshness
and intolerance Tocqueville describes in Mather's ecclesiastical history,
justified by the Puritans' belief in God's election and their subsequent
mission to turn New England into "a *refuge* for many, whom he means
to save out of the *General Destruction*."[55] This apocalyptic zeal was ultimately intended to foster "Protestant hegemony in a worldwide battle
with Catholic tyranny."[56]

In 1699, amid England's and Protestantism's global battle against Catholic forces, Cotton Mather wrote and published what is widely recognized
as the first Spanish-language publication in what would eventually become the United States, *La Fe del Christiano* (The faith of the Christian),
a short catechism modeled on Calvin's 1538 catechism. Mather taught
himself Spanish in order to undertake this evangelical endeavor, directed
at the Catholic Spanish-speaking colonies of the New World, in hopes
of sparking "a blaze of Protestant conviction across the vast zones of the
Americas to the south."[57] Undergirding this missionary undertaking was
Mather's sincere belief that Protestantism represented truth in a battle
"between his God's revealed truth and an array of other religious faiths
he regarded as false, chief among them Roman Catholicism."[58] Mather's
role in shaping the ideology that gave rise to the new nation is unquestioned given his role as "one of the principal instigators of the New
England Revolt of 1689, likely authoring the collective manifesto that

53. Tocqueville, *Democracy in America*, 848.
54. Tocqueville, *Democracy in America*, 848.
55. Tocqueville, *Democracy in America*, 847 (emphasis original).
56. Valeri, "Calvin and the Social Order," 28.
57. Kirsten Silva Gruesz, *Cotton Mather's Spanish Lessons: A Story of Language, Race, and Belonging in the Early Americas* (Cambridge, MA: Belknap, 2022), 2.
58. Gruesz, *Cotton Mather's Spanish Lessons*, 2.

some have seen as a forerunner of the Declaration of Independence."[59] While Mather's impact on the cultural and political development of the American colonies is unquestioned, and his collected sermons and major tracts like his *Magnalia Christi Americana* are considered foundational works of American literature, his Spanish-language catechism is a little-known and forgotten tract.

Much of the history about the writing, publication, and dissemination of this text is lost. From the few surviving copies, experts deduce that it was an amateurish printing made in Boston, likely done by an apprentice learning the craft, since the name of the printer is not listed on the title page, and obviously made using English-language type since the ñ in the title *ESPANOLES* lacks a tilde (though it has been hand-inked in some extant copies). Mather himself described the catechism as one of his "Little Books"—small, printed copies of sermons, shorter treatises, psalm books, or poetry mass-produced in New England for primarily devotional purposes. Given that scholars and historians have tended to focus on major published works, little "of his work that is not what we think of as 'book-length' is available in any printed edition."[60] It is believed that only a few hundred copies of the Spanish-language catechism were produced, and while only three extant copies remain, this is common for these lesser tracts, since "many of Mather's other 'Little Books,' as he called them, have vanished altogether."[61]

There is no way of knowing what impact, if any, Cotton Mather's Spanish-language works had on the propagation of Protestantism in Latin America.[62] But Mather was clear about his intentions. His ecclesiastical history provides a detailed account of New England's missionary efforts to evangelize North America's Indigenous populations, and he maintained a mutually beneficial correspondence with Protestant (Anglican, Moravian, and Lutheran) missionaries in New England, London, and India, keeping one another informed about their progress in evangelizing both "East" and "West" India. Mather wrote to August Hermann Francke, leader of the Protestant Lutheran mission in East India, complaining about the lack of

59. Gruesz, *Cotton Mather's Spanish Lessons*, 7.
60. Gruesz, *Cotton Mather's Spanish Lessons*, 20.
61. Gruesz, *Cotton Mather's Spanish Lessons*, 21.
62. The catechism was printed alongside another short work called *La Religión Pura* (The pure religion), a summary of the Reformed (Calvinist) faith in twelve articles.

support from Protestant churches for global missionary efforts: "It is to be considered a great and heavy scandal in the Protestant churches, which should deeply disturb us, that so little or almost nothing happens which serves to spread Christian faith, for this faith contains so much wisdom and kindness that no legitimate objection can be made to it. For it is by this faith that the kingdom of God came to the world which was bound and subjected by Satan with chains of darkness, Satan whose kingdom and works are everywhere."[63] Even more telling were Mather's concerns for the unchecked spread of Catholicism in the New World: "Meanwhile the Roman Catholic Church throws herself into propagating the idolatry and superstition of the Anti-Christ and into establishing the Kingdom of Satan. This whore is sending out thousands of people so that, as the proverb says, not one ship can carry them all together. How they do burn with zeal! How indefatigable they are in their undertakings! How fervently do they struggle for the crown, which in their opinion is faithful suffering accepted out of love for truth."[64]

In a journal entry dated October 2, 1696, Mather details his work to launch missionary efforts in the Spanish-speaking New World and speaks of his motivation to learn Spanish, a motivation that would culminate in the publication of *La Fe del Christiano* (1699) and *La Religión Pura* (1699): "I find in myself, a strong Inclination to learn the Spanish Language, and in that Language transmitt Catechisms, and Confessions, and other vehicles of the Protestant-Religion, into the Spanish Indies."[65] In an entry dated two years later, Mather writes, "Understanding that the way for our communication with the Spanish Indies, opens more and more, I sett myself to learn the Spanish Language," noting that in three weeks he had learned to write "very good Spanish."[66] And in April 1699: "About this time, I sett myself to draw up a compleat System of the *Christian Religion*. When this was done, I turn'd it into the Spanish Tongue, and printed it (along with my, *La Religión Pura*) under the title of LA FE DEL CHRISTIANO."[67]

63. Quoted in Ernst Benz, "Pietist and Puritan Sources of Early Protestant World Missions (Cotton Mather and A. H. Francke)," *Church History* 20, no. 2 (June 1951): 43.

64. Quoted in Benz, "Pietist and Puritan Sources," 43.

65. Quoted in Thomas E. Johnston, "A Translation of Cotton Mather's Spanish Works: *La Fe del Christiano* and *La Religión Pura*," *Early American Literature Newsletter* 2, no. 2 (Autumn 1967): 7.

66. Quoted in Johnston, "Spanish Works," 7.

67. Quoted in Johnston, "Spanish Works," 7.

The finished tract, whose English-language title, *System of the Christian Religion*, is an obvious allusion to Calvin's *Institutes of the Christian Religion*, is a short catechetical work patterned after Luther's and Calvin's short question-and-answer catechisms that played such a crucial role in spreading the Protestant faith across Europe in the sixteenth century.[68] Mather is the only writer in colonial Anglo-America to have published in Spanish, and his journal entries reveal a missionary zeal that was clearly not shared by most of his fellow New Englanders but was more in keeping with his missionary peers in East India.[69] Reflecting his Calvinist belief in divine providence and election, Mather describes his missionary efforts in Latin America in prophetic terms: "I had Advice from Heaven, that a glorious Reformation is near to the Nation. And more than so; that the Light of the Gospel of my Lord Jesus Christ, shall bee carried into the Spanish Indies; and that my Composures, my Endeavoures, will bee used, irradiating the Dark Recesses of America, with the knowledge of the Glorious Lord."[70] A sincere desire to bring the gospel of Jesus Christ to the Catholic settlers and Indigenous peoples of Latin America motivated the writing of this catechism, and while a few hundred were printed, it is not known how many of these forbidden texts made their way into the hands of Spanish-speaking people in the Caribbean and Latin America. It is known, however, from Cotton Mather's diary, that the Spanish-language catechism was being used by the considerable exiled Spanish population of Catholic converts to Protestantism living in the Netherlands and that the Dutch Reformed had colonial interests in South America in the seventeenth century.

Few copies of the text survive in the present. And outside of mentions in Mather's diary and his correspondence with missionaries in Europe, New England, and Asia, there is no evidence that Mather's evangelical push ever reached its intended audience. *La Fe del Christiano* is not even mentioned in the list of banned books published by the Spanish Inquisition in the New World. Yet the text provides valuable insights into the mindset of

---

68. See Mark A. Noll, ed., *Confessions and Catechisms of the Reformation* (Vancouver, BC: Regent College Publishing, 2004); Lyle D. Bierma, *The Theology of the Heidelberg Catechism: A Reformation Synthesis* (Louisville: Westminster John Knox, 2013); I. John Hesselink, ed., *Calvin's First Catechism: A Commentary* (Louisville: Westminster John Knox, 1997); and Timothy J. Wengert, *Martin Luther's Catechisms: Forming the Faith* (Minneapolis: Fortress, 2009).
69. Quoted in Johnston, "Spanish Works," 8.
70. Quoted in Johnston, "Spanish Works," 8.

Calvinists in the New World, locating their efforts within a global strategy to spread the Reformed faith to all peoples and all nations (Matt. 28:19). It also speaks to the far-reaching impact of Calvin's theology in the English-speaking world. Like Calvin's 1538 catechism, Mather's attempt to evangelize the Spanish-speaking Americas began with education and translation, reinforcing the sixteenth-century reformers' priority to translate the Bible into the vernacular. In writing his Spanish-language tracts, Mather had access to the Spanish translation of the Bible by Cipriano de Valera, the definitive seventeenth-century translation. Furthermore, like Calvin's 1538 catechism, Mather's *La Fe del Christiano* is a concise (nine pamphlet-sized pages) summary of the Christian religion that covers all the major themes of Christian theology: the nature of Scripture, God, predestination, creation, providence, angels, theological anthropology, sin, remission of sin, Christ, Christ's second coming, resurrection, salvation, justification, obedience, the Christian life, the Ten Commandments, the Lord's Prayer, church discipline, and the sacraments. The accompanying tract, *La Religión Pura*, serves as an apologetic companion to the more evangelical catechism, providing a critique and condemnation of Roman Catholic faith. The writing, publication, and dissemination of Mather's Spanish-language catechism was not some flight of fancy by the New England preacher but a well-planned, multiyear undertaking to evangelize and convert the Spanish-speaking nations of the New World. Mather himself knew the odds were against its success, and yet he hoped it would increase the Protestant religion in the Western Hemisphere. "Who can tell whether for our Lord's taking Possession of those Countreyes the sett Time for it, bee not come? This Matter I solemnly pray'd over; beseeching the Lord, that He accept of my Service in it."[71]

For Further Reading

Calvin, John. "The Catechism of the Church in Geneva (1545)." In *Calvin: Theological Treatises*, edited and translated by J. K. S. Reid, 83–139. Philadelphia: Westminster, 1954.

———. "1538 Catechism." In *Calvin's First Catechism: A Commentary*, edited by I. John Hesselink, translated by Ford Lewis Battles, 1–38. Louisville: Westminster John Knox, 1997.

71. Quoted in Johnston, "Spanish Works," 8.

————. "The Genevan Confession (1536)." In *Calvin: Theological Treatises*, 25–33.

————. "The Sum of the Christian Life: The Denial of Ourselves." In *Institutes of the Christian Religion*, vol. 1, edited by John T. McNeill, translated by Ford Lewis Battles, bk. 3, chap. 7, 689–701. Philadelphia: Westminster John Knox, 1960.

————. "The Things Spoken concerning Christ Profit Us by the Secret Working of the Spirit." In *Institutes of the Christian Religion*, vol. 1, bk. 3, chap. 1, 537–42.

Calvin against
Apartheid Calvinism

We must then really receive in the Supper the body and blood of Jesus Christ, since the Lord there represents to us the communion of both. For otherwise what would it mean that we eat the bread and drink the wine as a sign that his flesh is our food and his blood our drink, if he gave only bread and wine and left the spiritual reality behind? Would it not be under false colours that he had instituted this mystery? We have then to confess that if the representation which God grants in the Supper is veracious, the internal substance of the sacrament is joined with the visible signs; and as the bread is distributed by hand, so the body of Christ is communicated to us, so that we are made partakers of it. If there were nothing more, we have good reason to be satisfied when we realize that Jesus Christ gives us in the Supper the real substance of his body and his blood, so that we may possess him fully, and, possessing him, have part in all his blessings.

—John Calvin[1]

The tensions within the Reformed theological tradition between John Calvin's emphasis on the prophetic role of the church in civil society and

1. John Calvin, "Short Treatise on the Holy Supper of Our Lord and Only Saviour Jesus Christ," in *Calvin: Theological Treatises*, ed. and trans. J. K. S. Reid (Philadelphia: Westminster, 1954), 148.

his social conservatism, accepting of rigid social hierarchies, is nowhere more evident than in the history of Calvinism in South Africa. The history of Christianity in South Africa is the history of White European colonialism, with all that entails, contributing to a theology that reflected the interests and prejudices of the nineteenth-century European missionaries and the colonial powers that funded their missions.[2] The European settlers of South Africa were predominately Protestant. Though the first colonial excursions were led by the Portuguese in the sixteenth century, the dominant settler culture of South Africa coalesced in the seventeenth century with the arrival of the Dutch Reformed, French Huguenots, and German Lutherans, eclipsing and replacing the Portuguese Catholic presence. While the German Lutheran minority was able to maintain its distinct identity, the Huguenots were eventually assimilated into the Dutch Reformed Church, known as the Nederduitse Gereformeerde Kerk (NGK), which soon became the establishment church of South Africa. While the growth and expansion of Christianity in the eighteenth century was limited primarily to White settler congregations, with the advent of the nineteenth-century global missionary movement more intentional efforts were undertaken by the NGK to evangelize the Indigenous, "heathen" populations of South Africa.

Not surprisingly, the NGK churches reflected the White European attitude of cultural superiority over the colonized Indigenous peoples, which eventually led to a theological crisis as the racial prejudice of Afrikaners (descendants of the predominantly Dutch settlers who first arrived at the Cape of Good Hope in 1652) conflicted with the Calvinist theology affirmed at the Synod of 1829 that proclaimed the sacrament of Communion was to be administered "simultaneously to all members without distinction of colour or origin."[3] The social rift between the White settlers and the Indigenous Black population, many of whom were enslaved by the White settlers, contributed to the defeat of the more prophetic strain of Calvinism by the hegemonizing White nationalism that eventually birthed apartheid theology and the apartheid state. While the term *apartheid*, meaning "separateness," was not adopted by the Afrikaner National Party

---

2. For an overview of the history and development of South African Christendom and its role in the creation of the apartheid state, see John W. de Gruchy and Steve de Gruchy, *The Church Struggle in South Africa*, 25th anniversary ed. (Minneapolis: Fortress, 2005), 1–100.

3. Quoted in de Gruchy and de Gruchy, *Church Struggle*, 7.

until the election of 1948, the ideology of apartheid had long saturated all major cultural institutions—civil and ecclesiastical—reflecting the racial segregation that had characterized South Africa's colonial history since the arrival of Europeans in the sixteenth century. Despite a long and troubled history of political resistance to apartheid, often marked by domestic political violence (which prompted isolationist policies by the international community designed to undermine the apartheid state), the White regime managed to hold on to power and continued to mandate segregation until February 1991. South Africa then held its first elections under universal suffrage in 1994.

While the history of racism and apartheid in South Africa stands as a shameful example of Reformed theology's compromise with nationalism and White supremacy, a 1977 editorial in *Kairos*, the monthly news publication of the South African Council of Churches, proclaimed, "No State can prevail against a mass spiritual movement in the long run."[4] While the dominant theology among the White settler population was the theology of apartheid, a theology of resistance informed by Calvin's theology existed alongside it and was eventually embraced by Indigenous Black Christians in their struggles to overcome apartheid. Accordingly, in educating and empowering Black Christians to resist White supremacy, Allan Boesak, a Black Reformed pastor and theologian, accused White Christian nationalism of forcing "Jesus and his message into a western, white mould," degrading "him to a servant of mere self-interest," and identifying him with racial oppression; "it makes the gospel an instrument of injustice instead of the expectation of the poor."[5] Succinctly, if more confrontationally, Boesak also described South African Christendom as White Christian nationalism: "Whites have claimed the gospel for themselves. They have made the gospel the servant of their own lust for power."[6]

By looking at the rise and development of the Black church and Black theology in twentieth-century South Africa, focusing on Allan Boesak's leadership and key contributions, it is possible to trace the impact of

4. *Kairos* 9, no. 10 (November 1977), quoted in de Gruchy and de Gruchy, *Church Struggle*, 171.

5. Allan A. Boesak, *Farewell to Innocence: A Social-Ethical Study of Black Theology and Black Power* (Maryknoll, NY: Orbis Books, 1969), 23.

6. Allan A. Boesak, "The Courage to Be Black: Black Theology and the Struggle for Liberation," in *Black and Reformed: Apartheid, Liberation, and the Calvinist Tradition*, ed. Leonard Sweetman (1984; repr., Eugene, OR: Wipf & Stock, 2015), 4.

Calvin's theology in the struggle against apartheid. Boesak trusted Calvin's prophetic voice, despite the Calvinism that created apartheid and inflicted it on South Africa's Black citizens, because he "always knew that the God of the exodus and the covenant, the God of Jesus Christ, was different from the God whom whites were proclaiming."[7] According to Boesak, it was none other than Calvin who reminded the Black church of this fundamental truth—that Christ identifies with the oppressed amid their struggles.[8]

Black Resistance to Apartheid

The history of the church struggle in South Africa in the twentieth century can be distilled to two major protests, Sharpeville in 1960 and Soweto in 1976, and the ensuing violent crackdowns by the state. The protests in Sharpeville were prompted by a 1957 bill designed to make it difficult for Black people to attend church worship in White areas of South Africa. This bill was met with strongly worded opposition by Black and White church leaders, including the Anglican archbishop of Cape Town, Geoffrey Clayton, who wrote a letter of protest to the minister who proposed the legislation: "We feel bound to state that if the Bill were to become law in its present form we should ourselves be unable to obey it or counsel our clergy and people to do so."[9] This was a clear case of the state encroaching on religious freedom, and the archbishop's dissent was soon joined by a chorus from other churches, including the Baptist Union, which unequivocally stated its position by calling for acts of civil disobedience: "The proposed bill will compel law-abiding Baptists, together with members of many other Churches, to violate the law."[10] The NGK was also opposed to the bill, primarily because it encroached on the church's religious freedom, but rather than publish their opposition publicly, the leaders of the NGK chose to meet with the minister privately. Reassured that the final form of the bill would not trespass on the church's freedom,

7. Allan A. Boesak, "The Black Church and the Future," in Sweetman, *Black and Reformed*, 21.
8. Boesak, "Black Church," 23.
9. Geoffrey Clayton, "Open Letter to the Prime Minister (6 March 1957)," in *Apartheid and the Archbishop: The Life and Times of Geoffrey Clayton*, ed. Alan Paton (Cape Town: David Philip, 1973), 279, quoted in de Gruchy and de Gruchy, *Church Struggle*, 59.
10. A statement from the Baptist Union of South Africa, dated March 1957, quoted in de Gruchy and de Gruchy, *Church Struggle*, 59.

NGK leaders opted not to publish their critique and thus were seen as tacitly approving the state's action to limit multiracial worship in South Africa.[11]

While the state rarely acted to impede multiracial worship, there were incidents of police terminating Black worship services (sometimes violently) in "White areas," and while the denomination never officially published its opposition to the so-called "church clause" in the bill, individual clergy spoke out against it, including A. J. van der Merwe, the moderator of the NGK in Cape Town, who said in a newspaper interview, "It would have been better if it had not been introduced."[12] The crackdown against Black worship services in White areas, and the implied dislike of multiracial worship services, not only signaled the apartheid government's intrusion into the religious lives of its citizens but also exacerbated tensions between church members and churches that favored apartheid and those actively resisting apartheid. Accordingly, the imposition of the church clause drove the churches into action by taking part in nonviolent acts of civil disobedience that were quickly snuffed out by the authorities. On March 21, 1960, the eyes of the world turned to events in Sharpeville, a small town in South Africa, where 69 Black people, most of them women, were shot and killed by police at a demonstration, and 186 others were wounded. The demonstration was sponsored by the recently formed Pan African Congress, whose leaders insisted that it was a peaceful protest and that the only violence was by the police. The fact that many of the dead were shot in the back favors the accounts by Black protesters.[13]

The events in Sharpeville soon led to a national state of emergency during which thousands of Black South Africans were arrested. Police targeted the leadership of the African National Congress and the Pan African Congress, which included such figures as Albert Luthuli, Nelson Mandela, and Robert Sobukwe, imprisoning them for five months without charge in the unsanitary conditions of the Pretoria Local Prison. These organizations were then declared illegal. Other Black leaders fled the country, joining anti-apartheid exile movements abroad, while still others chose to go underground to continue the struggle against the increasingly

11. De Gruchy and de Gruchy, *Church Struggle*, 60.
12. From an interview in the *Cape Times*, April 30, 1957, quoted in de Gruchy and de Gruchy, *Church Struggle*, 60.
13. De Gruchy and de Gruchy, *Church Struggle*, 61.

authoritarian apartheid government. Geoffrey Clayton's successor, Anglican archbishop Joost de Blank, leveled a critique at the NGK for its complicity in the perpetuation of apartheid through its tacit acceptance of the church clause that had triggered the protests, demanding they either join in the struggle to dismantle apartheid or be removed from the World Council of Churches (WCC): "The future of Christianity in this country demands our complete dissociation from the Dutch Reformed attitude. . . . Either they must be expelled or we shall be compelled to withdraw."[14] The leadership of the WCC in 1960 was unhappy with Archbishop de Blank's ultimatum and did not want to add "ecclesiastical apartheid" to what was already an international ecumenical crisis, but they did agree to organize an international consultation on "Christian race relations and social problems in South Africa."[15]

However, it was the protests in Soweto in 1976 that forever shifted public opinion against the White apartheid government—especially abroad—and strengthened the resolve of Black and White anti-apartheid church leaders to commit without compromise to ending apartheid. Most agree that the "Soweto Uprising in 1976 was a watershed in the struggle for liberation in South Africa."[16] The uprising, a series of demonstrations and protests led by Black schoolchildren, began on the morning of June 16, 1976, when students from various schools began to protest in the streets of the Soweto township in response to the introduction of Afrikaans as the official language of instruction in Black schools. Soon Black students were joined in solidarity by "Coloured" and "Indian" students across South Africa,[17] reaching the townships of the eastern and western Cape and signaling to the ruling government that the younger generation was united in resisting apartheid. These student protests—a veritable children's crusade—were met with brutal police force, and 176 high school students were shot and killed by police. The Soweto Uprising not only solidified international opposition to the apartheid state; it also coalesced domestic resistance

14. Quoted in de Gruchy and de Gruchy, *Church Struggle*, 62.
15. De Gruchy and de Gruchy, *Church Struggle*, 62.
16. De Gruchy and de Gruchy, *Church Struggle*, 184.
17. In South Africa's complex racial politics, Black South Africans were not the only ethnic group affected by apartheid policies, as people were divided into "Whites," "Blacks," "Coloureds," and "Indians." Under apartheid, *Coloured* referred to people of multiracial heritage (any combination of Black, White, Asian, etc.), while *Indian* referred to descendants of South Asian indentured laborers and free migrants from British colonial India.

movements under the broad umbrella of the Black Consciousness Movement, a grassroots anti-apartheid movement that emerged in South Africa in the mid-1960s from the political vacuum created by the outlawing of the African National Congress and the Pan African Congress after the Sharpeville Massacre in 1960.[18]

John W. de Gruchy identifies five ways in which the Soweto Uprising came to symbolize the Black liberation struggle in South Africa and led to the unification of disparate resistance movements in a nationwide and multiracial effort to end the apartheid state: Soweto (1) became the international symbol for the anti-apartheid struggle; (2) energized a younger generation of activists in South Africa; (3) exposed the failure of "separate development" (segregation), which was still supported by some White liberals; (4) revealed the authoritarian and draconian practices of the ruling National Party for all the world to see; and (5) focused Black protest against the church itself insofar as church leaders and church bodies continued to support (implicitly or explicitly) the ideology of White supremacy.[19] Unlike the leaders of other denominational bodies, including the Anglican and Roman Catholic communions, who had condemned the state's actions in no uncertain terms, the leaders of the NGK publicly disavowed the police violence but did little to address the underlying social realities that caused Black South Africans to unite in protest. Still, while the NGK remained uncommitted to resisting apartheid, historically Black churches, the younger generation of church leaders (with ties to the Black Consciousness Movement), and the (mostly Black) South African Council of Churches (SACC) made unequivocal statements against apartheid and the ruling National Party, affirming Black Consciousness as "directly in line with the Biblical doctrine of creation—that all men are created in the image of God." They insisted: out of "Christian convictions we and others will continue to accept Black consciousness as naturally as we breathe. No State can prevail against a mass spiritual movement in the long run."[20]

18. See de Gruchy and de Gruchy, *Church Struggle*, 164–71, 175–81. Also see Noor Nieftagodien, *The Soweto Uprising* (Athens: Ohio University Press, 2014); and South African Democracy Education Trust, *The Road to Democracy in South Africa: 1970–1980* (Pretoria: Unisa, 2004), 317–70.

19. De Gruchy and de Gruchy, *Church Struggle*, 165–67.

20. *Kairos* 9, no. 10 (November 1977), quoted in de Gruchy and de Gruchy, *Church Struggle*, 170–71.

After the Soweto Uprising, violent police action continued unabated, prompting more protests and school boycotts, eventually generating counterviolence like the burning of public buildings by the protesters. While Black leaders attempted to organize resistance and minimize the violence, police continued to arrest and detain protesters without trial, and the violence continued for over a year, finally grinding to a halt with the death of student leader Steve Biko (1946–77) on September 12, 1977. Biko's high-profile murder while in police custody prompted the arrests of many Black community leaders, culminating in the "banning order" of October 19, 1977. Banning was a repressive extrajudicial practice used by the apartheid-era South African government to quell opposition. It involved a series of legislative orders censoring free speech and protests; labeling any opposition to the ruling National Party seditious and communist; and identifying leaders of anti-apartheid resistance movements and, under the guise of legislation, limiting their freedom of movement in the country and making them subject to arrest at any moment. Furthermore, a banned person was forbidden contact with other banned persons and was prohibited from engaging in political activity or would face up to five years in prison (without trial).[21]

Not only did Steve Biko's death contribute to the consolidation of the Black Consciousness Movement, but it also provided a crucial link between the more secular and communist protest movements and the ongoing church struggles. Biko was raised Anglican, and his funeral became an international event, with media covering the spectacle of twenty thousand people marching and singing freedom songs as they processed into Victoria Stadium in King William's Town, Biko's hometown. The Anglican service lasted five hours, with foreign diplomats from thirteen countries and an Anglican delegation, headed by Bishop Desmond Tutu, in attendance. Many speakers eulogized Biko, and the Reverend Xundu, a Transkei Anglican priest, presided over the funeral. In his message, Xundu appealed to God to take sides with the oppressed of South Africa to overthrow apartheid. While Biko's coffin was decorated with the images of Black Power and Pan Africanism, it was very much a religious service. During his imprisonment, Biko had been supported by the growing Christian

---

21. See Lawyers Committee for Human Rights (US) and the Human Rights Commission, *Fact Paper: South Africa; A Discussion of Current Human Rights Issues in South Africa, Issues 1–4* (Braamfontein: Lawyers Committee, 1989).

confessing movement converging around the work of the Christian Institute of Southern Africa, one of the political groups banned by the South African government after Biko's death.

However, White church leaders—especially those in the NGK in South Africa—had little credibility with the younger generation of Black students, as evidenced by the increased radicalization of young Reformed Black clergy and the increased frustration among the members of the SACC with NGK leadership. In the aftermath of the Soweto Uprising and in the months before Steve Biko's arrest, one journalist reported on the attitudes of Black youth toward the church and its institutions: "Most blacks regard the Church in South Africa as an irrelevant institution if not an extension of the status quo."[22] Not surprisingly, Black South Africans began to identify Christianity with apartheid, and during the Soweto Uprising church buildings were targeted by protesters. Sadly, the "NGK and the other Afrikaans Reformed Churches remained solidly in support of the government," but thankfully critical voices began to challenge the NGK from within.[23] During this period Black Reformed pastors and theologians took decisive action to join their church struggles to the nation's struggle against apartheid, decisively linking the Christian gospel with Black liberation via meaningful engagement with Black Power and Black Consciousness. Unlike Latin American liberation theologians, however, they did not actively pursue an alliance with Marxism. Instead, the Alliance of Black Reformed Christians in South Africa, under Boesak's leadership, raised its voice to condemn apartheid as a heresy and unite Christians in opposition to the apartheid state and those in the NGK who refused to join in the struggle for Black liberation.

Calvin's Role in the Church Struggles

Allan Boesak, who received his PhD in theology from the Protestant Theological University of the Netherlands the same year as the Soweto Uprising, was ordained in the Nederduitse Gereformeerde Zendingkerk, or NG Mission Church, the Black church established by the NGK in the nineteenth century in keeping with the doctrine of separate development

22. Revelation Ntoula, "Church Must Reach Out to Youth," *The Voice*, October/November 1976, 16, quoted in de Gruchy and de Gruchy, *Church Struggle*, 175.
23. De Gruchy and de Gruchy, *Church Struggle*, 190.

that characterized the White Reformed churches of South Africa. In the aftermath of Soweto and Biko's killing, the NG Mission Church cut ties with the White NGK and took up the mantle in the struggle against apartheid by representing Black Reformed Christians in the SACC. By 1982, Boesak had become the voice of Black Reformed churches in South Africa, and that year at the meeting of the General Council of the World Alliance of Reformed Churches (WARC) in Ottawa, Canada, he was elected president of the council and played a pivotal role in convincing the WARC to recognize that a *status confessionis* prevailed in South Africa.[24]

Status confessionis (state or stance of confession) is an ecclesiastical practice originating in the Lutheran tradition when debate over the adiaphora controversy led to the writing of the Formula of Concord (1577), which became part of *The Book of Concord* (1580), the historical creedal documents recognized as authoritative for Lutheranism since the sixteenth century. At stake was the difference between gospel truth (essential beliefs without which there is no church) and adiaphora (meaning "things indifferent"), matters of church order and practice about which believers can differ but that do not define the church. When Holy Roman emperor Charles V sought to establish religious unity by driving out the Lutheran "heresy" after militarily defeating the Protestant German princes, he reinstated Catholic liturgical practices in the Lutheran churches of various German principalities. This set off the adiaphora controversy among Lutherans, who argued over the role of the state in legislating church order and practice. The Lutheran churches were divided on this matter, creating a crisis in which those Lutherans opposed to Charles V's overreach declared that the issue at hand was not an indifferent matter but one of doctrinal faithfulness to the gospel, requiring the churches to resist this imposition by the state on matters of belief through an act of public confession.[25] The Formula of Concord reaffirmed Luther's doctrine of the two kingdoms, which states that temporal governments have no authority over spiritual matters.

Dietrich Bonhoeffer (1906–45), the German Lutheran pastor and theologian who became a leader of the underground Confessing Church movement in Germany during Nazi rule in the 1930s and 1940s, drew upon the Formula of Concord and the adiaphora controversy in his use of *status*

---

24. De Gruchy and de Gruchy, *Church Struggle*, 193.
25. See Michael P. DeJonge, "Bonhoeffer, *status confessionis*, and the Lutheran Tradition," *Stellenbosch Theological Journal* 3, no. 2 (2017): 41–60.

confessionis when resisting the German Reich. The Confessing Church was a resistance movement within German Protestantism during the Nazi regime that brought together Lutheran, Reformed, and United Churches in confessional consensus to oppose the pro-Nazi German Evangelical Church (1933–45). They adopted the Theological Declaration of Barmen in 1934, written mostly by the Swiss Reformed theologian Karl Barth, with some input from the Lutheran delegation. Barmen later became the template for *status confessionis* in South Africa (though the declaration itself never employs that language). While Bonhoeffer was influenced by Calvin's interpretation of Luther's two kingdoms theology, the concept of *status confessionis* began within the Lutheran tradition, and his use of it followed the arguments defended in the Formula of Concord, especially Article 10, on adiaphora, which decried any imposition by the state on the church—even on matters of little doctrinal importance. Bonhoeffer first used the language of *status confessionis* in his essay "The Church and the Jewish Question" (1933), in which he condemns the "Aryan paragraph," the Nazi legislation excluding Jews from certain offices and positions (including church offices). Bonhoeffer reasoned that by making "racial purity" a necessary qualification for access to the church and its ministry, the state elevated something indifferent to the status of dogma.[26] Since the gospel is clear that in Christ there is "neither Jew nor Greek" (Gal. 3:28), the state cannot impose its racial laws on the church, including by limiting who can serve in church offices, without contradicting the doctrine of the priesthood of all believers (1 Pet. 2:9; Rev. 5:10). According to Bonhoeffer, "The conditions of a *status confessionis* are met in this case when a faction within the church identifies an adiaphoron as central to the gospel. This happens when Aryan-ness is made into a precondition for full participation in the life of the gospel community."[27] The Barmen Declaration, while avoiding an explicit condemnation of National Socialism's Aryan policy, made its position on the relationship between church and state on matters of religious doctrine and practice quite clear: "We reject the false doctrine, as though the State, over and beyond its special commission, should and could become the single and totalitarian order of human life, thus fulfilling the church's vocation as well."[28]

---

26. DeJonge, "Bonhoeffer," 54.
27. DeJonge, "Bonhoeffer," 56.
28. "The Theological Declaration of Barmen," in *Book of Confessions*, part 1 of *The Constitution of the Presbyterian Church (U.S.A.)* (Louisville: Office of the General Assembly, 2016), 284.

In South Africa, Lutheran and Reformed clergy declared apartheid heretical and recognized the anti-apartheid struggle for Black liberation as a moment of *status confessionis*. In 1977, the Lutheran World Federation declared that the "situation in Southern Africa constitutes a *status confessionis*" that requires that the churches "publicly and unequivocally reject the existing apartheid system."[29] And as already mentioned, under Boesak's leadership, the WARC declared that the apartheid situation "constitutes a *status confessionis* for our churches, which means that we regard this as an issue on which it is not possible to differ without seriously jeopardising the integrity of our common confession as Reformed Churches."[30] The statement adopted by the WARC included words of solidarity with the Black Reformed Christians of South Africa, recognizing "that apartheid ('separate development') is a sin, and that the moral and theological justification of it is a travesty of the Gospel and, in its persistent disobedience to the Word of God, a theological heresy."[31] Not only did this draw a clear demarcation between White NGK churches and Black NG Mission Church churches (and their White allies); it also increased the ecumenical isolation of the White NGK in an effort by the worldwide Reformed communion to generate internal resistance to apartheid. This led directly to the drafting of the Belhar Confession by the NG Mission Church in 1982, the first "confession of faith adopted by a church within the Dutch Reformed tradition since the seventeenth century."[32] With the support of the WARC, the Mission Church became a confessing church on the belief that apartheid is contrary to the gospel of Jesus Christ, and this confessional affirmation by a church body within the Dutch Reformed tradition—with the support of the global Reformed communion—meant that any future relationship between the White NGK and the Black NG Mission Church "now depended on rejecting apartheid."[33]

When Allan Boesak addressed the first gathering of the Alliance of Black Reformed Christians in Southern Africa in 1981, he spoke on the

29. Lutheran World Federation, "South Africa: Confessional Integrity," in *Apartheid Is Heresy*, ed. John W. de Gruchy and Charles Villa-Vicencio (Grand Rapids: Eerdmans, 1983), 161.
30. Edmund Perret, ed., *Proceedings of the 21st General Council of the World Alliance of Reformed Churches, 17–27 August 1982* (Geneva: World Alliance of Reformed Churches, 1983), 177.
31. De Gruchy and Villa-Vicencio, *Apartheid Is Heresy*, 170.
32. De Gruchy and de Gruchy, *Church Struggle*, 193.
33. De Gruchy and de Gruchy, *Church Struggle*, 193.

subject "Black and Reformed: Contradiction or Challenge?" Without pulling any punches, Boesak delineated the history of Calvinism in South Africa imported by the Dutch Reformed, the French Huguenots, and the Scottish Presbyterians. These Europeans who brought Calvinism to South Africa also brought with them slavery, dehumanization, and violence. Boesak also affirmed that when his Khoi ancestors first accepted Christianity, three hundred years earlier, "they became the members of a reformed church."[34] In other words, the history of Calvinism in South Africa is a history of seemingly irreconcilable contradictions. Boesak did not romanticize this Reformed theological tradition, recognizing how Reformed Christians created the political, economic, and cultural conditions that gave rise to apartheid by imposing an ideology of White supremacy that exploited and enslaved Black South Africans. Boesak explained that, when it comes to racist regimes, "the uniqueness of apartheid lies in the fact that this system claims to be *based on Christian principles*. It is justified on the gospel of Jesus Christ."[35] For Black Reformed Christians in South Africa, who suffered under the totalitarian rule of White Reformed Christians, this contradiction was no longer bearable, so they had to ask themselves, "Does the Reformed church have a future in South Africa?"[36]

Perhaps surprisingly, Boesak found Calvin a powerful ally in his critique of South African Calvinism and undertook to construct an emancipatory Reformed theology that embraced the Black experience in South Africa. Boesak challenged other Black Reformed Christians to resist the idolatry that passed for Reformed theology in the White NGK churches and to make the Reformed tradition "truly their own" by making the tradition "once again become what it once was: a champion of the cause of the poor and oppressed, clinging to the confession of the lordship of Christ and to the supremacy of the word of God."[37] Boesak was quick to point out that for Calvin, Luther's two kingdoms theology implies that both the church and the state fall under God's sovereignty, so while the church is founded for the spiritual well-being of God's people, the state works to establish

34. Allan A. Boesak, "Black and Reformed: Contradiction or Challenge?," in Sweetman, *Black and Reformed*, 83.
35. Boesak, "Black and Reformed," 85.
36. Boesak, "Black and Reformed," 87.
37. Boesak, "Black and Reformed," 95.

the common good through just laws. When the state fails in its duty to care and provide for all—especially the poor and disenfranchised—it comes under the judgment of God's Word. Boesak thus concluded that "in terms of Calvin's understanding of legitimacy, the South African government is neither just nor legitimate,"[38] and he defended his argument by citing the closing chapter of Calvin's *Institutes of the Christian Religion* (1559), on civil governance: "But in that obedience which we have shown to be due to the authority of rulers, we are always to make this exception, indeed to observe it as primary, that such obedience is never to lead us away from obedience to him whose will the desires of all kings ought to be subject, to whose decrees all their commands ought to yield, to whose majesty their scepters ought to be submitted."[39]

Not only does Calvin exhibit the same Reformed emphasis on the lordship of Jesus Christ over all temporal authorities witnessed in the Barmen Declaration of 1934, condemning the Nazi Reich, but Boesak noted that this creedal point reflects the biblical truth that liberation theologians call God's preferential option for the poor. The tradition of the Hebrew prophets affirms that God hears the cry of the poor and oppressed in the same way God heard the cry of his enslaved people in Egypt and acted in human history to liberate them (Exod. 2:23–25). Commenting on the prophet Habakkuk, Calvin validates the cry of the poor and oppressed, acknowledging that "tyrants and their cruelty cannot be endured without great weariness and sorrow. . . . Hence almost the whole world sounds forth these words, How long, How long? . . . And this cry, proceeding as it does from the feeling of nature and the dictate of justice, is at length heard by the Lord. . . . And this feeling, is it not implanted in us by the Lord? It is then the same as though God heard himself, when he hears the cries and groanings of those who cannot bear injustice."[40] Calvin also offers this eye-opening commentary on Psalm 82:3–4, a text that reads, "Give justice to the weak and the orphan; maintain the right of the lowly and the destitute. Rescue the weak and the needy; deliver them from the hand of the wicked":

38. Boesak, "Black and Reformed," 93.
39. John Calvin, *Institutes of the Christian Religion*, ed. John T. McNeill, trans. Ford Lewis Battles, 2 vols. (Louisville: Westminster John Knox, 1960), 4.20.32.
40. John Calvin, *Calvin's Commentaries*, trans. Calvin Translation Society, 23 vols., 500th anniversary ed. (Grand Rapids: Baker Books, 2009), 15:93–94 (Hab. 2:6).

> We are here briefly taught that a just and well-regulated government will be distinguished for maintaining the rights of the poor and afflicted. . . . The end, therefore, for which judges bear the sword is to restrain the wicked, and thus to prevent violence from prevailing among men, who are so much disposed to become disorderly and outrageous. . . . From these remarks, it is very obvious why the cause of the poor and needy is here chiefly commended to rulers; for those who are exposed as easy prey to the cruelty and wrongs of the rich have no less need of the assistance and protection of magistrates than the sick have of the aid of the physician. Were the truth deeply fixed in the minds of kings and other judges, that they are appointed to be the guardians of the poor, and that a special part of this duty lies in resisting the wrongs which are done to them, and in repressing all unrighteous violence, perfect righteousness would become triumphant through the whole world.[41]

Boesak convincingly demonstrated that Calvin would see the apartheid state—and the NGK that supported it—as usurping Christ's lordship and would enjoin Reformed Christians in South Africa to resist both.

When Boesak addressed the World Alliance of Reformed Churches in 1982, where he was elected president of the council, he brought a challenge to the global Reformed communion from within the Black South African experience: "We realize that the racial situation in this country has reached a critical stage and that God is calling the church as a liberating and reconciling community to identify itself with the oppressed and the poor in their struggle for the dignity which is theirs as human persons created in the image of the Triune God."[42] While affirming Blackness and Black liberation, Boesak did so from within a deeply Calvinist understanding of God's grace that emphasizes the inherent dignity possessed by every human being solely by virtue of being created in the image of God. He did not claim that Black South Africans were more deserving of support than were others because of what they suffered under apartheid. In other words, he was not demanding special treatment for Black South Africans. Rather, he was demanding that which God has gifted to all human beings—regardless of race, color, or creed—but which had, for centuries,

---

41. Calvin, *Commentaries*, 5:332 (Ps. 82:3).

42. Allan A. Boesak, "God Made Us All, but . . . Racism and the World Alliance of Reformed Churches," in Sweetman, *Black and Reformed*, 108. Here Boesak cites a 1980 statement from the "Consultation on Racism" from the South African Council of Churches.

been systematically and tyrannically denied to Black South Africans by the White NGK and the Afrikaner National Party.

In making the case before the WARC, Boesak surrounded himself with Calvin's theology, which emphasizes the inherent dignity of every human being as the image of God: "Therefore, we have no reason to refuse any who come before us needing our help. If we say that he is a stranger, the Lord has stamped on him a sign that we know [the image of God]. . . . If we allege that he is contemptible and worthless, the Lord responds by showing us that he has honored him by making his own image to shine in him."[43] And Boesak closed his appeal by once again quoting Calvin: "That we have been redeemed by Christ at so great a price as our redemption cost him, so that we should not enslave ourselves to the wicked desires of men—much less be subject to their impiety."[44] Therefore, Boesak stands on strong Reformed theological ground—namely, because as Reformed theology Calvin's theology strives to proclaim the biblical message—when he asserts elsewhere, "For Reformed churches, the situation should constitute a *status confessionis*: Reformed churches should recognize that apartheid is heresy, contrary to the gospel and inconsistent with the Reformed tradition. Consequently the Reformed churches should reject apartheid as such."[45]

Sacramental Theology and Human Liberation

The core of Boesak's argument before the World Alliance of Reformed Churches is that racism—especially apartheid as a theologically justified dogma within South African Reformed Christianity—seriously undermines the unity of the church. The ideology of separate development is especially scandalous when celebrating the Lord's Supper. When the community gathers around the table to celebrate the sacrament of Communion, the many become one in Christ. In South Africa, where the NGK conspired with the state to limit multiracial worship, Boesak writes, "both white and black Reformed Christians are deprived of the meaning of the

43. John Calvin, *Calvin's New Testament Commentaries*, vol. 12, *The Epistle of Paul the Apostle to the Hebrews and the First and Second Epistles of St. Peter*, ed. T. F. Torrance (Grand Rapids: Eerdmans, 1994), 204–5.

44. Calvin, *Institutes*, 4.20.32.

45. Boesak, "God Made Us All, but . . . ," 109.

sacrament."[46] Once again, in resisting the apartheid church and state, Boesak turns to Calvin for guidance, grounding his argument in Calvin's understanding of the church as the body of Christ united with Christ and with one another via the sacrament of the Lord's Supper:

> Now since he has only one body, of which he makes us all partakers, it is necessary that all of us also be made one body by such participation. . . . We shall benefit very much from the Sacrament if this thought is impressed and engraved upon our minds: that none of the brethren can be injured, despised, rejected, abused, or in any kind offended by us, without at the same time, injuring, despising, and abusing Christ by the wrongs we do; that we cannot disagree with our brethren without at the same time disagreeing with Christ; that we cannot love Christ without loving him in the brethren; that we ought to take the same care of our brethren's bodies as we take care of our own; for they are members of our body; and that, as no part of our body is touched by any feeling of pain which is not spread among all the rest, so we ought not to allow a brother to be affected by any evil, without being touched with compassion for him.[47]

Much as Latin American theologian Gustavo Gutiérrez views the sacrament as a universal invitation extended to all humanity, regardless of race, color, or creed, Calvin cannot divorce participation in the sacrament from its real-world ethical consequences. Gutiérrez concludes, "Without a real commitment against exploitation and alienation and for a society of solidarity and justice, the Eucharistic celebration is an empty action, lacking any genuine endorsement by those who participate in it."[48] Similarly, Calvin asserts that we cannot love Christ without loving our neighbor.[49] The subsequent understanding of church as communion demands, says Gutiérrez, that the church "make the prophetic denunciation of every dehumanizing situation, which is contrary to fellowship, justice, and liberty,"[50] for any profanation of our neighbor—even the stranger in our midst—is an attack on Christ himself. Calvin comments, "It is to be noted that we

46. Boesak, "God Made Us All, but . . . ," 107.
47. Calvin, *Institutes*, 4.17.38.
48. Gustavo Gutiérrez, *A Theology of Liberation: History, Politics, and Salvation*, trans. and ed. Sister Caridad Inda and John Eagleson, rev. ed. (Maryknoll, NY: Orbis Books, 1988), 150.
49. See Calvin, *Institutes*, 4.17.38.
50. Gutiérrez, *Theology of Liberation*, 153.

cannot desire Jesus Christ without aspiring to the righteousness of God, which consists in self-denial and obedience to his will."[51] Consequently, Calvin cautions believers not to approach the Communion table unless they have first resolved that which divides them and keeps them from full fellowship with Christ and one another: "We must then not at all presume to approach, if we bear any hatred or rancour against living man, and especially any Christian who may be within the unity of the Church."[52]

Boesak leverages Calvin's sacramental theology against the apartheid doctrine of separate development to confront the heresy of apartheid, seeking to overthrow it through nonviolent means, and then work for reconciliation. However, genuine reconciliation comes at a cost: "Reconciliation is not feeling good; it is coming to grips with evil. In order to reconcile, Christ had to die. We must not deceive ourselves."[53] Citing Dietrich Bonhoeffer's analysis and critique of "cheap grace," Boesak warns that we must not rush to reconciliation without first securing liberation for South Africa's oppressed Black majority; then he reminds the White government that while Moses did speak with Pharaoh, it was "simply to convey the *Lord's* command: Let my people go!"[54] Black and White liberation are intertwined—Black South Africans seek freedom from the dehumanizing brutality of apartheid, and White South Africans need to be freed from the demonic idolatry of White supremacy. Therefore, Boesak insists, "we must not be afraid to say that in the South African situation Christian love between white and black must be translated into terms of political, social, and economic justice."[55]

While Calvin, a second-generation reformer, could hardly be called an innovator in the eucharistic debates—since "by the time Calvin issued his first word on the Lord's Supper in 1536, reformers had already issued countless words on the topic, in publications, disputations, correspondence, sermons, and even informal conversations"[56]—he nevertheless synthesizes and systematizes what the first generation, from Luther to

---

51. Calvin, "Short Treatise," 151.
52. Calvin, "Short Treatise," 151.
53. Boesak, "Black Church," 29.
54. Boesak, "Black Church," 28 (emphasis original).
55. Boesak, "Black Church," 30.
56. Sue A. Rozeboom, "Doctrine of the Lord's Supper: Calvin's Theology and Its Early Reception," in *Calvin's Theology and Its Reception: Disputes, Developments, and New Possibilities*, ed. J. Todd Billings and I. John Hesselink (Louisville: Westminster John Knox, 2012), 146.

Zwingli to Bucer, said on the matter while navigating the traditions of the church through the lens of Scripture. For Calvin, the various nuances of the different positions argued and defended—from the real presence of the Roman Catholic (transubstantiation) and Lutheran (consubstantiation) teachings, to the "symbolic memorialism" of Huldrych Zwingli (1484–1531), to his own understanding of the sacrament as *spiritually* real presence—seek to explain that which is, in essence, divine mystery. Ultimately, every theology of the Lord's Supper attempts to convey the mystery of Christ's union with the community of believers.[57] Yet, unlike most of his predecessors and contemporaries, Calvin was not fixated on rationalizing and dissecting this divine mystery but was more intent on celebrating and participating in this divine mystery as a gift of grace. Without minimizing the need for careful theological reflection guiding our administration of the sacraments, Calvin preferred to gloss over certain controversies for the sake of preserving our union with Christ: "I rather experience [the mystery] than understand it. Therefore, I here embrace without controversy the truth of God in which I may safely rest. [Christ] declares his flesh the food of my soul, his blood its drink. I offer my soul to him to be fed with such food. In his Sacred Supper he bids me take, eat, and drink his body and blood under the symbols of bread and wine. I do not doubt that he himself truly presents them, and that I receive them."[58]

Rooted in Saint Augustine's formulation of a sacrament as "an outward and visible sign of an inward and invisible grace," Calvin's exploration of the mystical union with Christ mediated by the sacrament of the Lord's Supper does not confine Christ's presence to the elements of Communion, nor does he treat the elements superstitiously, as if they contained any efficacy outside of the eucharistic celebration itself. Rather, Calvin affirms both ends of Augustine's analogy: the elements are the body and blood of Christ *because* they are the signs chosen by God to communicate grace and reaffirm our mystical union with Christ: "The bond of this connection is therefore the Spirit of Christ, with whom we are joined in unity, and is like a channel through which all that Christ himself is and has is conveyed to us."[59] Through the work of the Holy Spirit we are united with Christ, and it is the bond of that union that continually nourishes us as believers,

---

57. See Calvin, *Institutes*, 4.17.1.
58. Calvin, *Institutes*, 4.17.32.
59. Calvin, *Institutes*, 4.17.12.

but because as believers we are also trapped in a sinful fallen state, God accommodates our human limitations by providing the sacrament of the Lord's Supper as a reminder of our continual union with Christ. In other words, while Christ's act of justification on the cross is once and for all, "he who knows the baseness of his sin and the unhappiness of his state and condition while alienated from God, is so ashamed of it, that he is constrained to discontent with himself, to self-condemnation, and to groaning and sighing with great sadness."[60] Therefore, Christ has instituted the sacrament of the Lord's Supper so that we might better "recognize the blessings which we have received, and daily receive, from the Lord Jesus Christ, so that we may render him such offering of praise as is his due." One of the benefits of participating in the sacrament is "that it turns us from ingratitude, and does not allow us to forget the good our Lord did us in dying for us, but rather induces us to render thanks to him, and, as it were, by public confession, protest how much we are indebted to him."[61]

The sacrament symbolizes both our union in and with the body of Christ and the nourishment we receive as a benefit from our union with Christ: "We now understand the purpose of this mystical blessing, namely, to confirm for us the fact that the Lord's body was once for all so sacrificed for us that we may now feed upon it . . . and that his blood was once so shed for us in order to be our perpetual drink."[62] Therefore, it is correct and appropriate to refer to the elements (bread and wine) as Christ's body and blood, "because they are as it were instruments by which the Lord distributes them to us. . . . It is a spiritual mystery, which cannot be seen by the eye, nor comprehended by the human understanding. It is therefore symbolized by visible signs, as our infirmity requires, but in such a way that it is not a bare figure, but joined to its reality and substance."[63] Thus, the sacrament is not to be taken lightly, nor profaned by an unrepentant attitude; yet, as a sick person needs medicine, we ought neither to abstain from taking it when we fall short of perfection, for without it we lack the nourishment our faith needs to live and grow: "For if we allege as pretext for not coming to the Supper, that we are still weak in faith or in integrity

60. Calvin, "Short Treatise," 150.
61. Calvin, "Short Treatise," 148–49.
62. Calvin, *Institutes*, 4.17.1.
63. Calvin, "Short Treatise," 147.

of life, it is as if a man excuse himself from taking medicine because he is sick."[64]

Drawing on Calvin's theology of the Lord's Supper, Boesak framed the Belhar Confession (drafted in 1982, adopted by the NG Mission Church in 1986) around our union with Christ, which stands as both a gift of grace and a moral obligation proceeding from said grace. The confession affirms the Nicene marks of the church while highlighting that "the communion of saints [is] called from the entire human family," thus the need to work for unity even as we rely on God's grace—unity being "a reality which must be earnestly pursued and sought: one which the people of God must continually be built up to attain."[65] Echoed here is Calvin's concern that believers take seriously the ethical dimensions of union with Christ while also recognizing that it is only by grace—through the work of the Holy Spirit— that we become one body. Thus, sacramental participation is encouraged as much-needed medicine. Since we are called to live in community, and this community is one with Christ in Spirit, community is maintained by a series of intentional acts, the most central being our coming together as one people of God around the Communion table because we "have one God and Father, are filled with one Spirit, are baptized with one baptism, eat of one bread and drink of one cup, confess one name, are obedient to one Lord, work for one cause, and share one hope."[66] Because unity is so important to the life of the church, the Belhar Confession rejects as sinful any church practice or teaching that creates division within the body of Christ, rejecting any doctrine "which absolutizes either natural diversity or the sinful separation of people in such a way that this absolutization hinders or breaks the visible and active unity of the church, or even leads to the establishment of a separate church formation."[67]

Like Boesak's previous theological statements, the Belhar Confession does not seek to undermine the demand for justice with the desire for reconciliation; therefore, it insists that the concrete and historical liberation of the Black citizens of South Africa ought to precede any future talk of reconciliation and ecclesiastical reunification. Yet, as a Reformed statement of faith, the Belhar Confession recognizes that any hope of

---

64. Calvin, "Short Treatise," 153.
65. "Confession of Belhar," in *Book of Confessions*, 301.
66. "Confession of Belhar," 302.
67. "Confession of Belhar," 302.

reconciliation is made possible only by divine grace and forgiveness, firm in the knowledge that "where true human liberation takes place, it takes place because Christ is there."[68] Therefore, so long as apartheid remains the law of the land and a doctrine of the NGK, "the credibility of this message is seriously affected and its beneficial work obstructed when it is proclaimed in a land which professes to be Christian, but in which the enforced separation of people on a racial basis promotes and perpetuates alienation, hatred and enmity."[69]

Apartheid was abolished in South Africa in 1991, leading to the creation of a new Reformed body in 1994, the Uniting Reformed Church in Southern Africa (URCSA), which required member churches to adopt the Belhar Confession. Sadly, the NGK decided not to compel existing members to submit to the confession. The URCSA's position was that all members of the NGK should be required to profess the Belhar Confession or be expelled from the denomination. While the NGK has been accepted back into the World Alliance of Reformed Churches, it was only at the 2011 meeting of the General Assembly of the NGK that the denomination decided to begin the processes to make the Belhar Confession part of its confessional base. This suggests that the reconciliation desired by Boesak and other leaders of the Black Reformed churches remains elusive because vestiges of the White supremacist apartheid churches still linger.

The Belhar Confession stands as evidence of Black Reformed Christians' use of Calvin as an ally in the political struggle against racism in South Africa. Looking back on the writing and adoption of Belhar, Boesak describes his strategy to employ Calvin against apartheid Calvinists by emphasizing the unity of the church in Calvin's theology of the Lord's Supper. By demonstrating how the NGK policy of separate development in the life of the church exposed the heretical nature of apartheid, "Belhar understood Calvin as he spoke of Holy Communion. 'Christ has only one body of which he makes us all partakers.'"[70] Boesak also acknowledges that Black South Africans had no desire to unite with White South Africans, who had exploited, tortured, and killed so many of them. But they

68. Boesak, "Black Church," 24.

69. "Confession of Belhar," 303.

70. Gregg Brekke, "Allan Boesak Commends Belhar Confession," Presbyterian Church (USA), 222nd General Assembly (June 23, 2016), https://www.pcusa.org/news/2016/6/23/allan-boesak-commends-belhar-confession/.

were compelled to work for reconciliation because Christ calls all believers to justice *and* reconciliation: "So against our self-absorbed instinct for self-absorbed victimhood, the black church confessed God as a God who wants to bring forth peace and justice in the world."[71] Accordingly, despite Black Christians' unbending insistence on justice, accountability, and restorative justice in South Africa, Boesak finds Belhar "a unifying document" that "stirs us, humbles us, and inspires us."[72]

For Further Reading

Calvin, John. "Commentaries on the Prophet Habakkuk." In vol. 15 of *Calvin's Commentaries*, translated by Calvin Translation Society, 23 vols., 500th anniversary ed. Grand Rapids: Baker Books, 2009, esp. chap. 2, v. 6, pp. 93–94.

———. "Confession of Faith concerning the Eucharist." In *Calvin: Theological Treatises*, edited and translated by J. K. S. Reid, 167–69. Philadelphia: Westminster, 1954.

———. "The Sacraments." In *Institutes of the Christian Religion*, vol. 2, edited by John T. McNeill, translated by Ford Lewis Battles, bk. 4, chap. 14, 1276–303. Philadelphia: Westminster John Knox, 1960.

———. "The Sacred Supper of Christ, and What It Brings to Us." In *Institutes of the Christian Religion*, vol. 2, bk. 4, chap. 17, 1359–428.

———. "Short Treatise on the Holy Supper of Our Lord and Only Saviour Jesus Christ." In *Calvin: Theological Treatises*, 140–66.

———. "Summary of Doctrine concerning the Ministry of the Word and the Sacraments." In *Calvin: Theological Treatises*, 170–77.

71. Brekke, "Allan Boesak."
72. Brekke, "Allan Boesak."

Conclusion

As historian Carter Lindberg notes, "Few have been neutral about Calvin."[1] Why another book on John Calvin? It is my hope that, here at the end of our excursion, that question has been answered. As noted in chapter 3, one factor for Calvin's continuing relevance is his ability to speak to the experience of dislocation and migration—which, for historian Diarmaid MacCulloch, explains why (unlike Lutheranism) Reformed Christianity spread across multiple languages and cultures: because "so many of its leading figures had the same experience as Calvin, finding themselves forced to leave their native lands and to proclaim their message in new and alien settings."[2]

Yet, as anyone who has spent time with Calvin the theologian—engaging his *Institutes*, shorter treatises, biblical commentaries, sermons, and pastoral correspondence—knows, part of his appeal is the pastoral concern underlying his theological rigor: "Calvin's piety is the ethos and action of people who recognize through faith that they have been accepted in Christ and engrafted into His body by the sheer grace of God. . . . This relationship established by God with believers restores the joy of fellowship with God; it evokes and requires a response, and so re-creates their lives."[3] Still, beneath the practical guidance offered by Calvin the pastor,

---

1. Carter Lindberg, *The European Reformations* (Oxford: Blackwell, 1996), 235.

2. Diarmaid MacCulloch, *Christianity: The First Three Thousand Years* (New York: Penguin Books, 2011), 637.

3. Elsie Anne McKee, general introduction to *John Calvin: Writings on Pastoral Piety*, by John Calvin, ed. and trans. Elsie Anne McKee (New York: Paulist Press, 2001), 5.

there lie oceanic depths—the humble recognition of someone who has long wrestled with the divine mystery that, in the end, it is best to stand before the divine in worshipful submission. For example, he writes, "From our perspective the law may well be impossible to do, but it is possible for God to engrave it upon our hearts and to govern us by His Holy Spirit, indeed, so much so that it will seem like a gentle and light burden to us, involving no hardship that we cannot bear."[4]

Swiss Reformed theologian Karl Barth (1886–1968), arguably the most influential interpreter of Calvin's theology for the modern era, wrote to his friend and confidant Eduard Thurneysen (1888–1974) in a letter dated June 8, 1922, "[I could] gladly and profitably set myself down and spend all the rest of my life just with Calvin."[5] As Barth prepared to lecture on the Protestant reformers and the Reformed confessions at the University of Göttingen in 1922, he immersed himself in Calvin's theology and found himself awed by what he found: "Calvin is a cataract, a primeval forest, a demonic power, something directly down from Himalaya, absolutely Chinese, strange, mythological; I lack completely the means, the suction cups, even to assimilate this phenomenon, not to speak of presenting it adequately."[6] This fascination informed Barth's second edition of *The Epistle to the Romans* (*Der Römerbrief*) the same year, as later attested in his correspondence with his personal assistant Eberhard Busch (1937–): "Fortunately it turned out that my theology had become more Reformed, more Calvinistic than I had known, so I could pursue my special confessional task with delight and with a good conscience."[7]

In twenty years of teaching at Saint Louis University, a Jesuit Catholic university in the midwestern United States, I have used Calvin's *Golden Booklet of the True Christian Life* (1550) in my Theological Foundations class, a required course for all undergraduate students, and I have always been surprised by how students relate to and interact with this devotional classic. From the Muslim student who appreciated Calvin's understanding

4. John Calvin, "The Second Sermon on the Sabbath (Friday, June 21, 1555)," in Calvin, *Writings on Pastoral Piety*, 253.
5. Karl Barth and Eduard Thurneysen, *Revolutionary Theology in the Making: Barth-Thurneysen Correspondence, 1914–1925*, trans. James D. Smart (Richmond: John Knox, 1964), 10.
6. Barth and Thurneysen, *Revolutionary Theology*, 10.
7. Eberhard Busch, *Karl Barth: His Life from Letters and Autobiographical Texts* (Philadelphia: Fortress, 1976), 129.

of piety as humble submission to the will of God, to the Catholic semi-
narian who found himself closer to Calvin's understanding of the Lord's
Supper than to the Catholic doctrine of transubstantiation, to the community organizer who admired Calvin's social ethics in creating a social
welfare network in sixteenth-century Geneva, Calvin's theology continues
to resonate because it meets people where they live. Yet the verdict of history continues to weigh the scales against Calvin, always pointing accus-
ingly to his role in the execution of Michael Servetus and to his defense
of double predestination (which Calvin called that "dreadful decree"[8]) in
an attempt to cancel him. No matter that in his sixteenth-century context
"the execution of Servetus was lauded by Protestants and Catholics alike,"[9]
or that double predestination reinforces our human dependence on divine
grace, since "the belief that we are all sinners gives us excellent grounds for
forgiveness, and is kindlier than any expectation that we might be saints,
even while it affirms the standards all of us fail to attain."[10] Though, like
most of us in the modern world, Barth would have found life in Calvin's
Geneva personally restrictive and suffocating, he nevertheless challenges
modern Christians to continue to plumb the richness of Calvin's thought:
"In Calvin studies we cannot keep Calvin to what he once said as though
he had nothing more or new to say today! His work did not simply occur
then; it still occurs today. In what he once said he still speaks, saying what
he wanted to say. We may not speak merely of Calvin's historical impact;
Calvin himself has an ongoing history into which we insert ourselves when
we deal with him, in which we have a part to his honor or dishonor and
to our own good or ill."[11]

Have I overcome all objections? Hardly. Have I made the case that
Calvin is worth reading in 2024 and beyond? I hope so. Because, like so
many others, I find myself in deep waters with Calvin, and while I do little
more than tread water, I am not afraid of drowning because I have the
assurance of faith that in the end my own abilities have little impact on

8. John Calvin, *Institutes of the Christian Religion*, ed. John T. McNeill, trans. Ford Lewis
Battles, 2 vols. (Louisville: Westminster John Knox, 1960), 3.23.7.

9. Thomas J. Davis, "Introduction," in *John Calvin's American Legacy*, ed. Thomas J. Davis
(Oxford: Oxford University Press, 2010), 5.

10. Marilynne Robinson, "Puritans and Prigs," in *The Death of Adam: Essays on Modern
Thought* (New York: Picador, 2014), 156.

11. Karl Barth, *The Theology of John Calvin*, trans. Geoffrey W. Bromiley (Grand Rapids:
Eerdmans, 1995), 6–7.

the outcome. This is neither fatalism nor moral passivity. Rather, it is the same awe and wonder Calvin experienced when confronted with divine mystery. Like Calvin, I am convinced it is far better to enjoy and participate in this divine mystery than fully comprehend it: "I shall not be ashamed to confess that it is a secret too lofty for either my mind to comprehend or my words to declare. To speak more plainly, I rather experience than understand it."[12]

12. Calvin, *Institutes*, 4.17.32.

Scripture Index

167

Subject Index